Gaunty's
Best of British

Also by Jon Gaunt

Undaunted (available from Virgin Books)

Gaunty's
Best of British

It's Called Great Britain,
Not Rubbish Britain

Jon Gaunt

Published by Virgin Books 2009

2 4 6 8 10 9 7 5 3 1

First published in Great Britain in 2008 by
Virgin Books
Random House, 20 Vauxhall Bridge Road,
London SW1V 2SA

www.virginbooks.com
www.rbooks.co.uk

Addresses for companies within The Random House Group Limited can be found at:
www.randomhouse.co.uk/offices.htm

The Random House Group Limited Reg. No. 954009

A CIP catalogue record for this book is available from the British Library

ISBN 9780753515341

The Random House Group Limited supports The Forest Stewardship Council (FSC), the
leading international forest certification organisation. All our titles that are printed on
Greenpeace approved FSC certified paper carry the FSC logo.
Our paper procurement policy can be found at www.rbooks.co.uk/environment

Typeset by TW Typeseting, Plymouth, Devon
Printed and bound in Great Britain by CPI Bookmarque Ltd, Croydon CR0 4TD

TO LISA. MY FIRST, MY LAST, MY EVERYTHING.

Contents

CONTENTS

Acknowledgements

Once again I must thank my beautiful wife Lisa and my two gorgeous daughters Rosie and Bethany for all their love, support, encouragement but of course most of all patience while I wrote this book.

Thanks to Rebekah Wade at the *Sun* for giving me the opportunity to learn how to write what I believe every week and to Bill Ridley and Moz Dee at talkSPORT for giving me the airtime to talk to the British public.

Special thanks to my two radio producers, Sean Dilley and left-wing Laurie Palacio for their ideas and contributions to the book.

I am also really grateful to Chris Stevens, Paul Hudson and Graeme Frazer at the *Sun* for all their hard work on my *Sun* column every week.

I am immensely grateful to my agents Michael and Nick, my publisher Ed at Virgin and of course the fantastic work and advice put into this book by my editor, Martin Noble.

Most of all thanks to all the *Sun* readers, talkSPORT listeners and my colleagues who have argued, disagreed or agreed with my rants and have shaped my opinions.

Finally if after reading the book you want to continue the debate please get in touch with me at my official website at www.gaunty. com.

Foreword

What's so *Great* about Great Britain?

That's what this book's all about. It's now so unfashionable to be proud of our country that even our national flag, the Union Jack, has become a symbol of anti-patriotism – the most famous example probably being the way the punk movement used it to lampoon and tear down any respect or reverence for our national heritage.

I should know. I was one of them and back in the late Seventies, one of my most treasured possessions was a copy of the Sex Pistols' poster for 'Anarchy in the UK' which was a ripped and torn Union flag with safety pins all over it. You remember the one, it was designed by Jamie Reid who did the cover for the Pistols' 'God Save the Queen', which depicted Her Majesty with a safety pin through her nose. As a fully paid-up member of the punk community I proudly displayed my anti-establishment, anti-Royal Family attitude to all who visited a succession of grotty bedsits that I lived in. I was ready to spit on the flag and all it represented. Soon afterwards the Union Jack and the flag of St George were stolen by the Nazi boot boys of the National Front and the BNP and it became an embarrassment to wrap yourself in our flag.

However as I have grown up I've realised just how lucky I am to live in the greatest country in the world and I have come to appreciate that the flag actually represents all that is great about our nation. I also now understand that it is our flag, and I and millions of other true Brits should never have allowed the Far Right to hijack it. However, as much as I now love my country, I fear for it, and what is happening to it. And that's also what this book's about.

If you're a listener to talkSPORT or have read my column in the *Sun* you may already know at least some of my views about this great country of ours. If you disagree with them, I invite you to read on and who knows, on the Road to Damascus I may change your mind. I hope at least by the end of the book you may have come to realise what treasures Britain contains and to reconsider what we stand to lose if we don't revere and protect our great traditions.

The structure of *Gaunty's Best of British* is very simple.

In **Part I: What's So *Great* about Great Britain?** I start off by simply telling you about all the things that I love, appreciate and believe are truly great about Britain – and which I hope you do too.

Part II: How to Put the Great Back into Britain is the meat, where I tell you what has gone wrong, what's going wrong, and what might still go wrong in the future, if we continue to allow politicians to turn this Sceptred Isle into a Septic Isle. They have created a Disunited Kingdom and it is the duty of every true Brit to fight to get our country back. I want a country that respects and rewards the decent silent majority not the feral, the feckless, the foreigners, freeloaders and the long-term useless. If you've listened to me on talkSPORT, read my views in the *Sun* or watched me on Sky you know I will pull no punches and give it to you straight as I put the Great back into Britain.

Finally in **Part III: The Very Best of British** I celebrate all that's wonderful, magical, special, fun and ... of course *Great* about Britannia – and why it still really rules the waves – in a cornucopia of Best ofs. I know, you've seen all those Best ofs on Channel 4, but you *know* you love them – besides which I very much doubt whether Channel 4's politically correct producers will have anything quite like this on their schedules.

So here it is – *Gaunty's Best of British*. **This is Great Britain not rubbish Britain.**

I truly believe that now is the time to start shouting about this fantastic country from the mountaintops of Wales and Scotland through to the White Cliffs of Dover.

We need to remind ourselves that this is the country of Shakespeare, The Sex Pistols, Churchill, The Specials and Bobby Moore.

A land and people that invented football, rugby, the TV and telephone and revolutionised music, culture and the arts.

A small country that punches well above its weight with the greatest armed forces in the world, the home of democracy and defender of freedom.

A tolerant country. A fair country. A great nation and people.

It is time to rejoice in our culture, our history and our traditions and firmly put the Great back into Britain.

Jon Gaunt, August 2008

Introduction: Coventry is Great Britain

Most books have a beginning, middle and an end and they follow a familiar pattern but with this one I'm starting with the middle, the middle of this great country, my home town Coventry.

Coventry sums up all that has been, is and will be great about this fantastic country. It is a city that has refused either to be beaten or demolished whether by the Luftwaffe or the city planners and it has a population that is fiercely proud of its heritage. Coventry people may be critical of the city themselves but they would fight any outsider to the death who dares to knock the place.

To me that's part of the British character. We may well moan and groan but we know in the end this is still a great country, a country that could be a lot better but is still Great Britain not Rubbish Britain.

Coventry is a microcosm of Britain. It is a city that has had a chequered past and has brought some of its troubles on itself but it's a fiercely proud city that is now fighting back and reinventing itself while holding on to its past and history. Coventry has refused to be defeated and even now, if you drive into the city and see the vast open spaces filled with rubble from what was the recently demolished Peugeot car plant, you cannot fail to be also aware that the city is fighting back with two universities and new industry.

If you really want to know what it feels like to be British and to be proud of our heritage and history, just stand in the ruins of Coventry

Cathedral and stare for a moment at the cross of nails which stands proudly and defiantly in the bombed-out windows of the nave. Well, in fact it is a cross made of the charred roof timbers but, underneath it, is the cross made of nails from the timbers. Then turn your gaze to the left and look at the etched windows of the new cathedral and experience the hope and resilience of a whole city and country that stood against tyranny and fought back after destruction while at the same time placing peace and reconciliation firmly on the map.

Coventry was a great medieval city that many historians believe was more beautiful than York; in fact it was regarded before the war as one of the finest preserved medieval cities in Europe. But that was all to change on a beautiful moonlit night on 14 November 1940 as German bombers tore the heart out of the city.

Days before, on 8 November, the RAF had bombed Munich, the birthplace of the Nazi Party, and now Hitler wanted his revenge and Coventry was the target.

The operation was codenamed Operation Moonlight Sonata. The Blitz started at 7.20 p.m. with the dropping of parachute flares, which hung over the city centre in the clear sky, swiftly followed by phosphorus incendiaries, which started fires in the city centre buildings, including the Cathedral, to help guide in the heavy bombers.

Then the first of 500 bombers started to drop their deadly weapons on the city. By 7.40 p.m. the Cathedral was ablaze and the rescuers had to abandon all hope of saving it. By now there were over 200 fires raging with eyewitnesses saying that the flames were 100 foot high and that the approaching bombers could see the fires from over 150 miles away. The bombing continued relentlessly all night and it wasn't until 6.15 the next morning that the all-clear was sounded.

The raid had lasted at least eleven hours and over 30,000 incendiaries had been dropped along with 500 tons of high explosives. At least 554 Coventry citizens died that night and thousands were injured. Many bodies were never recovered from the rubble and many were unrecognisable. The Blitz destroyed over 60,000 buildings in the city and also destroyed the city's tram system and most of its infrastructure.

It has long been assumed that, in November 1940, Winston Churchill knew that Coventry would be bombed on the night of the next full moon, but he ordered no extra precautions to be taken in case it alerted Hitler that the boffins at Bletchley Park had cracked his Enigma code. So the city, almost undefended, was completely destroyed. However, the spirit of the Coventry people was not and never would be beaten. They would, phoenix-like, rise again from this nightmare.

Much of what remained of this great medieval city after the Blitz was torn down with overzealous rigour after the war and I have sympathy with the line that 'the council did more damage than the bloody Luftwaffe!' However the City Council already had dramatic plans to rebuild the city centre back in 1938 well before the Blitz. After the war these plans, led by a young architect called Donald Gibson, were put into practice.

But this destruction and regeneration is typical of what has made Coventry great and so resilient. Coventry had always been a forward-looking city and even though the world's first pedestrianised shopping precinct was perhaps, with hindsight, ugly – even an architectural carbuncle – it was at least unique and modern. It was a bold statement of a city determined to fight back and redefine itself while still linking with its past.

The original vision was for the precinct to have a clear view of the famous three spires of the city and was again echoed by the idea of linking the old and new as in the Cathedral. However the soulless nature of the precinct, especially during the recession of the late Seventies and Eighties, was to lead to accusations that the city was a concrete jungle, soulless and heartless, a description which most Cov Kids would argue with greatly. Just by demolishing the old buildings you do not and cannot rip the heart out of a place or community.

Coventry has always felt like a pioneer town. A place for new ideas and innovations. A place that whatever your background or place of birth you could come to and make something of yourself. In fact my old man said that when he arrived in the Sixties from Hull to join Coventry's police force it was like living in the Klondike with men being handsomely paid for working on the track or being skilled toolmakers. As a young copper he said that it was like a western town on a Friday and Saturday night when the lads and their wives would wash down their huge steak and chip dinners with gallons of ale before taking on allcomers in mass brawls in the city precinct.

This was a town that attracted the best from all over the country and then around the globe, attracted by huge wages on the factory floors and the opportunity to make something of themselves in this fast-developing city.

Fuelled by the wages they could earn, the carworkers in Coventry owned their own houses on vast estates across the city and by day they created some of the most famous vehicles in the world, everything from the Hillman Imp, the Triumph Stag through to the Jaguar.

There is a real sense of pride among Coventry people that they were the most skilled workers who made the greatest cars, armoured vehicles at Alvis or Rolls-Royce aircraft engines. There's a standing joke that the thick unskilled workers moved to Birmingham and this is emphasised in the Coventry joke: What does a Brummie call a spanner? Answer: a hammer.

I worked at the Standard Triumph for three months before I went to college and the factories were like major cities themselves where there was a tremendous sense of camaraderie and where you could buy or sell anything from one of the other workers. These factories underpinned everything the workers did: they had vast social clubs and recreation grounds and much of the leisure life of the lads on the track was directly connected to the car plant. The factories were who they played football for, where their lads went to boxing training or their daughters practised their Irish dancing. The factories were Coventry.

However this was a boomtown that unfortunately became a Ghost Town, as The Specials sang in 1981 as all the factories and the 'clubs closed down'.

Well, not all the factories but many of them. I remember going off to university in 1978 and most kids at my school walked straight into toolmaking apprenticeships or well-paid jobs on the track, but by the time I returned to live in the city three years later there was not only huge youth unemployment but also mass unemployment for all ages. The Triumph Standard factory had been closed down with the loss of thousands of jobs and soon other famous British manufacturing names were to follow including Alvis, Humber and eventually, years later, Massey Ferguson.

Coventry was a depressing place at the time and it was and still is a hard city but a city and a population that has and always will refuse to lie down and die. It is this bulldog spirit that needs to be echoed around this great country of ours. We should all be wrapping ourselves in our flag regardless of our colour, our creed or where our dads came from. We should be proud of our individual heritage or culture but united under one flag in our vision for a future.

Coventry was the Two Tone city but actually it has always been a city of many colours. With the exception of one or two isolated incidents it was a city that had been proud of its multiracial history and its ability to welcome allcomers. Starting with the Irish, who came in the postwar building boom; to the Asian doctors, who came in the Sixties to head up our health service; through to the West Indians, who gave the city its vitality.

It was this mix that was going to be the catalyst for the Two Tone movement that for an all too short period showed the country that black and white could unite, have a shared vision and view of the world, and also dance like crazy.

It was no coincidence that Two Tone was born in this particular city at a really difficult time in its history; however, the real pity is that there is no real legacy of this unity left either in the city or the country as a whole.

Two Tone was multiculturalism in practice without the New Labour labels or social engineering. It was young kids, black or white, university educated or not, joining together in a love of music that had been brought to the country from Jamaica with the first immigrants in the Sixties.

It was living proof of just how tolerant this country can be and just how non-racist most Brits are. Of course there were still racists around and skinheads did interrupt and try to kidnap the music and the movement, but I used to be so proud of The Specials when they would refuse to play on if the knuckle-dragging fascists started to Sieg Heil. I was even more proud when Cov Kids including some of the band would face down these fascists with fists and boots.

The Specials' guitarist, Lynval Golding, was stabbed in the eye in a vicious racist attack and as a result wrote a brilliant song that to me not only sums up why racism is so dumb but also why Two Tone was so important to Coventry and the nation as a whole.

The song was simply called 'Why?'

Why did you try to hurt me?
I got to know
Did you really want to kill me?
Tell me why, tell me why, tell me why

Why do we have to fight?
Why must we fight?
I have to defend myself
From attack last night

I know I am black
You know you are white
I'm proud of my black skin
And you are proud of your white, so

Why did you try to hurt me?
Tell me why, tell me why, tell me why
Did you really want to kill me?
Tell me why, tell me why, tell me why

We don't need no British Movement
Nor the Ku Klux Klan
Nor the National Front
It makes me an angry man

I just want to live in peace
Why can't you be the same?
Why should I live in fear?
This fussing and fighting's insane

With a Nazi salute and steel capped boot
A Nazi salute and a steel capped boot
You follow like sheep inna wolf clothes
You follow like sheep inna wolf clothes
We chase you out the dance hall, we chase you through the door
We chase you out the dance hall, we chase you through the door
Cos' we can't take no more of this at all
Cos' we can't take no more of this at all
With a Nazi salute and a steel capped boot
Tell me why, tell me why, tell me why
You follow like sheep inna wolf clothes
Tell me why, tell me why, tell me why

You're too scared to make a speech during the light
Without a thousand police protecting your rights
To threaten and abuse, incite or fight
But who will protect me from you in the night?

Why did you try to hurt me?
Tell me why, tell me why, tell me why
Did you really want to kill me?
Tell me why, tell me why, tell me why

With a Nazi salute and a steel capped boot
Tell me why, tell me why, tell me why
You follow like sheep inna wolf clothes
Tell me why, tell me why, tell me why.

As far as I'm concerned that song is as relevant today as it was over 25 years ago when Lynval wrote it. Things are getting tough again economically and the knuckle draggers are on the rise again but just like 25 years ago the solution to Britain's problems don't lie with the racists of the Far Right.

The Coventry mascot is a phoenix rising from the flames and it rightly symbolises this great city as it demonstrates the resilience and ability of Coventarians to rise again from the pits of destruction and despair, whether caused by German bombers or economic recession.

Recently I stood in the Jaguar Hall in the newly built Ricoh Arena and watched the future of Coventry in the shape of a young band called The Enemy. They played with passion and anger for just over an hour and over eight thousand Coventry kids shared their enthusiasm and pride in coming from the Two Tone city. The lads proudly displayed the Coventry City flag on one speaker and, on the other, the Union flag and it is this passion and patriotism that should be on open display right across this septic isle.

For too long we have been shouted down as little Englanders or, worse, racists if we dare to say that we are proud of our culture, our history and our traditions and customs but now is the time to fight back.

There is nothing racist about draping ourselves in the red, white and blue.

There is nothing racist about protecting our borders and wanting those who want to settle here to understand our culture and embrace our way of life and language.

There is nothing racist in saying you are proud to be British.

This is why we also don't need the very politicians who for years have been promoting and enforcing the failed dogma of multiculturalism on to us to suddenly give us permission to wave our flags or to say we should be proud of our country.

This miserable bunch of self-serving pigs in Westminster have opened up our borders to every Tom, Dick and Abdul without consulting us and sold our rights and country down the river to a European superstate without even giving us the chance to vote.

Now they want us to come up with sound bites about what it is to be British! Well, sod them.

I know what made this country great and so do you and in this book we are going to celebrate and rejoice in it.

This is Great Britain — not Rubbish Britain. The greatest country in the world.

PART I

What's so *Great* about Great Britain?

1

Simply the best: the Red Arrows

The world-famous Red Arrows have been banned from appearing at the 2012 London Olympics because they are deemed to be 'too British'.

Organisers of the event say that The Arrows' military background might be 'offensive' to other countries taking part in the Games.

The display team have performed at more than 4000 events worldwide, but the Department of Culture, Media and Sport have deemed the display team 'too militaristically British'.

Red Arrows pilots were said to be 'outraged', as they had hoped to put on a truly world-class display for the Games, something that had never been seen before.

Being axed from a British-based event for being 'too British' is an insult – The Arrows are a symbol of Britain.

The Red Arrows have been excellent ambassadors for British overseas trade, as they display their British-built Hawk aircraft all over the world.

> The Arrows performed a short flypast in 2005 when the winning bid was announced, but their flypast at the Games was to have been truly spectacular.
>
> It is to be hoped that common sense prevails, so if you disagree with this decision, please sign the petition on the link,
>
> http://petitions.pm.gov.uk/RedArrows2012/?ref=redArrows2012

Did you receive this email?

I did, about a thousand times, and over 365,000 true Brits went on to sign the petition.

After a bit of dithering, the Government, in the form of Olympic Minister Tessa Jowell, intervened and said the story was untrue and that no firm decision had been made.

In true politician style she passed the responsibility on to someone else by saying, 'This allegation is not true. The Government has not banned the Red Arrows from the London 2012 Olympic Games. The organising committee of London 2012 will decide what to include in the Opening Ceremony and other celebrations – but with almost five years to go, decisions are yet to be made on what these will look like.'

But the fact remains that so many people believed the story and signed the petition because it wouldn't surprise us for the Government to ban something like the Arrows for being too British. The fact that so many people don't believe the government about the Red Arrows is indicative of how little trust we have in them to reflect and cherish our way of life.

It would have been just another example of how the bleeding hearts that infest our Government, civil service and media want to constantly run down our history, our culture and our achievements.

To me, like the Changing of the Guard, the State Opening of Parliament or Big Ben, the Red Arrows symbolise everything that is great about Great Britain and I still get the same thrill now when I see them as I did as a boy.

Only just a few weeks ago I was finishing my show at talkSPORT and as the news jingle played in I heard the roar. Like the rest of the capital, I ran to the window and looked up to the skies and suddenly I was a little boy again as I stood in awe and stared as they flew down the Thames, painting the clear sky red, white and blue.

They were taking part in the ninetieth celebrations of the RAF but for a moment I wasn't in London, I was back in Cornwall at RAF Mawgan Porth watching the Arrows perform their artistry in the sky.

Like me you must remember staring up at the sky, oblivious to the fact that your ice cream was melting as you watched our heroes carry out their display.

Of course they symbolise everything that is great about Britain and yes, they celebrate our military at its best and that's because all nine Red Arrows display pilots are fast-jet pilots from frontline Royal Air Force squadrons. Many of the Red Arrows' pilots and support staff have recently returned from Afghanistan and Iraq and many will be temporarily detached on operations overseas during their time with the Red Arrows.

The team was formed in 1965, and has completed over 4,000 displays in 53 countries and they are the best because the selection process is tortuous with pilots having to meet strict criteria that include having a minimum of 1,500 flying hours, having completed a frontline tour, and being assessed as above average in their flying role. Eventually a shortlist of nine applicants is drawn up who are examined during a thorough selection week and then put through a gruelling flying test, formal interview and peer assessments. Once selected, pilots stay with the Red Arrows for a three-year tour of duty.

Three pilots are changed every year, so that there are always three first-year pilots, three second-year pilots, and three in their final year. There are no reserves as a spare pilot would not perform often enough to fly to the standard required. The team leader must have completed a three-year tour as a team pilot earlier in his career, and is appointed in a separate selection process.

The pilots spend six months from October to April practising for the coming display season. If one of the pilots is not able to fly, the team flies an eight-plane formation. However, if the team leader, 'Red 1', is unable to fly then the team does not display at all. Each pilot always flies the same position in a formation. Reds 1 to 5 form the front section known as 'Enid', and Reds 6 to 9 are known as 'Gypo'. The Synchro Pair, Reds 6 and 7, perform the highly popular opposition manoeuvres during the second half of the display sequence. During an aerobatics display, Red Arrows pilots experience forces up to five times that of gravity, and when performing the aerobatic manoeuvre 'Vixen Break', forces up to 7g can be reached, close to the

8g structural limit of the aircraft, a dual-control BAE Systems Hawk T1. This is the RAF's advanced trainer, and has been used by the Red Arrows since 1979, replacing the Folland Gnat.

The aircraft are essentially the same as those flown by Advanced Flying Training students at RAF Valley, with the exception of smoke-generation modifications and a slightly uprated engine giving a faster response time. The smoke-generation system pumps diesel mixed with appropriately coloured dye into the jet exhaust to produce the colourful vapour trails that enhance both visual effect and flight safety. This allows five minutes of white smoke, one minute of red and one of blue.

This is the awe-inspiring jaw-dropping spectacle that all of us love in the sky that virtually writes on the clouds 'Britain is great' and that's why the leftie pen-pushers at the Department of Culture, Media and Sport who *did* say that the finest aerobatic team in the world were 'unsuitable' and not in keeping with the event as they were 'too militaristically British' should hang their heads in shame or be sacked.

I am proud, and I'm sure you are too, of our military history and the brave boys who act like lions in Basra and Afghanistan to this day. We have a fantastic and glorious history and we shouldn't let these revisionists make us feel ashamed of it. Departments, councils and quangos like these always find the money to celebrate diversity and every immigrant's history but recoil at our flag and anything that remotely celebrates our glorious past.

These people actually despise not only our way of life but also the very men and women who are brave enough to pull on a uniform and try to defend it.

Colonel Tim Collins – the bloke who made the inspiring speech to his troops on the eve of battle in Iraq in 2003 – told me once that New Labour had always despised the military and this kind of comment about the Arrows just seems to illustrate it.

But hold on Gaunty, Tessa says everything is going to be all right! Well, not really because she hasn't clearly and unequivocally said that they will fly in 2012, has she? But I guess we all know we can trust Tessa, don't we? After all, she's the Labour Minister who, along with Ken Livingstone, produced the budget for the Olympics that was at least six billion short and counting.

She was also the woman who masterminded Ken's re-election campaign and didn't have anything to say after Livingstone bragged that 'I decided to bid for the Olympics not because of three weeks of sport but because I knew it was the only way of getting any government, Labour or Conservative, after thirty years of neglect, to invest billions of pounds in rebuilding the East End – and it worked a treat.'

When Ken made this outrageous statement on BBC1's *Question Time*, David Dimbleby exclaimed: 'You make it sound like a con trick.'

'It was!' Ken responded. 'Literally, absolutely!'

A spokesman for Ms Jowell refuted Ken's boast in the *London Evening Standard* by saying, 'We put the budget together with the best information possible and the best expert advice that we could get.'

Asked if there had been any kind of con, the spokesman retorted: 'Absolutely not. Ms Jowell always said that the budget would have to be revisited once we won the Games.'

There you have it then: it's either a con trick or they worked the budget out on the back of a fag packet or on little Leo Blair's abacus.

I can clearly remember interviewing Livingstone when I was working on BBC London when he told the people of London the Olympics would only cost the equivalent of a walnut whip, when it turns out he knew all along that it was going to cost the whole country the price of Willy Wonka's chocolate factory.

However just as with the Dome the worst thing is none of the *winkers* involved in this con trick have lost their jobs, let alone been put before the courts.

In Livingstone's worldview the Olympics are clearly a regeneration opportunity and just as with the *Doom* it's the rest of us mugs that are going to end up paying for it. But just like the Doom the Olympics are also not going to reflect the real Britain.

I knew that the moment that prat Peter Mandelson took over the running of the Dome, and wore those 3D glasses, that the politicians involved didn't have the vision to pull off this celebration of the Millennium and I was right.

The Millennium celebrations were a total flop and completely unrepresentative of why Britain is great and it is my greatest fear that the Olympics could go the same way. The Red Arrows could be just the start of the New Labour rebranding of our country.

We need more displays of our military might not less, and then perhaps we wouldn't have the ridiculous situation where an RAF commander tells her boys not to wear uniforms in Peterborough town centre in case they get attacked.

Perhaps then we wouldn't have Muslim extremists hurling insults at our boys in uniform in a Selly Oak hospital and perhaps then we would have political leaders who would take the time to welcome home the fallen when they return to Brize Norton.

In the dying days of Brown's Labour Government the unelected Scottish Prime Minister is now announcing plans to create an Armed Forces Day, to draft schoolchildren in to the Cadet Force, to tell service personnel to wear their uniforms when off duty and now to make it a criminal offence to insult a uniformed soldier.

All of which I broadly support but why do I smell a rat here and think this is just a cynical and cheap attempt to gain popularity and to glamorise military action abroad?

I would trust Brown and New Labour more if they provided decent homes for troops, the right gear when they go into battle and actually had the guts to be present when the fallen return home.

But I'm afraid that far from being a sign of respect for our troops, this is yet more propaganda by Gordon and his gofers at Number 10. They think they've duped us into thinking they're in touch with the public.

However this despicable attempt at a conjuring trick is transparent and spits in the face of every serving soldier as well as anyone who's ever worn a military uniform in service of the Crown and is the latest example of just how patronising and out of touch our unelected Prime Minister and his Government are with the British public.

They've spent the last eleven years trying to rebrand Britain and despite sending our boys into more battles than any government in modern times, they have treated our armed forces with disdain.

Britain doesn't need rebranding – it just needs its leaders to feel the same pride we possess in our brave boys, our military heritage and the traditions that made and are still making Britain Great.

2

Trooping the Colour . . . and all that (Royal) jazz

Let me make it clear – I am no great Royalist or monarchist. However I do know for certain that Her Majesty the Queen has served this country brilliantly and we should all support and thank her for over fifty years of dedicated service.

I don't subscribe to the old cliché that the Royal Family are great for tourism, as the French chopped the heads off their aristocracy years ago and the Palace of Versailles is still the most visited royal palace in Europe. However, our Royal Family and the Queen are more than dress-up Disney attractions. They are, or should be, the focal point and the glue that binds our country together.

When the pint-sized President of France visited us recently I would defy anyone not to be puffed up with pride at the show and the banquet the Queen laid on for him. Not only have we got the most magnificent fighting forces in the world but we also do pomp and ceremony better than anyone else. That's why Prince Charles is correct to remind us that when we marvel at the Trooping of the Colour we must bear in mind and never forget that these 1,400 marching men are also all fully trained soldiers who have all seen active service, some very recently.

This superb display of British pageantry always takes place on the second Saturday in June on the date of the Queen's official birthday and the custom of the Trooping of the Colour goes back to the time of Charles II in the seventeenth century. Essentially the colours of a regiment were used as a rallying point in battle and therefore the flags were trooped in front of the soldiers every day so that they could recognise them. However it wasn't until 1805 that the parade was first carried out to celebrate the Sovereign's birthday.

Obviously the Queen attends and takes the salute, nowadays arriving in a carriage, but in previous years she rode side-saddle. She always wears the uniform of the regiment whose colour is being trooped and the regiments take it in turn for this honour in a strict rotation. As well as 1,400 officers on parade there are 200 horses in attendance and over 400 musicians from several corps of drums who march and play.

As the clock on Horse Guards Parade strikes eleven the Royal Procession arrives and her Majesty takes the Royal Salute. The highlight of the day for many though is when, after the event, the Royal Family gather on the balcony of Buckingham Palace to watch an RAF flypast. Often as not by the Red Arrows. I would defy any true Brit not to be simultaneously proud and moved by this extraordinary display of history and military courage and honour. This is truly Britain at its best.

Years ago as a student I would pooh-pooh such tradition and pageantry. As an aspiring punk rocker I was even stupid enough to organise an anti-Jubilee party in 1977 when the rest of the nation was honouring the Queen with street parties. However, as the years go by and so much of our culture, tradition and history have been diluted, I have begun to be more and more embarrassed by my youthful stupidity while simultaneously recognising the importance of such symbols of national pride and unity.

I'll never forget one rainy day when Lisa and I and the kids visited the Royal Yacht *Britannia* in Edinburgh. For years I had argued that this was an anachronism and a total waste of money and a sign of excessive privilege, which exemplified why the Royal Family had to be scrapped. But on that rainy day I must admit I had one of those Road to Damascus moments where I suddenly realised that we had been diminished as a country by putting this old lady to rest and refusing to fund a replacement. As Lisa said, every tinpot country in the world has a royal boat but we, one of the greatest sea-faring nations on the globe, have refused to replace it. Yes the Queen would live in luxury but what does it say about our nation if we haven't got one?

I realised the scrapping of *Britannia* in December 1997 was a massive mistake and actually an attack on our Britishness by the ruling Government. Then Blair had the temerity to push for an equivalent to Airforce 1 to transport him around the globe. I am not suggesting that the former Prime Minister should have travelled on EasyJet but despite his delusion that he was President he was not and no prime minister ever should be our head of state.

I had the same feeling when I was invited to Buckingham Palace for a party to celebrate British broadcasting. Don't ask me why I was on the guest list – it was probably something to do with winning the three Sonys, which as you know I don't like to talk about! However, as I mingled with the great and the good of British broadcasting – and also some Radio1 DJs – I was impressed, perhaps even converted to the idea of having a constitutional monarch. Although I was somewhat taken aback when her Majesty asked me to say the phone number more slowly as she couldn't get it down (joke). Mind you I reckon Prince Philip would be a better stand-in for me than that rabble-rouser George Galloway.

Now I can here the sneers already. 'Gaunty's doing a Billy Connolly and selling out,' but I don't think I am. I just think that I'm growing up and moving away from the working-class prejudices that developed in my teenage and certainly student years. It's easy to condemn and criticise when you don't really know or have experience of the 'enemy'. But as I have grown older I've begun to realise that there's no need to fix something that isn't broken and I can't see what we would now replace the monarchy with. I certainly wouldn't want the usual bunch of self-serving pigs to put themselves up for election to be our ambassadors abroad and in the absence of any credible alternative I reckon we should stick with what we've got.

'The Firm' could certainly be trimmed down to size a bit and a lot of the minor royals could drop their cost to the taxpayer as well as their airs and graces – and yes Princess Pushy Michael of Kent and golfing Prince Andy Capp, I am talking about you – but the core of the Royal Family should remain.

3

'Play up, play up and play the game': in praise of cricket

I've got to admit that I am not a great cricket fan, or rather I should say I wasn't a great fan but as I've got older I've grown to enjoy it and appreciate it more and more. It will never replace football as my number one sport but on a warm typical British summer afternoon there's nothing better, even if it's only on the telly, than sitting back, kicking off the shoes, opening a can and losing yourself in hour after hour of this quintessentially British game.

Only the British could have invented a game that is so fiendishly complicated and that can also last five days and still not produce a winner. Many people say that is why the Yanks will never get it – and long may that continue, even if I must admit that's one of the reasons why I didn't take to the game when I was younger. But like all good things such as real ale, fine cheese and classical theatre, sometimes you have to be a little bit more mature to appreciate the intricacies and subtleties of a game that requires more than just shoving a ball into the back of a net. It's a clear case of educating either your sporting palate or taste buds.

I blame Lisa's dad, if anyone, for getting me into cricket – well, to be truthful it was Mike and an old West Indian bloke we met in Barbados one holiday.

We were staying at some pretty grotty apartments but there was an old nightwatchman called Holden who was employed to keep guard.

He was a bloke of about sixty-eight but he had the body and mind of a forty-year-old – it must have been all the rum, Banks' beer and sunshine! He also had a rather unorthodox way of keeping watch; he would fall asleep on our patio and snore in unison with the singing frogs. Still, as they say in Barbados, 'No problem'.

When he was awake in the early evening we would pass him the ubiquitous bottle of Banks' beer and he would sit and chat with my father-in-law about cricket. It was amazing to hear these two old-timers reminisce about test series between the Windies and England from years ago when they were both schoolkids, which these two, separated by thousands of miles of sea, would listen to simultaneously on their radios. Both knew all the fielding positions and unlike a moron like me can envisage and recall all the manoeuvres and tactics. Even though I had obviously never heard the games they were talking about I was pulled into their conversations. It was then I began to understand the tactics of the game, the chesslike strategy employed by the captains and the fierce but friendly rivalry between the teams.

The game of cricket is probably one of our greatest exports and surely something we should be proud of, even if the ungrateful colonial bastards are now usually much better than us at the game!

When I first visited Barbados twenty-odd years ago it was great to see all the young kids playing cricket on the beach. This was when Barbados was footballer-, wags- and probably Michael Winner-free, when there were no traffic jams and, more importantly, hardly any American influence via satellite TV. In those days Barbados really was 'Little England' and it was a great welcoming place to visit. The people made me feel humble because so many of them sounded and acted more English than Lisa and me.

I felt a kind of guilt when I remembered the reception that some British whites gave these people when they arrived on the *Windrush* and later ships during the late Fifties and Sixties. It made me, a twenty-six-year-old, again confront the horror of racism, not the overt thuggery of the NF or the BNP but the subtle and not subtle everyday racism these people must have felt when they first arrived in places like Coventry when I was a kid.

Fortunately times have changed in Britain but unfortunately for Barbados things have changed there too: the people are just as friendly but the American influence is everywhere, the creeping social cancer of American TV is spreading and cricket has been a casualty of this, with more and more kids forsaking the bat and ball in favour of basketball and other 'cruder' American sports.

However they still manage to give us a run for our money – and let's not mention the Aussies, for God's sake!

Later, when I started going to test matches, I would recall those conversations in Barbados on those warm balmy evenings and could almost still hear Holden's exaltations whenever there was a wicket and these memories, the great wine and company enabled me to begin to relax into this wonderful extravagant game. In a world that is so hurried, it is sometimes delightful to just let go and have a day at the cricket. I like the more relaxed atmosphere, even with the barmy army singing, in comparison with football and also, as I get older, I enjoy the slower pace of drinking!

Mind you, I have to admit I am beginning to be taken by the new Twenty/20 game and I can see the very real possibility of it making cricket both more accessible and popular. In fact my Bethany has become a real fan of this new game and really enjoys the odd evening at the Northamptonshire ground. I hope Twenty/20 does take off and I don't begrudge one penny of the fortunes the cricketers could potentially make as I feel they have been the poor relation to football for too long.

But for me nothing will ever replace the real game which has to be a test over five days, preferably with no rain to disrupt play, and it's a cliché but true: there is nothing more English than the sound of leather on willow.

4

'More strawberries, Vicar?' – the great British summer fete

I adore the traditional British fete, whether it's the large-scale affair organised by councils or the smaller event put together by a local community, church, village or scout group. I like the fact there is always the inevitable worry about the weather and the concerns about clashing with other events either nationally or local. It all adds to the atmosphere and anticipation.

When I was a kid I used to love the annual Coventry Carnival and the fair in the memorial park afterwards. This was back in the Sixties when every factory in Coventry and their apprentices would decorate the back of a low-loader and turn it in to a magical float. All the Scout and Brownie groups would get involved and either march or have a float of their own and the whole procession, which would snake in very slow progress through the city centre, would be led by Scout bands or brass or silver bands from the local factories.

As a child I can remember sitting on the kerb outside Boots in Corporation Street waiting for the procession to arrive. Then suddenly you would hear the band in the distance or perhaps a police motorcycle rider would roar up the road and then the magnificent cavalcade would come into view.

In later years when I was in the Eighth Coventry Cubs we all made a massive Loch Ness Monster and had to wear green tights and black pumps and get underneath this papier-mâché and fibre-glass construction and march in unison – it was brilliant and we won a prize when we arrived at the park.

The Memorial Park is on the poshest road in Coventry and there would always be a massive fair there including a wall of death and a huge display arena where the Red Falcons would land or the police dogs would perform.

I'm sure that Coventry wasn't unique and this was an event replicated all over the country but it seems like a tradition that is fading fast with the demise of the factories and the pits, and that's a shame, a tragedy.

Likewise smaller local fetes seem to be a dying trend and with their decline we could lose all those traditional games that we love: rat in a drainpipe, the tombola, guess the name of the teddy, the number of sweets in the jar, beat the buzz with that piece of wire and the bent coat hanger, even guess where the cow will poo in the field! Then there were the other attractions: the ice cream and candy floss, the lone police motorcycle to sit on for a photo or the visit by the local fire brigade. These fairs and these games were part of the British Summer.

One thing that both the big and small events had in common though was a sense of common purpose and giving a community a sense of identity, tradition and history. It was part of what made Britain great.

5

'For those in peril . . .': the RNLI

At my dad's funeral we had a collection for his favourite charity, the RNLI, and no book on Great Britain would be complete without a tribute to these brave men who risk everything to save those in peril at sea.

'Those in peril at sea' – that's a gloriously out-of-date cliché, isn't it? But how else do you describe what these brave men and women do? The Royal National Lifeboat Institution hold a very special, even unique, position in the hearts and minds of every Brit. I know we are an island nation but, let's face it, we are hardly a nation of sailors, are we? In fact I would hazard a guess that most of our sea legs were gained on a twenty-minute speedboat trip down the Camel estuary on that speedboat *Apollo* when we were kids holidaying in Padstow. However, as a child no visit to the seaside was complete without a visit to the lifeboat station and then my dad ordering us to empty out our small change and put it into the replica-lifeboat collection box on our exit.

It seems the Gaunts are not alone as when I asked *Sun* readers for their lists on what should be in this book the RNLI or the lifeboat men were mentioned again and again. Philip Kay's email was typical;

There is a group of people who, at a moment's notice, will stop what they're doing or leave their meal

17

unfinished or get out of a warm bed. They come from all walks of life and backgrounds. They may be postmen, shop assistants, bakers, electricians, doctors or solicitors. They will risk - and sometimes give - their lives for what they are doing. With few exceptions they are unpaid volunteers. The organization that they belong to is run entirely on voluntary contributions with no input or interference from central or local government. They define the adjective hero.

They are the men and women of the Royal National Lifeboat Institution.

Philip's right: these men and women are the equivalent of the firefighters of New York who rushed up the stairs of the World Trade Centre on 9/11 as thousands trooped downwards. I am sure just like me the haunting images of these firefighters are still clear in your mind as is the BBC documentary *Penlee: The Lifeboat Disaster*, which another reader Mike Simms reminded me of in this email:

Hi Gaunty

In your column on 4th April you asked for suggestions of what makes us proud to be British. My nomination would be the crew of the Penlee Lifeboat - *Solomon Brown* - who gave their lives to rescue 8 people on the coaster *Union Star* 26 years ago last December. This is an amazingly emotional incident that brought tears to the eyes of many who watched the BBC documentary last year - 'Penlee: The Lifeboat Disaster'.

The *Union Star* was drifting helplessly towards the rocks in weather that has never been seen like it before. Winds over 110 mph and waves over 60 feet high. Helicopter rescue was not possible and Penlee Lifeboat was asked if they would consider launching. Normally the Coxswain (Trevelyan Richards) would make the decision to launch, but this time realizing how bad things were gave the crew the option whether to launch or not and to a man they said, 'Yes'. One crewman said 'We have to go – they are expecting us to.'

Trevelyan selected his strongest crew and they launched, and those who remained behind thought they might not see them again. They fought through the horrific weather and eventually got to the ship, which by now was only 100 or so yards from the rocks. They pulled 2 women and 2 men off just as the ship was about to founder and onlookers thought they would accept that was all they could do, leaving the others to their fate in order to save what they had. But Trevelyan and his crew went around again to try and get the last 4 off, knowing it was almost impossible. Sadly the ship was swept onto the lifeboat and all were lost.

This [was an] unselfish and courageous action by such brave men, who knowing they were unlikely to make it still gave it one more try to save life and gave their own. To me they should be declared national heroes and an example of all that is left of pride and goodness in this country. It is well documented on the Internet – it makes emotional reading. Hope you consider them for your book.

How could I not consider it, Mike, and the incredible acts of similar bravery that are still going on today.

In fact 2006 was the RNLI's busiest year for the lads and lasses who man the 230 lifeboat stations around the UK and the most amazing thing is that all of the cost of this, at least £130 million, is supported entirely by public donations.

Some cynics argue that it is an extremely wealthy charity and that somehow it is less deserving of our support as a consequence. However, as a child of the Sixties and Seventies who spent many an hour collecting silver foil or foreign coins at the bequest of John Noakes and the *Blue Peter* team, I was and still am convinced that this vital work has to be supported.

The Royal National Lifeboat Institution is the Best of British.

6

Bountiful Brits: charity in the UK

One of the things that makes this country and its people great is the way we are all so willing, all of the time, to dip into our pockets and help others less fortunate than ourselves. We are definitely not a nation that believes that charity begins and ends at home.

There are over 168,000 registered charities in Great Britain and as a nation we donate more to charity than any other Western European country. Charities in turn spend £36 billion of our donations a year on a variety of projects that enhance all our lives and are literally lifesavers for some Brits.

Charities and charitable giving can be traced back to Elizabethan times and I never cease to be amazed at just how generous ordinary Brits are when they are asked to dip into their pockets and help out those fellow Brits and people around the globe who are less fortunate than themselves.

The Hospice movement is a prime example of this selfless giving with over 90 per cent of the funding of these vital institutions coming from the man in the street. Although I applaud and indeed have been very involved in the fundraising for these institutions I do think there is something sick in the heart of this great nation that we need so much charity and that hospices in particular have to rely on public donations. There will always be a need for charitable donations to help fund the extras in the Hospice movement but the basic core funding should surely come from direct taxation.

I will also never forget my daughter Bethany's birth where on a casual inspection around the delivery room it appeared that most of the equipment had been donated by a local charity, Baby Lifeline. This was a charity set up years ago by an ordinary Coventry housewife, Judy Ledger – indeed, many charities are set up by ordinary people – to help babies and mothers. It was wonderful that so many local people had been inspired by Judy to fund-raise and donate money; however, is it right that, in a modern democracy and in a society with one of the strongest economies in the world, we rely so much on charity? I don't think it is.

Which is why I have always objected in any way, shape or form to Lottery money being used to fund essential services like the NHS. That said, the Lottery profits should be more geared to funding grassroots organisations and smaller, less glamorous projects rather than being pumped into the black hole that has become the Olympic budget. We need less grandiose building projects, especially for the middle-class elite who don't even buy a bloody ticket, and we need more spent on grassroots and community-based arts and sports projects.

With the amount the Lottery has raised I cannot really understand why we haven't got a swimming pool in every neighbourhood, parks with free football pitches and football and sports equipment for every child in the land. I am constantly being asked by youth teams to supply either books or other memorabilia to help them raise much-needed funds for basics like kits or ground fees, and I often oblige, but surely this should be available as a matter of right in a country that has such a successful lottery.

I also sense a mood in the country that many charities are duplicating resources and competing with each other for both donations and supporters. I think the whole sector would benefit from amalgamation and a subsequent cut in administration and wage bills. Don't get me wrong – you do need to pay decent and competitive wages to attract the best executives to the charitable sector, but at the same time one has to be constantly aware of the main target of any charity, which should be about getting the cash to those most in need.

However, despite these reservations, us Brits should never lose sight of the fact that we are a really generous nation who should be proud of what we achieve together when we decide to act. With our collective efforts we can and have changed individual lives and the fates of millions and that is something to shout about.

7

Leader of the pack: the great British fox hunt

It's a crisp autumn morning when suddenly my dog's ears prick up, she stands and points, and then you just about hear the horn in the distance, a slight pause and then you see it, one of the most spectacular sights in Britain. First a flash of brown and then the lead hound with the pack in pursuit and then the horses and their riders begin to emerge from the mist. It's the hunt in full flight. It is Britain at its best and most traditional. It's an image that sums up the British countryside and it's a tradition that should be celebrated and protected not banned.

I'm a townie by birth but have lived most of my married life in the country and I absolutely adore our green and pleasant land.

There is no more magnificent sight than the hunt emerging from the mist or a wood and then galloping across a field; this is an image that is as uniquely British as a pint of beer or a bag of chips and it is outrageous that this centuries-old tradition has been banned.

The anti-hunting lobby in Parliament, which is stuffed full of urban backbench class warriors, should never have been allowed to try and ban hunting with hounds let alone succeed. If this had been a tradition brought in by an ethnic minority they would never have dared to attack it but as it is something quintessentially British the New Labour social engineers attacked it with glee.

However in multicultural, multiracial Britain, some minorities are obviously more equal than others because over 700 parliamentary hours were wasted debating the banning of a true British tradition that started in 1534. Eventually these urbanites won and this undemocratic ban was enforced in November 2004 with the clear intention of wiping out one of the greatest British countryside traditions.

I lived with a hunt saboteur when I was at university and I can quite honestly say she was the most loathsome creature I have ever had the misfortune to spend time with. Just like the townie MPs she was full of self-righteous indignation about the plight of the poor fox and absolutely no knowledge of the countryside, its people or its economy.

I'll be straight with you, it probably is cruel to chase and kill a fox, but it could also be said that it's also pretty cruel to trawl for fish and let them suffocate on the deck of a boat, but I don't see fat urban MPs wanting to ban fish and chips. But no doubt fishing and shooting will soon be in the sights of the anti-blood sports mob now they've got their way with hunting. It's also pretty cruel when a fox gets in a chicken coop and kills everything in it.

However, this is all immaterial because a fox is vermin, it's just a rat with a bushy tail. Plus most townies don't really understand just how large a hunting hound is. Once the lead hound has the fox in his jaws, nine times out of ten with one swift shake of the head the fox is dead. All the emotional claptrap and propaganda about the fox being torn apart alive by the pack is rubbish and the idea that the huntsmen are as bloodthirsty as the pack is frankly ludicrous. These people actually love animals – that's why they ride. I only half jokingly put the blame for this emotional childish anti-hunt feeling on the late, great Johnny Morris and his TV show, *Animal Magic*, with his silly voices which seems to have convinced a whole generation that foxes have emotions and rights.

What these urbanites do not understand is that the hunt provides a tremendous service for the country and the idea that it is stuffed full of chinless wonders and Hooray Henrys is wide of the mark. I must admit some of the upper-class berks who follow the hunt and actually act as spokesmen don't do their cause much good, as they can come over as right snobs, but to think that the hunt is only followed by people like this is stupidity at least and misplaced class warfare at worse. I repeat, hunting is not something that I will ever do but I will defend the right of others to continue to hunt to the end.

In my village the hunt is followed by loads of people from all backgrounds and also the stereotype that all country folk support it is a misnomer too. There are hunt supporters and those against it but at least those who live in the country understand the pros and cons.

The great irony of course is that since the ban more foxes have been killed than ever before. The idea that you can actually ban it is ludicrous anyway. I mean, you can hardly get a copper to investigate a burglary where I live so are they really going to come out to look after Basil bloody Brush? Unfortunately in the topsy-turvy, target-led, policing culture we are inflicted with today they probably would hunt the hunt rather than chase down the burglar or mugger!

So much anti-hunting feeling is really misguided, inverted class snobbery from townies and students whose only experience of the countryside is the annual dope-fuelled visit to the Glastonbury Festival.

These urbanites and the animal-rights idiots make me want to vomit. With their immature, emotional Johnny Morris influenced opinions they've managed to keep the banning of fox hunting at the top of the political agenda.

The ban is completely unworkable and a total flop because despite the legislation, the net result is that more people than ever were hunting on Boxing Day, 2007.

If only our glorious leaders had defended our borders with the same vigour as they have protected Basil Brush. Maybe we wouldn't be in a position where one bloke from the Congo could rip off the Post Office to the tune of 20 million quid and a quarter of the suspected terrorists that have been detained are asylum seekers.

And before you start sending in the hate mail, of course fox-hunting is bloody cruel. But so is putting a bolt through a cow's head, but that isn't going to stop me eating a rare steak. How about you?

Yes, I know it's different because we don't eat a fox but the fact remains that Charlie or Basil is vermin and if you'd ever seen the wanton destruction caused by a fox in a chicken coop you would agree.

If townies want to have the wonderful unique British countryside to visit at the weekend and enjoy then for God's sake leave the management of it to people who understand and actually live in it.

In fact if most people had ever seen a chicken without it being in a Tesco freezer then perhaps we would have had a more mature debate on the whole subject.

However instead we have had an emotional sixth-form-style discourse and one of the finest British traditions has been put under tremendous threat and the people who have followed the hunt for years have been tarred as animal haters at least and criminalised or beaten up by the police at worse.

This is a tragedy because if the British countryside is something that all of us Brits cherish, then those living in towns have to let the people who live in rural areas manage the land the way they see fit. The Hunt is as British as the Sunday roast, church bells in the morning, a pint and red pillar boxes. It will never die but the attacks on this great British tradition must cease. Let's celebrate the Hunt not condemn it.

8

'We few, we happy few': stand up for Shakespeare

When I owned my nightclub one of the best and most profitable nights of the year was St Patrick's Night. Yes, in the heart of County Coventry the plastic paddies let their hair down and all found a little bit of Irish in them or certainly got a bit later in the night!

I know Coventry's biggest ethnic minority is the Irish but my point is the whole city got behind this day and night and if I'm honest I am envious of the way our Celtic cousins, including the Scots, seem to celebrate their national days and culture and tradition, while we English just moan from the sidelines.

When I was on BBC London you could almost set your watch to the day and hour when the moans would start about Ken Livingstone funding a St Patrick's Day celebration but refusing to fund a St George's Day event. Ken would always of course deny this and say that he didn't fund St George's because nobody had asked him to. However ordinary Londoners had long memories and could recall this creep having tea and biscuits with the IRA leadership while they bombed the capital and therefore suspected him of being anti-English. Whatever the truth is or was I couldn't help siding with Ken because it shouldn't be for the councils and authorities to organise these days but for the English themselves.

There's a great line in one of my favourite Dexy's Midnight Runners songs, 'Burn It Down', where Kevin Rowland lists all the great writers to come out of Ireland.

Never heard about, won't think about.
Oscar Wilde and Brendan Behan,
Sean O'Casey, George Bernard Shaw, Samuel Beckett,
Eugene O'Neil, Edna O'Brian and Lawrence Stern . . .

Do you suppose an Englishman could ever sing a list of our writers with such passion? Most English people I know think that George Eliot was a fella and we don't even celebrate Shakespeare's birthday, which coincidently falls on the same day as St George's, 23 April.

The bottom line is we should be demanding a bank holiday on this day and celebrating our culture, heritage and traditions and the world's greatest ever playwright at the same time, but for that to happen we have to start watching, reading and enjoying Shakespeare.

My talkSPORT colleague and former Ipswich and Scotland footballer, Alan Brazil, is always having a go at me when I've been down to Stratford to see a play, making out that I am a snob or up myself, but his playground taunts are the literary equivalent of the child who says he doesn't like sprouts but when pressed admits he has never tried them. So Brazil and his ilk would rather push the sprouts to the side of the plate or Shakespeare to the margins of his own existence and revel in his own ignorance.

But it's probably not Alan's fault, he was almost definitely put off the Bard by poor teaching at school or being forced to watch some crappy Shakespeare production in a regional repertory theatre. I always tell him that if he was to watch one of the recent history cycles at the RSC he would become an overnight convert. I've told Alan to a chorus of giggles from his production staff that some of these productions have been as athletic and exciting as a great football game and I mean it.

This cycle of plays has probably been one of the RSC's greatest triumphs and Lisa, the kids and I have seen the lot. For the first time since Shakespeare's day the plays have been performed in the order they were written in and they give a brilliant insight into our history. The productions are highly visual, bloody and extremely relevant to today as well as illustrating what a great country this is.

However the real tragedy isn't on the stage, it's in the audience, as some performances have not been sold out. Why? I'll tell you why. Because there are too many Brazils in this country who won't or can't try it. Too many people who feel that it's not for them and that theatre is for snobs. But it's not and it isn't. The RSC receives millions in subsidy and that's millions of your money and mine and we all have a right to see what they are spending it on.

Years ago when I was running the Tic Toc Theatre Company I rebelled, rather childishly in retrospect, against the funding of these major companies but it is only with maturity that I have realised that this is where arts funding should go. So that you can see Shakespeare the way he would have wanted it performed, and you can't get that with small-scale companies performing in village halls or schools. Instead of trying to bypass these massive institutions with small-scale touring, it's important – no, vital – that ordinary working-class people have access to them and the great work they do.

To be fair, the RSC are doing an awful lot to encourage new audiences and although the top seats are expensive they still offer standby tickets and student concessions. So there's no real excuse for trying it, is there? Are you listening, Mr Brazil?

The RSC should also be applauded for their campaign, 'Stand up for Shakespeare', which is attempting to get kids as young as four into the themes and plots of the plays. That's the point: Shakespeare's stories and themes are as relevant today and in some cases even more so than when he wrote them. Almost all soap operas and many films have stolen or borrowed his themes of jealousy, revenge, love and obsession and family conflict. There's been a real effort by Hollywood to popularise Shakespeare and even films like *Shakespeare in Love* have appealed to a mass market but still many working-class English folk are reluctant to give the real stuff a go.

So the onus has to be on us parents. You need to pack away your prejudices, perhaps even fears, and realise the whole world is a stage and that the Bard is as relevant today as he was years ago.

RSC website: **www.rsc.org.uk**

9

In praise of Blighty: what makes Britain truly great

If you wanted to invent the perfect country from scratch then you would probably end up with Great Britain.

Of course there is a lot wrong with Great Britain at the moment and yes I've got both gripes and solutions to our problems but, just like in a family, if an outsider dares to criticise my country I will come down on them like a ton of bricks and I am sure every true Brit feels exactly the same.

Writing this book has made me reassess what I think about this country, my country. It's easy to trot out the line, 'This is Great Britain not Rubbish Britain', but what is it that makes it great? Just what exactly is it that makes this tiny country so special?

Well, first of all it's got to be the geography and location of the place. Yes we are part of Europe but we are separate by the very physical presence of the English Channel. This 22-mile divide is what makes us what we are, an island race. It sets us apart from our European neighbours and gives us our unique British character.

That doesn't mean over the years we haven't either invited or welcomed other nationalities to join us and in fact I truly believe we are the most tolerant and welcoming nation in the world. We have a proud tradition of providing a safe haven for those fleeing persecution and long may that continue. Of course it is true to say that in recent years, through our chaotic immigration controls, we have let in people who are playing the system or abusing our hospitality but I would never want us to turn away the genuine refugee.

This provision of a safe haven is a direct result of our belief in a sense of fair play. This is the very essence of our character and that's why we are the mother of all democracies and why we have one of the fairest and most honest criminal justice systems.

The right to be considered innocent until proven guilty by twelve good men and true is a fundamental British value that we should cherish and preserve. Although at times I have ranted about the bewigged buffoons and their ludicrous liberal sentencing the fact remains that in Britain, Great Britain, you are guaranteed a fair trial. Yes of course there have been miscarriages of justice and abuses of power, as there would be in any system, but at least in Britain we believe in the right of appeal and we thoroughly investigate any such abuses.

This British sense of fair play of course begins with the way our police force police by consent not force. There is a partnership between the bobby on the beat and the general public and it is, or has only been, when this trust has broken down that the system has failed to protect us. That's why I welcome the return to community policing, my old man would call it a bobby on the beat, and I am all for power being devolved downwards to the community so that they can be actively involved in how their area is policed and governed. However even in its present form I still maintain that the British police force is the best in the world.

It was also our sense of fair play that led us to be the first country to call for the abolition of slavery and we should be immensely proud of this too. It was also us who were the founders of the trade union movement who have improved the lives and working conditions of generations, and of course it was this fair and tolerant nation that created an NHS and a welfare state that would become a safety net for all Brits who fell on hard times or were ill.

These are massive achievements, which we should talk about more, rather than allow the lefties who infest Government and our educational bodies to dictate the agenda and somehow make us want to feel ashamed of our history. Without doubt there are aspects of our history that are shameful and our kids should be taught about them too but at the same time they need to know why and how Britain ruled the waves. Not everything about the atlas being painted pink was bad. We did export our justice system and our form of parliamentary democracy around the globe and again we should be proud of these achievements or at least judge them in the round, not condemn them as if we were just an all-conquering force intent on rape and pillage. It was this spirit, this tenacity, that led to us rescuing Europe in two world wars. It was this little island race who stood up and led the fight against Nazi tyranny and it was the sacrifice of ordinary Brits on the fields of the Somme and the beaches of France and further afield in the Far East that led to the development of a great country being fit for heroes and a free world.

Likewise today we still have the most magnificent fighting forces on the planet. We have a non-political army that doesn't question its orders but just gets on with the politicians' bidding. In recent years of course these brave boys and girls have been stretched to the limit in Iraq and Afghanistan and to be honest they have been treated appallingly by our present Labour Government, often sent to war without the right equipment or uniform and then treated with disdain when they return injured or worse from the battlefield. I know I keep banging on about it on the radio and in the column but it is a bloody outrage that neither Blair nor Brown has found time to welcome the fallen home even once during the past five years. If you have the courage to take the decision to send your fellow countrymen to war then surely you owe them the duty and respect to kit them out correctly and be there when they return. Instead many soldiers have had to rely on another great British trait, our capacity to be charitable both in time and money. Without the aid of the Royal British Legion and the Help for Heroes campaign, many soldiers and their families would be in a lot worse state. But still our lions fight on despite the fact that their donkeys of political leaders pay them a pittance, house them in slums and treat them with complete disdain.

Then the press and particularly the BBC have been all too eager to highlight abuses or bad behaviour by our boys and condemn every man who wears the uniform rather than see these horrific abuses as isolated incidents. The *Daily Mirror*, or The Daily Taliban as I call it, even printed false pictures of abuse but never mind – Piers Morgan got the sack and went on to a high-profile celebrity career. Unfortunately that's one of the downsides of modern Britain: anyone can become famous for anything.

However it's too easy to just blame the press or the politicians – we the public have our part to play too and when you compare the way we have reacted when our troops come home we should hang our heads in shame. Not enough of us have turned out at parades although I'm glad to see there appears to be a sea change at the moment. The sad fact remains though that there have been far too many stories of soldiers being abused, even spat on, when they wear their uniforms in public and not enough has been done to honour and respect their sacrifice.

Despite all this provocation, neglect and abuse, the boys continue to do their duty and I for one am truly grateful for their sacrifice and commitment to democracy and the security of our island race. The British armed forces are truly one of the greatest things about Great Britain and I salute and respect every single member of them. They are the true defenders and protectors of our democracy.

Our parliamentary democracy should also ensure that we have real political debate in this country and that we have the real power to elect directly those who we wish to serve us. Those people then need to remember that they are our servants and we are not their slaves, which of course in recent years has been muddied by the rows over cash for honours, MP expenses and sleaze, but even amongst all this our Parliament stands tall when you even compare it with our European neighbours. Yes of course there have been scandals like Profumo but our Government hasn't been mired in corruption, blackmail or bribery to the extent that some of their colleagues have across the water.

One of the greatest protectors of this has been our belief in a free press and the right of free speech and again these are almost uniquely British characteristics that make our country great. I believe it is absolutely essential that our press and broadcasters are as free and separate as they can be from government. It's absolutely essential that there is a broad spectrum of ideology and political beliefs across the whole range of newspapers in this country and even though I despise and mock certain leftie papers I would defend to the last breath their right to publish their interpretation of events.

That's why the 'weapons of mass destruction' row was so damaging to our democracy. As many of you know, I believed our prime minister when he made the 45-minute claim, as did the majority in the country. The subsequent sackings of top BBC executives over the affair was a very sad day for democracy. Whether Blair lied or the intelligence was wrong will probably only be decided by history but the simple bottom line is that Andrew Gilligan was right and no weapons have been found. Don't get me wrong, I still believe regime change was necessary and I am glad Hussein did the Saddam shuffle but he wasn't the only casualty in this sorry saga. One can't forget Dr David Kelly and his family and of course our brave boys who have had to try and sort this mess out. But the capitulation of the BBC and the crowing of Alistair Campbell were both tragic attacks on our free press and our democracy. The BBC, which incidentally I believe is one of the greatest British institutions, was cowed that day and I believe has never fully recovered and is now little more than a propaganda arm of the Labour Government.

Of course this is a tragedy when we actually consider the fantastic history and legacy of programme making from the Beeb. I'm the first to criticise it and state there is no real place for an organisation of its size funded by a compulsory poll tax in the modern multi-platform world but even I can't deny the brilliance of its programmes and its importance to British life. The BBC has been there to commemorate and report on every major event in this great nation's history, it has educated and entertained us and it was without doubt in the Seventies the greatest broadcasting organisation in the world. It had a range of programmes from news through sport to light entertainment that no other broadcaster could match. Those days are over but a trimmed-down BBC still has a vital role to play in our society. However, it must be free of left-wing infiltration and government influence.

We need a free press just as we need a police force and a judiciary free from political interference or influence, but during the last twenty years or so this separation has been diminished. Without a shadow of doubt Mrs Thatcher used the police force as a political tool during the miners' strike and, whatever the rights and wrongs of that fool Scargill not having a second ballot, the facts are that the damage and consequent lack of trust between these mining communities and the British police force has still not been repaired to this day.

I should know – I hear it every time we discuss the legacy of Mrs T. The strike still remains an open sore in our modern history and although I largely agree with the approach Maggie took to the ridiculous power the unions had created for themselves I still feel we lost something as a nation when she viciously attacked our industrial base. But it's not a black and white issue, is it? The unions were too powerful: there were ridiculous Spanish practices in factories, secondary picketing was an abuse of power and the union block vote and closed shop was one step away from a Marxist state. Scargill was no hero and neither was Red Robbo at Longbridge but, by the same token, the managers at British Leyland and in other industries were a joke too.

Maggie was right after the winter of discontent in 1979 to take them on and I applaud her transformation of Britain into a property-owning democracy. I'm not one of these middle-class, silver spoon in the gob lefties who think there is something almost heroic about being working class and living in a damp council flat that you will never own. Let me tell you there is nothing heroic or romantic about that life. Just like there wasn't anything heroic about working in heavy industry, on a boring assembly line, or down a pit, but unfortunately there's also not too much to shout about flipping burgers or living in a country that has become so service based.

I know all the arguments about living in a global marketplace but to me it's tragic that we have lost our industrial base and with that loss it is easy to forget our heritage. This is the nation that started the industrial revolution, the country that built those magnificent bridges, viaducts, railways and canals. A nation of innovators and inventors in every field of industry, commerce and science. I won't bore you with a long list of everything this country and its people have invented, built or developed as there are plenty of books which have detailed this and that isn't the purpose of my book, but when you consider the amount of inventions and innovations that should have the label 'Made in Britain' attached to them, it is endless.

We have also played a major part in art, culture and literature. I don't need to remind you that Shakespeare was British but look at the roll call of other great writers from these islands, and then there's our poets and filmmakers before we even begin to consider our painters and sculptors.

British theatre led the way in bringing social realism to the stage with the ground-breaking work of writers like John Osborne with *Look Back in Anger*. These kitchen-sink dramas led to the creation of a really vibrant film sector in the Sixties and Seventies that produced classic movies like *This Sporting Life*, *The Loneliness of the Long Distance Runner* and later *Kes*. Then there's the innovative TV that was largely produced by the BBC, the nature programmes, the Plays for Today and then the creation of a vibrant commercial TV sector, which bred programmes like *Coronation Street*.

IN PRAISE OF BLIGHTY: WHAT MAKES BRITAIN TRULY GREAT

The creation of our brilliant TV was helped by the British tradition of music hall and working men's clubs that were the breeding grounds for the great British comics from Max Miller through Tommy Cooper to Bruce Forsyth, Ken Dodd and of course Morecambe and Wise. This sense of humour extended to our great TV writers like Carla Lane, Galton and Simpson, Johnny Speight and John Sullivan who took ordinary working-class characters and their lives and put them into our living rooms for the first time in classic series like *The Liver Birds*, *Steptoe and Son*, *Till Death Us Do Part* and of course *Only Fools and Horses*.

On the music front we have a great heritage that not only encompasses orchestras and classical music but also working-class traditions like brass or silver bands and we have an enviable history of providing peripatetic musical teaching so that all of our kids have the chance to learn to play a musical instrument.

When it comes to pop music it might be true to say that the Yanks stole the blues from poor blacks and created rock and roll but it has been the British and their peculiar take on the world and life that has really shaped pop music.

It was the Swinging Sixties that created The Beatles, it was Birmingham and the Black Country that created heavy rock with Black Sabbath and Led Zeppelin, and only Britain could have created punk rock. The subcultures that accompanied these musical movements were also uniquely British from the working-class pride of the mohair-suited Mods through to the Greabo head-banging of the rockers to the fashion and creative industries of London that created the dress code of punk.

Our music may be made in Britain but it has been exported around the globe, the fashion and attitude that accompanied it has been copied by kids on the streets of LA through to the suburbs of Tokyo. The influence of our music and the subculture fashions that have accompanied it cannot be understated and that is why Britain still leads the way in fashion, modern art and design as we hurtle through the twenty-first century.

This is why I love my country and why I hate those both within and outside who want to change it or wreck it. This has and will always be a country worth fighting and even dying for and that is why I am determined to join with you and fight to get our country back. This will be Great Britain not Rubbish Britain and the fightback starts now.

PART II

How to Put the Great Back into Britain

10

The red, white and blue

Can we please stop discussing what it is to be British and just wrap ourselves in the flag and tell anyone who doesn't like it to get lost and get out.

Labour are probably right to say we need a day to celebrate Great Britain but what we don't need is a New Labour revisionist version of Great Britain, which is what these clowns are suggesting.

When the day was first mooted back in 2007 by the then Communities Secretary Ruth Kelly, she said, 'It isn't going to be about standing around and saluting the flag.' Why not? What's wrong with our flag, Ruth?

This was the moment when I first suspected that this day was going to be just a con trick on the indigenous people of this island.

It was clear that their Britishness day had nothing to do with celebrating our glorious history, culture or traditions and everything to do with celebrating their failed experiment of multiculturalism and diversity.

So what would it be then – dancing in the streets because we all love Chicken Tikka Masala after a few bevvies?

It's also deeply ironic that a Labour politician who is a member of a party that has systematically denied us the right to rally round our flag should come out with such piffle.

It got worse when Margaret Hodge, the then so-called Culture Minister, said that the Government 'is keen to make the Union Jack a positive symbol of Britishness reflecting the diversity of our country today and encouraging people to take pride in our flag'. However, most Brits already have great pride in our flag and, just like Bottler Brown asking for a catchphrase to sum up Britain, most of us don't need Labour to tell us how to feel. We already have immense pride in our nation, our history and our culture.

You should also take the word 'diversity' to mean that before too long we'll be incorporating the Polish flag into the Union Jack. In fact, due to Labour's nonexistent border control, we may as well forget the Union Jack and hoist the white flag as they have surrendered our country to the immigrants of the world and the unrepresentative self-serving pigs of Europe.

If Labour really wanted to promote a real sense of British identity and prevent communities becoming more divided, they would start by securing our borders and stopping the unchecked immigration that has fundamentally changed this green and pleasant land.

I'm not talking about the managed immigration of the Sixties and Seventies, which, I believe, has benefited this country but I'm talking about the 'Immigrants R Us' policy that New Labour has allowed to fester.

Whether it's the illegals jumping out of the lorry at Watford Gap or the ridiculous decision to be in Europe and allow everyone freedom of movement, it is these two things that have changed Britain for the worse and have now made us have to question what it is to be British.

Most Brits just want to get on with their lives, educate their kids, earn a few bob, buy a nicer house and have a holiday or two. What they don't want is a situation where every Tom, Dick and Abdul can come into our country without the need to have a medical, learn our language or respect our customs, traditions and way of life.

This is what the immigrants of the Sixties and Seventies realised and coupled with their strong work ethic this has enabled them to become full British citizens who now share the same concerns as me.

Politicians need to realise that this is not a black and white issue in any sense of the word and many British-born second- and third-generation immigrants have the same concerns. They too see the massive queue in the doctor's surgery, the queue jumping in the housing office and the hands stretched out at the benefits counter and they too are sick of this New Labour Britain.

Now with the mood of the country turning against an unelected Scottish prime minister, Labour are trying to subtly change tack with the Bottler Brown suggesting that a Union flag should fly from every public building. But when I want tips on being British from a government that has systematically disunited this kingdom, I'll ask.

Let's face it, we no longer live in a democracy but a 'Jockocracy' where there is one rule for us mugs in England and a completely different set for the subsidised Scottish who then have the gall to try and run the whole of the 'Disunited Kingdom'.

Scotland is a great country but I am afraid that it's getting greater off the back of our English sweat and our subsidies. They should either be a part of the Union or completely out of it but this political halfway house has as much life left in it as a Scottish World Cup journey and it makes me sick.

I love Scotland but I can't stand the Scottish MPs who not only want to run their country but also dictate to us English how we should live our lives. That's why David Cameron is bang on the money when he says Jock MPs shouldn't have a vote on English matters. Those in the Labour Party who are now accusing him of wrecking the Union need to wake up and smell the coffee and realise it's their misrule that has demolished the Union with their pathetic half-hearted attempts at devolution.

How can we have a United Kingdom where Wales and Scotland can decide to have free prescriptions, no tuition charges and free central heating for pensioners while the rest of us in the economic powerhouse that is England are meant to subsidise their schemes?

As a consequence us English might stop being treated like a minority in our own land and perhaps the Government would deign to spend more than £230 in five years on St George's Day and celebrating the English.

How much longer is this ludicrous situation going to be tolerated by us English mugs and when are the Tartan mafia that run the UK going to realise that we English want to be called *English* and are proud to be *English* and want to celebrate that fact on St George's Day on 23 April?

I don't know how Jack Straw can keep a straight face when he tells us to reclaim St George's Day from the 'bigots'. This is the man who is down on his knees more than your average worshipper in a mosque, trying to appease his largely Muslim constituency.

The Union is already fractured, and probably beyond repair, so the time is right to give them full independence and allow those of us who are English to wrap ourselves in the flag of St George, those of you who are Scottish to wrap yourselves in the flag of St Andrew, and those of you who are Welsh to wrap yourselves in the flag of St David.

Oh and by the way McBrown, we don't need permission or tips from you on being English, let alone British.

11

Part of Europe but not owned by Europe

You can't write a book about Great Britain without talking about Europe (sorry!) and Britain's place in it both in the past, the present and the future.

I'm proud that along with a little American help this small country has been the liberator of our continental cousins on two occasions. The sacrifices of our brave heroes on the beaches of Dunkirk and the battlefields of Europe must never be forgotten both by ourselves or the rest of Europe.

I don't subscribe to the theory of many of my callers who say we might have won the war, Gaunty, but we are losing the peace and that Germany is now ruling the roost through the back door of the EU. Believe it or not I am not anti-Europe but I am vehemently opposed to any more of our laws, rules, defences or control of our sovereignty being given over to Europe.

I love Europe and I like holidaying there like most Brits and I want to trade with our nearest neighbours but I definitely don't want a single currency or our laws being made by faceless bureaucrats in Strasbourg or Brussels. I am old enough to remember Ted Heath taking us into the Common Market and I well remember the rows and discussions my mum and dad had over the referendum, as did most households of the time. However I am positive that most Brits, as my old man used to say up to his dying day, thought the vote was about joining a common market not forming a United States of Europe.

I don't think wanting to keep control of your borders, your armed forces, your laws and sovereignty and even your imperial measures is a sign of being either a racist or a little Englander. It's just proof that you are proud of being an island race, proud of your culture and history and want to remain resolutely British.

Final confirmation for me that I am British – well, English actually, first and European second – came when Sean my radio producer and I were invited to the European Parliament in Brussels to broadcast a programme from the building about the merits, myths and strengths and weaknesses of being more integrated in Europe. We were invited over by Labour MEP Claude Moress and I have to say both he and the Parliament were excellent hosts, but then again they had to be as they were after positive publicity!

The first thing that hits you when you see the building is both the sheer size of it and just how ugly, bland and architecturally uninspiring – is that a symbol, my friend? To get into the building you have to go through a very extensive security and vetting procedure including airport-style X-ray machines and human searching. This process can take up quite some time so as per usual the MEPS have sorted out a nifty little system for themselves. They get paid an attendance allowance for every day that they attend the building but guess which side of the security system the book is that they have to sign to pick up their wedge? Yes that's right, before the long security check! I wonder why?

Once inside the building we set up our temporary studio right outside the voting chamber itself. We had a lively programme discussing the pros and cons of Europe and of course whether or not Britain should sign the Lisbon Treaty, which was a very live issue at the time. You will remember that this was called a treaty not a constitution and therefore both Blair and then Brown insisted that they were not breaking a manifesto commitment by refusing to allow the British public a vote on the issue.

This of course was a despicable act of smoke and mirrors and a clear act of betrayal of the British people by New Labour. Brown even scuttled off to Lisbon the day after all the other European leaders to sign the wretched document so as not to be photographed with them.

Clearly the British public didn't and still don't want further integration but still the pro-Europeans force it through. Thank God for the Irish, who even as net beneficiaries of Europe, unlike us who are net contributors, decided in a referendum to say no to this treaty in June 2008. As a result they have probably scuttled this European superstate for the while at least.

It's always puzzled me that if Europe is so great then why didn't Blair and why doesn't Brown spend a fortune on adverts and public information films and documentaries outlining the pros and cons and allow the British people the same constitutional right as the Irish to decide just how tied into Europe they want to be? If Europe were such a good idea and so popular then surely the pro-Europeans would win? Of course they don't allow the referendum, even though it was a clear manifesto promise, no matter what they call it, because they know the British, although not being anti-European, are firmly against any further integration or dilution of our sovereignty and nation.

Back to the outside broadcast – so there we are, having a right ding-dong about Europe with guests from all sides including the vehemently anti-European UKIP who delight in telling me how the place is full of conmen, shysters and crooks and repeating the oft-quoted line about how the accounts haven't been signed off for years, when I am suddenly presented with a very pro-European MEP from Finland to argue the case for further integration.

He was called Alexander Stubb and I started with what I thought was a fairly innocuous question asking him to name five things that Europe has done for us.

He started his reply by saying that the freedom of movement for work was a positive. I just had to interrupt him and said, 'That's not how most British people see it.'

He asked what I meant and I talked about the fact that when people like myself and other columnists said that the opening of our borders to new European countries like Poland would mean that our country would be swamped with cheaper workers we were shouted down as racists. Labour attacked us as scaremongers and stated categorically that only 13,000 would come, not the hundreds of thousands I and other commentators were suggesting.

However I was right and they must have been doing their figures on Leo Blair's abacus again because so far 670,000 Poles alone have come to Britain and there were over 13,000 babies born to Polish mothers in 2007 alone.

Alex replied with an implication that I was racist but I deflected this by stating that we in Britain were finding it hard to cope with this unprecedented and largely unwelcome invasion of foreigners. I told him I was no longer alone in this view as a headteachers' union had made the point only the week before that schools needed extra resources to cope with the amount of kids who had English as a second language. Not only that but recently senior police officers had raised worries about immigrant crime.

As per usual on my show the atmosphere got tenser and tenser until both of us were saved by the bell or rather the news jingle being played in. I shook the MEP's hand but held firmly on to it and told him it was rude to come on my show and infer that either my listeners or I were racist just because we were concerned about immigration.

He pulled away and said, 'I did not call you a racist, but you are one.'

I replied, 'I am not a racist.'

'Yes you are, you are a filthy racist.'

Now at this point I should have turned the other cheek and ignored the Finnish fool but in a clear example of the truism that you can take the boy out of Coventry but not the Coventry out of the boy I replied, 'Fuck *off!*'

He then complained to the Parliament and the little-read *Independent* newspaper wrote an article trying to imply that I was indeed racist; however, Stubb issued a grovelling apology within hours.

The point is I wasn't being racist and if anything the following months have proved my point: we are a small island and there is no way we can continue with this massive influx of people, not only from the ever expanding Europe but from around the globe.

Our health service is at breaking point. Police are continuing to voice concerns about immigrants, with the Chief Constable of Cambridgeshire, Julie Spence, taking the lead. Our schools are facing real problems with resources and support for immigrant children and without a shadow of doubt wages for our tradesmen have been deflated.

I reiterate that it is *not* racist to be concerned about this, especially when one considers the British people have never been asked or consulted about this massive wave of immigration. As I have said on numerous occasions and in other places in this book, most people haven't got a problem with well-controlled and managed immigration but it is this 'Immigrants R Us' policy of New Labour that is fundamentally changing the structure and make-up of this green and pleasant land that people are getting increasingly angry about.

It doesn't help either when it is revealed that new European entrants have a right to claim child benefits for dependent children even if they don't live in the UK and it appears that the hated Human Rights Act protects newcomers more than the indigenous population.

However, at last mainstream politicians seem to be waking up to the problems, but unfortunately border controls and stricter immigration rules for non-Europeans will do nothing to stop the flow of immigrants from Europe. As our Finnish friend says, the freedom of movement is enshrined in the European constitution, or is it a treaty?

This is however one of the major reasons why Brits want no further expansion of Europe and certainly why they don't want to cede any more control to Brussels. A sovereign nation must have the right to control its own borders and protect its own people and an expanded Europe would not allow that.

Back to our friend, Stubb. When we got back to London Sean investigated Finland's attitude to immigration and discovered that they had much tougher controls than us. This has led me to the very reasonable conclusion that when I want tips on immigration from a man who probably eats rollmop herrings for breakfast and spends half the year in darkness I'll ask.

Finally when we the British people are expected to give our country to the faceless bureaucrats of Brussels and Strasbourg the least our poxy Government should do is *ask* us if we want to.

12

The lead swingers and what to do about them

My radio producer, Sean, is completely blind.

Every morning he wakes up early in his home in Stevenage, walks for twenty minutes, catches a train into London and then a bus to talkSPORT Towers. On this journey he is aided and abetted by his guide dog Chip but once in the radio studio he holds down one of the most difficult jobs in British broadcasting – massaging my ego.

Seriously, he does perform a really difficult job and if someone had told me years ago that I would be working with a completely blind bloke I would have laughed them out of court, saying there was no way somebody with a disability could hold down such a job. However I would have been a prejudiced prat because the truth is Sean is the best producer I have ever had and is better at the job than most able-bodied people I've met.

He reads the papers and wires on his computer at double the speed I can listen to audio, he can check the time with his specially adapted watch and his knowledge of politics is second to none. Not only that, he can drive the mixing desk with its vast array of knobs, buttons and switches and most guests don't realise when they first meet him that he is actually blind.

Once we had to have lunch with David Cameron's adviser and on the way back to the studio, as the polite conversation was drying up, he remarked, 'Sean, I hope you don't mind me saying, but when I first met you I didn't realise you were blind.'

'That's because you don't wear sunglasses, Sean,' I chipped in.

'What do you mean?' said Sean.

'Glasses, like most blind people do.'

Sean was indignant. 'Most blind people don't wear sunglasses!'

'Yes, they do!'

'No, they don't.'

'They do, Sean.'

'They don't!'

'How the fuck would you know?'

There was silence, I swear I actually heard the political adviser's bum cheeks clang, and then the silence was broken as Sean burst into laughter, quickly followed by everyone else.

That's the point – I wasn't being nasty to Sean. I wasn't putting him down. I was just having a joke at his expense and in today's politically correct world that should be allowed. Sean wants to and should be treated equally, and the moment we pussyfoot around with our language or jokes we may as well start treating him as an unequal and asking if he takes sugar. There was no nasty intent in my joke. It was just a laugh. Sean and I are equal but different.

But one thing puzzles me. If my blind mate can get up every day, get dressed, travel miles to work and hold down such a difficult job, how come there are four and a half million scrounging lead-swinging leeches who can't get out of their stinking pits and get to work too!

I'll tell you why: because successive governments have bred a dependency culture in this country that is now costing the rest of us, the decent silent majority who work and pay our taxes, *18 billion* a year in sickness benefits.

Whole towns and whole generations have got used to lying in their stinking beds while the rest of us pay for their slothfulness.

Let me be clear: there is no way that anyone needs to be on the dole for more than six months and there are plenty of jobs out there. Not great jobs, I grant you, but jobs and the only way to get the job of your dreams is to start from a position of having a job, any job.

That's why I believe that benefits have to be time-limited and tapered so that they force people back into work, and doctors should be given financial incentives to sign people back on to work not off it.

I have never understood why if you've got a bad back you can't work in a call centre.

Former Social Security Minister Frank Field was asked to think the unthinkable in terms of benefit reform, did so and subsequently Tony Blair sacked him, but Field seems to me to be the only politician with the balls and vision to get Britain working again.

He wants to cut the two-tier benefit system which encourages people to register as incapacitated so as to pick up an extra seventy quid a week. It doesn't take a rocket scientist to realise that if you offer this kind of incentive then millions more will suddenly develop depression or stress.

Allowing these people to work the system clearly does society no favours but equally doesn't do the benefit scrounger any good either, as they fall into a cycle of real depression as they become more and more separated from the rest of working society.

And, by the way, I do know what I'm talking about. After my business went bust and I had worked in Scotland for a while I returned to Coventry and spent about six or seven months on the dole. Looking back now, I don't know how Lisa and I survived both on a day-to-day basis or as a marriage, let alone how we managed to cope with our newborn baby, Rosie.

I was one of those lazy bastards, lying in my pit or spending hours and hours in the bath moaning about my predicament and wallowing in both increasingly tepid water and my own self-pity. It was easier to nip over the offie or the supermarket and stock up with cheap lager than actually confront the fact that the only one who was going to get me out of this mess was myself. Looking back, I am ashamed that I took so long to get my act together.

I was lucky: I managed to get a break into radio by sheer chance but once that small opportunity was offered, something kicked in and I made the most of it. I've had mates though who have gone the other way; one lost his job due to the classic bad back. Now the back injury was legitimate but he took the quack signing him off as a green light for a life of scrounging and leeching off the rest of us.

At the time he was living in a council flat and when he was working it was a little palace and extremely clean and tidy, but a chance meeting with another doleite living above him, in my opinion, wrecked his life. This waster told him that if he could convince the doctor that he was depressed or stressed he would qualify for an extra benefit.

I can still remember my mate bragging that he was going to go down this route, for the extra cash. It didn't occur to him that he could actually get more cash if he got back into work – any work.

However, despite warnings from friends and family not to mess with his mental health, before long he was cutting himself and pretending to self-harm and as quick as the blade nicked his arms, the doctor wrote out the sick note.

He lived like this for years and spiralled further and further into real depression as his own horizons became more and more limited. Yes, it was his choice and his personal responsibility, but where was the help, the tough love that should have been reassessing him and realising that he was a lead swinger before he hit rock bottom? Why was there a financial incentive for him to go down this self-destructive path? He should have been forced back into work or retraining so he could rebuild his self-esteem.

I am not suggesting that everyone on benefits is a scrounger or cheat but clearly a massive proportion of that 18 billion a year could be saved. However with Labour it seems to be a case of another day and another initiative or gimmick to get the unemployed and the long-term useless back to work. All of which are half-measures and therefore doomed to fail.

The latest idea is that if someone doesn't work for a year they will be forced to do voluntary work for – wait for it – four weeks or lose their benefits.

Oooh, what a threat! I bet the layabouts are quaking in their pits at the thought of that.

Why doesn't Labour wake up, smell the coffee and realise that the stick has got to be a lot bloody bigger than that?

They have created a benefit and dependency culture where whole swathes of people don't want to work and don't see any shame in not doing so. Either that or they blame everyone else for their idleness.

Prime example was Gill from Wolverhampton who phoned my radio show to moan that her 27-year-old son – or was that mummy's boy? – hadn't had a job for over a year and that this new 'get tough' policy would penalise the innocent like him. She expected sympathy but she got quite the opposite from me.

I asked why he hadn't worked and she said there were no jobs. When I suggested McDonalds, Tesco's or any other number of jobs that I see advertised every day, she responded by saying those jobs were on the minimum wage and beneath her little Timothy or whatever the pampered prat is called.

Sean immediately got on the computer and googled jobs in the Black Country and discovered that there were over 5,000 jobs in her immediate area. Go figure, Gill!

Her and her son's attitude stinks but then she proceeded to blame all the foreigners who have come into the country and taken the jobs. It was everyone's fault except her useless son's idleness.

No wonder politicians make us swallow the lie that we need all these immigrants because they do the jobs that Brits won't do.

The liberal elite has created this underclass by excusing their slothfulness and criminality and by creating a benefit system that rewards them and discourages them from looking for work. This underclass is not too thick to realise that they can get more by scrounging on the dole rather than working. They've sussed that even with a minimum wage they can lie in their pits until the afternoon and still pick up a nice wedge, especially if their feet become pen pals and they keep pushing out babies.

These scroungers are shameless but the rest of us aren't blameless as we have allowed the Guardinistas and social services to create a new Britain where we are no longer allowed to be judgemental and we must accept all forms of 'families and lifestyles'.

Let's get tough on these parasites. We need to immediately remove the two-tier benefit system where by just claiming that you are 'stressed' you can pick up 70 quid more a week. We need to cut the connection between getting pregnant at sixteen and getting the keys to a council flat and hot and cold running benefits. We need to have benefits time-limited and force people back into work, because I don't know about you but I'm fed up of working to pay for their useless lifestyles.

13

'Time, gentlemen, please': when the puking has to stop

If Britain is ever going to be truly great again we have to reclaim our streets from the feral and the feckless yobs that infest our city centres at night.

Let's be clear though, the trouble isn't with 24-hour licensing, the fault lies with the individual mindless morons who can't hold their drink and the lawmakers and enforcers who have ceded control to these drunken louts. I don't know about you but I want to buy and drink an alcoholic drink whenever I fancy and I don't see why I shouldn't be able to.

Years ago when I was working on the radio in Luton I used to do a really mad late-night show on a Friday, which finished at ten in the evening. I would book a hotel room and stay over as I had to do an early-morning show on the Saturday. As a result the team and I would go for a few jars after the show. But that's the point – it was only a few jars, because the local across the road had to shut at eleven due to the ridiculously outdated and draconian drink laws of the time.

We were then left with the choice of relocating to a nightclub or a so-called fun pub, which had an extension because they had a disco or entertainment. Of course this was a ludicrous situation where decent drinkers were effectively barred from drinking whereas the youngsters were free to drink, vomit and fight at will.

Therefore I welcomed the relaxation of licensing and I truly believe that with time we will all develop a more mature attitude to drinking.

I actually buy into the idea that we can become more like our European cousins. I know our climate doesn't lend itself to café or pavement culture but I think over time our attitude to drinking will change.

Years ago Lisa and I visited an old friend from Coventry who had moved to Utrecht in the Netherlands. As per usual I was clock watching and necking back the beers when he said, 'Gaunty, you're drinking on Coventry time, slow down and do it the Dutch way.' He was right: there was no rush, no enforced rigid chucking-out time and a much more civilised attitude to drink.

It was a far cry from when I was a lad and the ten-to-eleven rush to the bar before last orders which led to us all downing three or four pints and a short or two quicker than Druggie Dwain Chambers knocked back the anabolic steroids. This of course led us inevitably to the taxi or late bus queue in the Burges in Coventry city centre and then to getting involved in the Friday night fracas outside the chippy or takeaways. A scene which I am sure would have been repeated the length and breadth of this 'septic isle'.

When I was running my nightclub I learned a couple of valuable lessons about drink, which the headline punch-drunk writers of Fleet Street could well learn from too. The more relaxed the atmosphere, preferably with live entertainment, the more beer you sold but the less trouble you had. Relaxation of stupid dress codes – 'sorry, lads, no trainers or football shirts!' – meant you actually encouraged a nicer, more responsible, albeit scruffy crowd. But when you're lying on the ground getting a kick in, does it really concern you if the lad is in torn jeans or a cheap 'smart suit' from Man at C&A! Finally, staggered opening and closing times actually reduced pressure outside clubs and takeaways and actually stopped trouble brewing. (Sorry about the pun!)

So that's why we needed, and have now got, more liberal licensing laws but we need tougher action on the yobs, the licencees and the braindead who want to kick off.

How about coppers getting out of their cars and patrolling our city centres and instead of videoing the yobbos fighting actually 'break a few skulls' and get them off the street? If a yob was arrested and put before the courts before the puke of the chilli sauce from last night's kebab had actually dried on his Fred Perry shirt, then maybe, just maybe, they would think again about fighting, urinating or shouting in the street.

If the courts then sentenced them to a minimum of seven days' hard labour on real community sentence programmes like picking up litter or cleaning up graffiti in chain-gang style then maybe, just maybe, the streets would be safer for the majority. Justice needs to be swift and hard and effective. We've tried the softly-softly approach and it has failed miserably so now it's time for swift affirmative action.

We also don't need any more new laws around drink. We just need to enforce the ones we have already got. If someone is holding a licence and running a pub in an incorrect manner, serving drunks or underage drinkers, then their licence needs to be revoked. However it is a fact, and a disgraceful one too, that in the past three years since Labour introduced so-called new draconian licensing measures not one single licensee has lost his licence for serving underage drinkers.

One of the major problems is that the lawmakers and politicians have never held a licence themselves so they don't understand the problem. But I have run loads of bars and clubs and I know that the answer lies in swift punishment and affirmative action.

Outside of pubs let's see corner shops and off licences absolutely caned if they sell to underage drinkers, but there is no need to raise the tax on drink – we already pay the highest rate of duty on alcohol in the western world.

When you visit Spain or Cyprus you see young people drinking but there is nowhere near the same level of violence or drunken behaviour because they know that the coppers will not hesitate in coming down hard, probably on their skulls with a baton, if they step out of line. On the continent there also seems to be a healthier respect for drinking because they are more family orientated and I can't be the only one to have noticed whole families drinking and eating together.

It seems ludicrous to me that the decent silent majority are treated as kids when it comes to drink whereas the mindless drunken morons are treated with kid gloves, and this has to change – and change fast.

14

Want to know about respect?
Ask Mrs Morgan

I was busy signing copies of my first book in a bookshop in Coventry when I was suddenly disturbed by a voice that I hadn't heard in thirty years but that was instantly recognisable.

'You don't remember me, do you, Jonathan?'

I looked up from the copy of my book that I was signing to be confronted by my yobbish past.

The voice belonged to Mrs Morgan, a neighbour from over thirty-five years ago, who proceeded to tell the assembled fans in the queue that she had told me off in no uncertain terms when I was a lad for using the F word on the bus.

I was embarrassed and remembered the incident as if it were only yesterday but the most important part of her tale was still to come when she turned to the queue and said, 'Of course, that was in the days when you could tell other people's kids off.'

And in that one single simple sentence Mrs Morgan summed up all that has gone wrong in British society and illustrates how we have gone from Great Britain to Rubbish Britain.

I was brought up in a working-class area of Coventry where everyone knew everyone and looked out for each other. I guess along with the local vicar's family we were the centre of this community because my dad and his neighbours were the local beat bobbies. However these were the days when there was discipline and respect instilled into kids at home, backed up by school and church, and reinforced by neighbours who had a pride in their area and community.

As a result in those days we didn't have children arriving at school not being able to recite the basic nursery rhymes and even know how to hold a knife and fork or in possession of the basic manners of please and thank you. But now it doesn't seem a week goes by without another survey that tells us that children don't have any manners or that some new wacky educational or parenting initiative is announced by the Government to combat this.

When all we really need is a simple return to basics. It seems to me that we have forgotten the basics of parenting and parental responsibility that clearly we possessed in the Sixties.

In my opinion family is and has to be the bedrock of any society. If I promise to bring up my children correctly and teach them manners and respect and my neighbours do the same and you do too, then surely we have the basis for creating a more decent and stable society. Back in the Sixties, as Mrs Morgan said at that book signing, you could tell off other people's kids and their parents would listen to and believe the other adult. I know for a fact that when she told me off all those years ago, I was petrified that she would then tell my dad and all hell would break out. I didn't answer her back. I apologised and was both humiliated and scared. Not telling your mum and dad that you had got the cane at school because if you did then it would only result in another smack off the old man may have been a cliché but was nonetheless true.

I'm not suggesting a return to the systematic beating of children or of course any form of child abuse, but we have lost something in our rush to call children young people and treat them as mini adults. The pendulum has clearly swung too far to the liberal left and children, families and indeed society in general are being damaged.

Lisa's mum has been a godsend in helping us to bring up our two and guiding us along the way as we have learned how to be parents. The most important lesson she taught us both was that children have to be set clearly defined boundaries. They have to know the limits they can push you to and the rules of the house. That's why I always say our house is not a workers' co-operative but a clear social hierarchy with Lisa and me at the top. That old cliché of my dad's comes to mind, which no doubt your old man trotted out as well, 'You can have a say in this house when you bring a bloody wage in!'

Hard but true, isn't it? Of course kids will test you, it's part of growing up and becoming an adult to push the boundaries, but should they cross the line, they do need to know the consequences. That's why the single most important word in any parent's vocabulary must be 'No'. But how many kids do you see of all social classes who clearly haven't been shown this? The ones who have had the privilege of being brought up by the electronic babysitter, the TV, rather than being read to in bed or eventually reading back to a parent. I also can't believe just how many so-called parents allow a TV let alone the Internet into their children's bedrooms and don't realise or are too afraid to accept the damage they are creating.

In my live one-man show people always ask why I end every radio programme by saying, 'If you've got kids, give them a kiss, give them a hug and don't forget to tell them that you love them.'

Well, the answer is simple, because giving a child love and security is the single most important thing any parent can give a child. I guess I know what it's like to be alone – completely alone – as I was in care as a child. I went from having a mum and a dad, especially a mum who took an absolute interest in everything I had done or was about to do, to suddenly having no one to whom I was special.

When I was in care, I was no one's child. I was just a child who needed caring for and there's a world of difference. That's why I say to blokes, if you are lying on the bed reading to your child, and it's the same story that you've read to them a million times and there's that moment when you are sure that they are falling asleep, so you skip a section of the story, and then they wake and say, 'Dad, you've missed out the bit about the elephant on the bus!' don't lie and say, 'No, I haven't,' just accept it and start the story again – and it doesn't matter if the football has just started or if you're knackered or stressed or want a drink. All of those things can wait, the football will be on again sometime but one thing's for certain: this moment with your child will never, ever happen again, so you have got to make the most of it.

I'm not trying to make out I'm the perfect father because I'm not, far from it. But I'm just trying to illustrate the point that you only get back out what you have put in to a child. Too many children in twenty-first-century Britain clearly haven't had enough of that input and that is why teachers too often have to try and pick up the pieces rather than getting on with the job of educating them.

Added to this is the simple plain fact that kids no longer have any sense of fear and as a result they have no sense of right and wrong. In fact many kids haven't been told the difference between right and wrong and without a shadow of a doubt too many children, especially boys, are being damaged irreparably by not having a male role model in their life.

This is why I am always wary of just attacking single mums for the state of our youth because, let's face it, it takes two to tango and too many blokes think their responsibility to their offspring ends as they roll off the woman and light up a fag. That's why the Government is correct in demanding from now on that the father's name should be on all birth certificates and these men should be hunted down and forced to pay for their children. If the CSA spent less time chasing and persecuting those dads who want to or are supporting their kids and more time pursuing these irresponsible breeders, Britain would be a greater country for it.

That said, we have to cut the umbilical cord between a young girl getting pregnant and being rewarded with a council flat. Mistakes happen, of course they do, but the responsibility for that mistake and definitely for any further 'mistakes' should rest with the extended family of the teenage slapper and not with society in general. I am sick and tired, and so is most of the country, with being expected to support the feral offspring of these irresponsible morons.

Of course I don't want a return to the bad old days of the Fifties and Sixties where girls who got pregnant out of marriage were shunned and in some extreme cases shunted out of sight and their kids forcibly removed and adopted. However, I do feel again that the pendulum has swung too far the other way and we have ended up with a 'do anything you wanna do' society where the decent silent majority are not expected to judge but still pay for the largely irresponsible lives and breeding of this underclass.

What hope do these kids have then if life begins like this for them, and if and when they enter the education system there are no clear boundaries and structure and expectations set down for them within school? Not only that, but how many incidents have we heard of and discussed on my radio show where a child has been told off by a teacher, only for the parent to march up to the school and at least shout the odds with the teacher if not physically or verbally abuse them? Again it's the cliché of butter wouldn't melt in little Johnny's mouth.

So in simple terms, compare and contrast my reaction to Mrs Morgan as an eleven-year-old in 1973 with the reaction you would get from an eleven-year-old 'Gaunty' today. He would at least argue the toss, perhaps flick a sign or at worst physically attack the adult.

Because many children haven't been set boundaries by their parents or parent they do not even know how they are meant to behave. If then the school system is so busy recognising all kinds of family and desperately not trying to be judgemental, the child is again left to his own devices and we end up with the chaos in the education system we have today where 50,000 children a day are playing truant and many are leaving school without being able to read and write.

That's why we need a return to real discipline in the classroom and that has to start with school uniform being compulsory in every single school. Teachers need to be addressed by their surnames and it wouldn't be a bad thing if, like at my comprehensive, children were expected to stand when a teacher enters a room and address them as Sir or Ma'am.

I also believe there needs to be a clear discipline structure and I am afraid to say to you liberals that does mean a return of the ultimate deterrent, the cane. I know the cane didn't and won't work for everyone. In fact there was one lad at my school who was constantly standing outside the headmaster's office waiting for the cane – he seemed to enjoy it and probably went on to be an MP! However, for the rest of us who were or could be easily led, it only took one of us to be caned for the rest of us to fall into line.

There's also a desperate need to bring back real streaming into schools and I would go even further and say that there is a need to return to selection at eleven. I speak as someone, by the way, who failed his Eleven Plus and unlike my elder brother, who went free of charge to the local grammar school, I went to a Church of England comprehensive. I was lucky, although I didn't feel so at the time, because this was a school run on grammar-school discipline principles and with a very firm sense of identity and an even firmer head-master.

The worst aspect of the comprehensive system is this leftie notion that we are all equally good at everything. Clearly we are not. There is a difference between equality and equality of opportunity and us all being the same and we need to recognise this. It is this misplaced and ill-thought-out social engineering that has led to the ridiculous position where Tony Blair had a vision of 50 per cent of all school kids going on to university. *Why?*

Meanwhile we opened the stopcock of immigration and let in thousands of Polish plumbers to fill a trade's craft gap. Can the Government not add 2 and 2 and get 4? Clearly not! The plain facts are that some people are academic and others are more practically gifted. Rather than trying to get everyone to go to 'uni' (God, I hate that word) and be faced with record numbers of university dropouts, how about recognising that we need skilled plumbers, sparks, mechanics and chippies and start encouraging more vocational training and work placements at the age of fourteen for those so minded?

However instead this Government has made a pledge to get most kids to stay on to the age of 18 as way of counteracting the 200,000 or so called NEETS. That's youths who are not in education, employment or training. These teenagers at present are left to their own devices, funded of course by our money in the form of handouts, to infest our estates in the daylight hours causing mayhem. The annual cost to the UK of so many NEETS is a mind-blowing £3.65 *billion*. Just stop for a moment and think how many teachers, nurses or coppers that would actually pay for if these kids were gainfully employed?

But forcing them to stay on at school is not the answer. The only result of such an ill-thought-out idea will be more kids in the school system that will disrupt those who do want to study.

Our education system should be and was the envy of the world. However, there is a drastic need for root-and-branch reform as evidenced by the ever-increasing number of parents who are voting with their wallets and sending their kids to private schools or with their feet and a little with their wallets and moving to areas where the better schools are situated.

This leads me to the conclusion: you either ban all private schools (clearly impossible in a democracy) and therefore remove all so-called parental choice and make every kid go to their local community school. Of course this will never happen as parental choice does only exist for those who can afford to pay for it, or con a priest that they've found God, or play the system like smart MPs including former PM Tony Blair whose children travelled halfway across London to be educated in what just happened to be one of the best schools in the country.

Alternatively you can just display the breathtaking cheek of Labour MP Diane Abbot and use the excuse that the state system fails black boys like her son and send him to private school and flash two fingers to your opponents and constituents.

I'll be straight with you, I've sent my two to private school and as a working-class comprehensive boy who didn't do too badly out of the comp or state system I sometimes wonder why. Until that is I visit the school and see and hear how well mannered the pupils are, realise my kids aren't sharing school textbooks or fighting over computers and that finally the headmistress hasn't had to fit a metal knife and gun detector next to the tuck shop. Joking aside, though, this is the tragedy of our education system: the education my children are getting should be available to all but it clearly isn't.

Now politicians of all parties are beginning to realise the jungle some of our schools have turned into and are suggesting radical initiatives like introducing cadet corps in all schools. Which actually isn't a bad idea but I would take it further and suggest that there is a real need for some leadership and tough male role models in schools and we have the perfect opportunity now to employ ex-squaddies or forces personnel to act as both mentors and role models for kids. Why not employ these people to instil discipline but also work on team sports and character-building programmes like outward-bound courses?

Of course a fundamental issue that has to be addressed is that one in five schools is also failing to get enough of its pupils five GCSE passes or more. That's why it's essential that the government stops meddling in schools and actually cedes control and budgets back to individual headmasters. These people must also have the right to expel troublesome pupils without fear of their being readmitted by some quango. Likewise referral centres for these 'troubled' children need to be expanded and reopened to deal with these kids.

We have tried the all-inclusive, cuddly, softly-softly approach and it has singularly failed. We need a return to decent solid discipline not only in schools but also in society in general.

But it would be too easy to pin all the blame on schools, teachers, councils and the Government. We as adults must take our share of the blame as well. We all need to become more like Mrs Morgan and be willing to tell off other people's kids without fear of retribution. Britain is so broken we can no longer afford to walk on by on the other side of the road. Of course we need to be helped in this by the police and the judiciary and whether it be a simple case of an adult telling some kids to calm down or the tragic cases of people like Gary Newlove or Kevin Johnson who lost their lives when they intervened, the law should be on the side of the adult and the presumption of guilt on the yobbo.

However the Mrs Morgans of this world won't intervene if they think that reprimanding a yobbo – like Jeremy Clarkson did in Milton Keynes a few months ago, or Gary Newlove did in front of his twelve-year-old daughter – could result in them ending up in court with a criminal record or worse on a mortuary slab. Instead these good decent people will walk on by and the decline in their communities will continue.

However, when the country is crying out for discipline from birth, Labour seem to be hoisting the white flag and continuing down the path to anarchy. Their latest decision to introduce the turkey-baster law, which will give equal rights to single women for IVF without the need of a father, is a clear example of this lunacy. Children need a mum and a dad, and that is the best way of both bringing up children and creating a better Britain. Obviously couples do break up and some single parents and women who become lesbians after having kids can bring them up as well as the traditional couple, but to actually contemplate bringing new children into the world without a dad is social lunacy.

Children are not a commodity, a material good or vanity purchase. They are a gift and as well as needing hugs, kisses and love they need guidance, discipline and role models and security to develop into mature adults.

Politicians would be better off listening to Mrs Morgan than the do-gooders and human-rights loonies that have allowed our society to descend into the gutter.

15

Great British icons under attack

There are certain iconic symbols that shout 'You are in Britain, Great Britain' and by God we Brits should be doing everything we humanly can to preserve them.

The red telephone box

In an age of every home having a phone and 98 per cent of Brits owning a mobile, the iconic red box is clearly under threat. Without doubt the red telephone box, first designed by Giles Gilbert Scott in the 1920s, is one of the most instantly recognisable symbols of Britain.

I can still remember as a kid growing up in Coventry and the whole family being marched over the road en masse to ring Nana or an auntie in Hull. Standing outside in all weather waiting for our turn to cram inside and tell her 'Yes we are behaving ourselves and yes the jumper you knitted last Christmas nearly fits now, as you said Nana I've grown into it.' The pips going, Dad groping for another coin, while neighbours tapped on the glass for us all to hurry up and finish. Happy days!

The death knell for the red box began with the introduction of those horrible steel and plastic mini bus shelters that started to appear in the Nineties but the spread of the use of mobiles has obviously hastened their decline.

Tom Jones has one in his garden in LA and I've been in several boozers and nightclubs where they have them in the foyer but surely we need to make sure that at least some of these absolute British design classics are kept *in situ* in tourist locations.

The red Routemaster bus

The Routemaster bus, which by the way was built in my home town of Coventry, first appeared in London in the Fifties and although the red buses are true London icons these buses were also used right across the country. I can still fondly remember jumping on to the number 16 from Radford in Coventry and trying to hop off again before the clippie had chance to charge me.

Seriously though, I believe the phasing out of the much-loved Routemaster in London by former mayor Ken Livingstone was one of his greatest mistakes. The Routemaster along with the black cab and the Beefeaters *are* London. I know there were concerns about disabled access but the nondescript self-destruct bendy buses are not right for modern London either.

Another important aspect of the Routemaster was the presence of a conductor, who I believe gave added security to travelling by bus. I am convinced that the reintroduction of clippies would not only cut down on fare dodging but would also act as a visual deterrent to graffiti and general vandalism.

In inner-city London's crowded streets the bendy buses are a traffic hazard and that's before the air-conditioning fails or they decided to self-ignite. Whereas the Routemaster, which you could hop on and off, were ideal for the centre of town.

It's an absolute certainty that the New Mayor Boris could guarantee himself re-election if he got the Routemasters or a modern equivalent back on the road.

The black cab

Obviously many of my listeners are cabbies and of course this iconic British vehicle is built in my home town of Coventry but even so there is no disputing that the black cab and the traditional cabbie is under threat from private hire vehicles, legislation and political correctness.

I love jumping into a cab in London and I have never understood celebs or comics who moan about cabbies talking to them on the journey. If you don't want conversation and instead value ignorance get on a bus or a tube.

Former mayor Ken Livingstone, along with scrapping Routemaster, seemed to have a pathological hatred for the men who drive cabs. He hardly ever consulted the cab trade on the real transport issues facing London and then he attacked them again by saying there were not enough women and ethnic-minority drivers in the trade.

Citizen Ken's (and his cronies at the London Development Agency) solution to this 'problem' was to set up knowledge schools to encourage these poor under-represented groups to become cabbies. These 'schools' provided free helmets, mopeds, childcare and even fuel to help them in their ambition and caring Ken even offered extra tuition including English lessons to help them through the process.

Meanwhile fat white blokes from Essex still had to plant their lardy arses on scooters, pay their own way and do it in the traditional manner. And they call that equality.

Forget equality though. Surely this will lead to a dumbing down of the trade and clearly speaking English has to be a pre-requisite for the job. If the new Mayor doesn't do a swift handbrake turn on this politically correct lunacy then we will end up with a cab trade as useless as New York's.

The Sunday roast

I know it sounds stupid but I actually think that the traditional Sunday roast, which of course has to mean rare rib of beef, Yorkshire pudding and all the trimmings, is seriously under threat.

Knocked by health warnings on the danger of red meat in the diet through to the real and imagined health scares of mad cow disease and CJD roast dinners, the traditional British butcher has been taking a hammering for the past decade.

But can there be anything better than sitting down at a table groaning under the weight of a huge lump of meat, a mountain of roasties and Yorkshire puddings the size of Ben Nevis? Answer – no.

However, more and more families are no longer carrying out this ritual on a Sunday and certainly not during the week. A combination of our so-called busy lives and a decline in teaching girls how to cook has led to a situation where the traditional sound of church bells ringing on a Sunday has almost been replaced by the ping of millions of microwaves.

I'm only half joking. My girls do cooking at school but now it's called food technology and instead of learning how to cook the proverbial cheese scones or how to cook meat, they have to learn how to design a hamburger box, food hygiene or are indoctrinated in the perils of eating the wrong kinds of food. All-important, I am sure, but wouldn't it be good if we actually taught our young people to cook?

Not only that but I'm a firm believer that a family that eats together sticks together. Meals should be a time for reflection and conversation and the base camp where manners are taught. Is it any wonder that kids are turning up at primary school without the ability to use a knife and fork or know the basics of manners, like not eating with your mouth open, asking permission to leave the table and the simple please and thank-yous that make us civilised?

I also believe that one of the reasons some children are such faddy eaters is because they haven't been involved in the preparation and cooking of a family meal. If you get your kids to help prepare the food – and at the risk of sounding all New Labour they actually become stakeholders in the meal – they are much more likely to eat what's put in front of them.

OK, reluctantly I will take on board that not every family including my own can sit down at the table and eat together every night of the week, but surely come a Sunday they can? It's time to reinstate the traditional Sunday roast if we ever want to make Britain great again.

The traditional butcher

Following on from the roast, of course, is the necessity to preserve the traditional British butcher's shop.

In 2000 there were 9,081 in Britain, but by 2007 this had dropped to 7,186 – with 23 butchers closing every month according to the *Meat Trades Journal*. Industry leaders say the decline has been caused by the march of the supermarkets, by cheap foreign imports, increased overheads, and changes in shopping habits, but we need to reverse this trend.

I am a great believer in the idea that kids need to know from an early age where meat comes from and also to realise that it doesn't miraculously appear wrapped in plastic in a supermarket fridge.

I wrote a glowing piece in the *Sun* about Gordon Ramsay when he decided to rear turkeys for Christmas in his garden and let his children help him with the full knowledge that come Christmas Day they would be eating what they had raised from chicks. To my way of thinking this was an excellent life lesson for his kids.

Now I am not suggesting that we all need to model ourselves on Felicity Kendal and Richard Briers in *The Good Life* but surely we must let our kids realise where meat comes from.

I love the traditional butcher where you can ask for advice on what cuts to buy and how to prepare and cook them. I love looking at the various joints displayed in the fridge and I actually enjoy watching the skill and artistry of my butcher as he bones out a carcass.

I go to a great family butcher in Coventry called John Taylor & Son. Here the skills of butchery have been handed down through the generations and just how good Taylor's meat is can be demonstrated by the queue around the block on a Saturday morning. I also love the fact that John has the certificates of the beasts that he is selling displayed on the wall behind the fridges and, as with most butchers, John will sell you any quantity, however big or small, that you require. What money can't buy though is that cheery hello and the personal service that you get when you enter the shop.

I also love the fact that when you buy sausages, meat pies or bacon from a traditional butcher there will be subtle differences in taste, depending on who has made them. Each has a regional twist so that you never get the bland homogenous taste of supermarket produce.

Yes it might cost a few pennies more, but surely it's worth the expense to keep your shopping choice unique and varied? Support your local butcher. And not just your butcher but all the other truly local and unique shops in your community, otherwise we are going to end up with identikit high streets the length and breadth of the country that may give us choice but no real variety or surprise. I like my coffee and I have been known to eat a burger but I don't know about you, I don't want a high street full of Starbucks and McDonalds. For my money you can't beat the unique smell of a traditional cobblers as you enter or a quirky gift or toy shop where you might find that toy that you loved as a kid but which wouldn't be given shelf space in one of those out-of-town toy sheds.

It was Napoleon who said we were a nation of shopkeepers and I don't see anything wrong with that. One thing's for sure – it's preferable to becoming a nation of franchisees.

16

The great British motorist – and how green has become the new red

Ford may have invented the modern motor car but it was Britain and Brits who styled the Jaguar, the Roller, the Mini and dreamed up the Aston Martin. Mr Ford gave you it in any colour as long as it was black, but British engineering gave the motoring world flair, culture, design classics and a motoring heritage that most countries would die for. Then there are the British motoring heroes from Stirling Moss through Jackie Stewart and Roger Clarke to Colin Macrae and now Lewis Hamilton. And only Britain could create a programme like *Top Gear* where three petrol heads can command an audience of millions (350 million in fact – it's one of our most successful TV exports and also one of the most popular TV shows anywhere in the world). Us Brits are proud of our motoring history and love our motors.

So that's why for a nation whose economic strength is largely built on our heavy industrial heritage and the motor industry in particular, I find it amazing the way the British motorist is treated by politicians of all parties.

Instead of being seen as a potential electoral force motorists are treated as cash cows and pariahs by the self-serving pigs of Westminster.

However, if a political party actually became the motorists ally they would be bound to win the next election, but instead they just continue to burden us with ever-increasing taxes and regulation which we have plenty of time to think about when we are stuck in traffic jams in gridlocked Britain.

According to the AA there are 27 *million* motorists in the UK who pay on average £1,811 a year in fuel duty, car tax and VAT on fuel to the taxman. This is an increase of £652 since Labour came to power ten years ago. In simple petrol terms this means at least 64 pence in every pound goes straight into the Chancellor's pocket. It gets worse because if the Government get away with raising car taxes and then re-imposes the 2 pence a litre rise in petrol duty then the total amount paid by the British motorists could top £48 *billion* this year!

So what do we get for this largest example of highway robbery since Dick Turpin hung up his mask? Not much according to the AA as only £8 billion of the £48 billion we pay actually comes back to the roads. That's less than 20 per cent! No wonder we are driving on surfaces with more potholes than downtown Baghdad and that roads like the M25 are swiftly being turned into Europe's largest car park even out of rush hour.

It's hard to argue with the President of the AA, Edmund King, who says that it

> appears the car is seen and taxed as a luxury rather than a necessity. Motorists are now taxed at a higher rate than champagne drinkers but for the vast majority of people driving is an absolute necessity. The high taxes are now affecting people's lives and families are having to cut back on other areas of spending to pay for their cars.

I guess we wouldn't mind too much if the trains and public transport infrastructure were in place to take the strain, but let's face it, they are in a pretty miserable state themselves. Why can't these moronic ministers see that you can't tax the motorists out of a car and on to public transport if the system isn't up to scratch?

Politicians, who are largely based in London, don't understand that the majority of us haven't got any choice but to use our cars; we haven't got chauffeur-driven cars or even the tube or late night buses to transport us to and from our workplaces.

I commute into London every day from Milton Keynes and I'll be honest the service is pretty reliable, but to guarantee a seat –

and in my opinion therefore my safety – I am forced effectively to buy a first-class season ticket. Either that or be transported in conditions that loopy animal-rights protestors would be bombing scientists' homes for if animals were forced to travel like that. I also live in a rural environment where the bus service, along with the police and every other public service, is woefully inadequate. For my neighbours and myself the car is definitely a necessity – for some even a lifesaver – and without a shadow of a doubt never a luxury.

However, even if you live in the city, why is it such a sin to want to drive? The car was and is the liberator of the working class. It allowed, for the first time in the early Sixties, ordinary working-class people to get into the car and get out and about without the necessity of having Mussolini's standard of understanding of a rail timetable. Just as cheap budget airlines are now opening up major European cities to families that would have been previously out of reach for ordinary working-class people, the car fulfilled the same role and still does.

That's why Labour's new and retrospective taxes on so-called 'gas guzzlers' is so unfair on the decent silent majority of this country who haven't got luxury cars but people-carriers and 4 × 4s which they use to transport the whole family. It's even unfair on those of us who choose, or have the economic wherewithal to choose, to buy a luxury car with an engine bigger than the size of a sewing machine. Surely the bigger the car the more VAT you have paid when you bought it, the more duty you pay on the extra fuel you buy and, of course, Gordon Brown screws us for more road tax.

Clearly the unrepresentative greens have seized too much of the agenda and for those of us with more important and urgent issues to worry about, such as immigration, law and order, and knife and gun crime, they are dictating social and taxation policy. That's why I believe that green has become the new red. It's just a new way of screwing more and more money out of us who are working and already contributing to British society. If you don't believe me let's have another fact: did you know that the environmental costs associated with motoring are less than £6 billion a year? So again, if you deduct that £6 billion from the £48 billion we are all paying you can still see there is a massive imbalance and that motorists are clearly paying through the nose for other public spending initiatives that have nothing to do with motoring or motorists.

I might not even mind this rip-off if I actually thought that green issues were as high up on the political agenda of most ordinary Brits as pompous politicians and of course the Biased Broadcasting Corporation would have us believe. But green issues are clearly not our biggest concern because if they were we would have more of the lentil-eating, yoghurt-knitting 2CV drivers in Parliament, getting their noses into the no doubt organic trough.

The reality of course is that for the majority of us feeding the kids, keeping a roof over our heads and protecting both our borders and our loved ones are of much more importance than whether or not a polar bear is having to take swimming lessons or not.

The political elite are so far removed from the real-life experience of the rest of us and they must start listening to motorists and our concerns. Instead of tinkering at the edges of our transport problems with congestion charges, road pricing or the ridiculous idea of using the hard shoulder, they need to fund a massive road-building programme.

I'm not talking about concreting over large tracts of Britain. I agree with Edmund King who made the very sensible point on my radio show that when you fly into the country and look down, it's a patchwork of fields you see, not an LA sprawl. So let's get real.

Government needs to stop listening to the unrepresentative voices and protests of the pompous pious prats of the so-called eco warriors and road-building protestors like Swampy and his ilk. As a side issue, did you hear Swampy passed away? He had a heart attack but refused a bypass!

Seriously, the point is we have a planning system that is thorough and once the democratic process has been followed and permission granted for a bypass or a new road the first noise we should hear after any bleats from unelected protestors should be the sound of the fire hydrants being switched on and then the sight of the soap dodgers getting a well-deserved wash-down.

Why do we tolerate these berks and why should we the taxpayers be forced to pay for their clearly undemocratic actions and protests? Just like that scruffy dole-scrounging Herbert, Brian Haw on Parliament Green, we should take the French attitude and wash the dreadlocked smelly gits off the highways and byways of Britain. What do these people contribute to the greatness of Britain? Absolutely nothing and it's about time if we are getting tough on the unemployed that the Government start with their own backyard, or should I say frontyard, and Iraq war demonstrator Haw. How the hell can he be available for work if he's sitting outside a tent rolling up fags and shouting through a loudhailer about our boys murdering innocent civilians in Iraq every day?

My point is that it appears that in twenty-first-century Britain it is these demonstrators who not only get an inordinate amount of publicity but also too much of our hard-earned taxes to make their pathetic sixth-form points whereas the decent silent majority and their wishes are largely ignored.

Then again, perhaps we only have ourselves to blame because we have allowed the Government and local councils and the coppers to treat us like sponges that can be squeezed again and again until every last penny is extracted. And what do we do? Apart from a one-day fuel strike and a couple of lorry drivers putting down their Yorkies and raising their foot off the accelerator to block the motorway, sweet FA is the answer. In France they would be burning sheep or at least fishing boats. In Spain they blockaded the supermarket warehouses but in Britain we pick up the phone, moan to Gaunty and his imitators and do sod all.

This has to change. It is essential now that we the British motorist stand up and be counted and demand fair and equitable treatment. We need a massive road-building initiative and we need it now. We need to slash speed limits to 20mph outside schools but lift them on motorways altogether. There should not be an increase in either fuel duty or road tax but a decrease and the car and the drivers of Great Britain should be respected rather than treated as pariahs.

17

Stand up and be accountable: the battle for the Beeb

The BBC is a great British institution and I never want to see it scrapped but I do want the Bloated Broadcasting Corporation cut down to size.

In the multi-platform age it is becoming increasingly difficult to justify funding this British Leyland of broadcasting by means of a punitive poll tax which one has to pay or face jail.

In essence the BBC should be only providing services and programmes that the market can't or won't produce. They have no right to infest every sector of broadcasting with their leftie over-funded propaganda.

In an age when it is perfectly possible to watch the news, be entertained, follow the sport and surf the Net without ever using the state monopoly's services why on earth should we all still be forced to pay for this dinosaur?

I am not calling for the BBC to be completely privatised, I'm not even calling for the licence fee to be scrapped. I just want the BBC to be dragged kicking and spitting if necessary into the real world and I want it to be forced to both earn and justify its existence.

When I worked for the BBC I must admit, next to saying you drove a Jaguar, it was a sure-fire way of impressing people in the States. Of course the BBC is held in high esteem around the globe and it has obviously produced some brilliant radio and TV but unfortunately at home its presence in all media is far too dominant. As a state broadcaster it has tremendous privileges and rights but it should also have enormous responsibilities to the very people who are forced to pay for it.

Furthermore, after being found guilty of ripping off and conning children and charities, the only phone vote the BBC should now be conducting is one that asks if the Corporation can still be funded by a compulsory poll tax. A few sackings should not enable the Beeb to escape the more serious discussion of its future.

I have long argued that Radio 1 and Radio 2 should be immediately sold to the highest bidder. The Corporation's argument that both stations bring on new talent or champion minority causes can be easily satisfied by opening up sections of the licence fee for both the BBC and private companies to bid for to put on these type of shows.

However I don't see how or why I should have to pay the enormous salaries of Jonathan Ross (£18 million over three years) or even 630 grand a year for that fat tub of humourless lard, Chris Moyles, to play pop songs and make masturbation jokes as my wife drives my kids to school. If these two are soooooo incredibly talented and popular I am sure the market will provide them with their huge salaries and the licence feepayer can see their money spent on other things.

When it comes to BBC Five Dead, why should they be allowed to use *your* money to bid for Premiership football rights and effectively outbid commercial stations and then use the football to build their brand?

Likewise the BBC has no role to play in the Internet. It is an absolute disgrace the way they have been allowed to use licence fee-payers' money to dominate this new media and undoubtedly they have used their state-funded monopoly and brand positioning to push out smaller operators.

As for all those BBC digital channels that no one watches or listens to, they should be scrapped.

Can you give me one good reason why popular programmes such as *EastEnders*, *Strictly Come Dancing* and the plethora of programmes that are sorting out Andrew Lloyd Webber's pension pot can't be sponsored in the same way as *Coronation Street* is by Cadbury's? I am not suggesting advertising interrupting the shows, but surely they could flog credits at the beginning and the end. Again, revenue attracted in this manner would free up cash.

All of this money saved could then be used to fund BBC core activities that will not be provided by the private sector, such as speech-based local radio, but even here financial excesses must be reined in.

I will give you a classic example. My radio career started in my home town of Coventry and without the guidance of the station manager Andy Wright I wouldn't be where I am today and I wouldn't have won my three Sonys – which of course I don't like to talk about!

However the BBC in their wisdom decided to merge Coventry with Birmingham. Obviously some over-educated jerk in London looked over the rim of their skinny latte and saw that the two cities were close to each other and made the classic metropolitan mistake of assuming that the people must be similar.

Wrong!

It took them ten long years to realise their mistake and they decided to spend another three million pounds of your cash on building new studios in Coventry and employing new staff, including yours truly.

Now as a licence feepayer I am sure that you will be delighted to know that the project came in £9,000 under budget.

However you might not be so delighted by this email that the senior management sent out to all staff in 2005 asking for their views on how to spend *your money*.

```
-----Original Message-----
To: Cov & Warks All
Subject: Staff money

Hi

Here is the shortlist for spending our £9,000 on.
Thanks to everyone for some great ideas. As an earlier
email made clear some of the plans for lavish Christ-
mas parties and the like aren't possible because we
have been told we can't spend the money that way.
However we have been able to incorporate most of the
other ideas.

We will now get cracking on spending the money. Until
we have placed the orders, we can't be sure how much
```

everything will cost so we'll report back later once
we know.

Artwork
2 infrared patio heaters
Play equipment – table football, darts, etc.
Health treatments, experts to come for one day a month
to provide a range of treatments such as Indian head
massage.
Fresh Fruit daily
Contribution to the Project party.
Radios to allow everyone to listen to output at his or
her desks
Sky TV
****
Any comments to me ASAP
Cheers

*Try the new radio station everyone is talking about: BBC
Coventry and Warwickshire on 94.8, 103.7 and 104 FM.*

You will notice of course that it doesn't cross their minds to spend it
on programmes or, God forbid, give it back to the licence payers.

No, this kind of publicly funded, not in the real world, kind of
thinking is just so typical of the BBC and must be stamped out. There
needs to be a sea change within the Corporation and a realisation that
the days of corporate profligacy are well and truly over. If this is
happening in just one local radio station, imagine what else is going
on higher up the food chain?

Of course the BBC is something we Brits should all be proud of
but as we pay for it the Corporation needs to be forced to cut down
on its excesses.

The licence fee should also be available, as the Tories are now
proposing, for other media companies to apply for to produce public
service broadcasting. I found it deeply ironic that while the Beeb was
being called the Baghdad Broadcasting Corporation for its biased
reporting on the Iraq campaign, it was left to Sky to broadcast a show
with Ross Kemp to illustrate just what a great job our boys are doing
in Afghanistan. Surely this is exactly the kind of programme that
should have been funded by a licence fee available to all?

Talking of which, the soft leftie bias of the BBC has also got to stop and the state broadcaster should realise that one season of programmes on the majority culture, i.e. the white season, is not enough to cover all the bases of political correctness.

I think the BBC is rightly seen as a great symbol of all that is great in Britain but it has to be cut down to size, more accountable to the British Public who are forced to pay for it and more supportive of the British way of life. It should reflect our shared values not be an organ of propaganda for those who would seek to destroy our way of life or change it without even consulting us.

18

'Evenin' all': whatever happened to the great British bobby?

Despite being led by politically correct clowns the British police force is still the best in the world.

Did you notice my ever so politically correct crime there? Yes, I actually called the police a force and not a service! Charlie Caroli of the constabulary, Sir Ian Blair, and the rest of the politically correct, over-educated, wet behind the ears, top coppers will be after me. But that's the basic problem: the police should not be a service but a force, a force to be reckoned with.

My old man was a copper in Coventry for thirty years and he was definitely of the old school. In fact I joke in my one-man show that he was so old-fashioned he made DCI Gene Hunt from *Life on Mars* look like Brian, *let them smoke weed*, Paddick. But the truth is of course that he was old-style. He just wanted to nick bad 'uns rather than take diversity courses or understand why little Johnny was a toe-rag and as he used to say, at least in those days, 'We actually got people sent down.'

As a kid I lived in a police house right in the heart of the community and that made my dad, my mum and the rest of the family an integral part of that community. Dad and our neighbours in the other three police houses would sort out trouble when it flared in the chippie or the pub and our mums would act almost like vicars' wives or counsellors to other women in the neighbourhood.

The cliché of the clip around the ear was a cliché because it was true but it meant that people knew my dad and clearly understood what would happen if they stepped out of line. There was respect but there was also fear and we need a bit more of that today. You can't police the streets from a Panda car and my old man would swear that the streets became more dangerous once coppers like him were taken off the beat and the old police boxes were demolished.

My dad didn't want to understand or know why a criminal committed a crime, he wasn't interested, it wasn't his job; all he wanted to do was nick them and get them off the street. That's what most of us want, isn't it? Real coppers who will police. That's why the growth of 'Plastic Plods' is so dangerous and why the Police Federation are right to be concerned about the number of real coppers being slashed and replaced by these community officers who have no more powers of arrest than you and me. The kind of health and safety experts who stand by and let kids drown rather than risk their own necks to save them.

What we need is real coppers working the same area day in day out for year after year. Britain was a safer, friendlier, less crime-ridden and, yes, greater country back when my dad and his sort were on the streets and if we ever want to put the great back into Britain we need a return to some of these values and practices.

I know there can't and there shouldn't be a complete return to the *Dixon of Dock Green* Sixties with coppers in police houses living on the breadline, but we do need our police officers to come from and be part of the community they serve. That's why I support the recruitment of ethnic minorities and even gays into the police, but I am afraid the pendulum has swung too far and we now have too many stories of white heterosexuals being turned down purely on the grounds of their colour or sexuality. This is political correctness gone mad.

I knew a young white lad who was over six feet tall with a solid working-class background of a loving family. He had never been in trouble with the law. He had excellent qualifications, including a degree in criminology, and although he got accepted as a 'Plastic Plod' he was told that there were no places in the real 'service' and that he should apply again the following year. I can still remember my old man laughing his nuts off when he told the youngster, 'Eh lad, you should have told them you were a shirt-lifter and you would have been straight in.'

Not very politically correct, I know, but I *did* tell you that Dad was more Gene Hunt than Ian Blair! However, despite the old man's language I can't help but wonder if he had told them that he was gay then would he have been straight through the door and been measured up for the uniform and long baton before *The Sweeney*'s Jack Regan could shout, 'Get your trousers on! You're nicked!'.

This young lad a few months earlier had also asked Dad for advice about joining up and I'll never forget the cynical old bastard's reply: 'I wouldn't bother son!' Those four words are the most damning indictment of how we are losing the war on crime and we the British public are being let down by the politically correct buffoons who infest Parliament, the criminal justice system and the police force. If my dad had lost confidence and support for the police, what hope is there for the rest of us?

Of course one of the biggest strengths of the British bobby is that they do police by consent, but if the relationship between the copper and the public continues to deteriorate then this consent will disappear and we will have no choice but to arm them. Don't believe me? Well, how come the Police Federation is already calling for all their members to be issued with Tasers?

The simple fact is that too many people's experience of coppers or the law is when they are fined for speeding or when the civilian at the end of a line says that the police will not be coming out to investigate the theft of your car radio or your burglary and just hand you an insurance number instead. This dereliction of duty leads to a breakdown in trust between the decent silent majority and those who are paid to protect them.

But I don't blame the rank and file. I know just how dedicated these men and women are and every year I am privileged to be a guest at the Police Bravery Awards where the Police Federation and the *Sun* recognise the incredible work and dangers our boys and girls do and face every single day. The event has so many video re-enactments of real crimes and acts of bravery by police officers that it is almost unfair to single out any but last year I was extremely moved and thankful for the story of the two coppers who actually defused the car bomb that had been towed to Park Lane. When you speak to the winners of these awards later over a pint they are so unassuming and modest about their bravery it is actually quite humbling to be in their company.

So it's not the coppers on the beat that are the problem. They are just like my dad – they just want to police – and so I put the blame fairly and squarely on the shoulders of politically correct prats like Ian Blair and his other Oxford University chums. These are the berks who direct operations and set priorities and it is these twerps who need to be removed or at least we should be able to vote for the kind of senior officer we want and the kind of policing that your city requires. Before anyone shouts out that this will politicise the police just hang on a minute, the police force – sorry, service – is already politicised and infested with like-minded liberals.

Forget *Life on Mars*, what planet is politically correct Ian Blair from? He acts like an inverted racist, and couldn't run a bath let alone the police. When he was at Oxford he wanted to be an actor but wasn't up to the grade so a careers teacher suggested the police. His thespian tendencies don't surprise me, as he seems strangely drawn to the media like a moth to a light.

On 7 July 2005 – 7/7 – despite the advice of his press and PR team, his first instinct was to get on TV and reassure us that he was firmly in control. This was a bit ironic because only a few days earlier he had downgraded the terrorist threat. To be fair to him he didn't do a bad job and the officers under him did a sterling job in the days that followed, but the real Ian Blair re-emerged when he appeared for his regular phone-in session on my radio show just days after the attack.

His first comment to me before we went on air was along the lines of 'I trust you're not going to put all the racist nutters on having a go at Muslims.' He obviously expected me to be in his politically correct camp but I hold the view that a phone-in is a phone-in and people, especially Londoners who had been bombed in their own city, had a right to ask their top cop whatever question they liked regardless of his political sensitivities.

It was interesting to compare him with his predecessor Sir John Stevens. With him there was no messing about: he took all questions and criticisms and answered them straight on. By the same token if someone rang in and Sir John felt their criticism was out of order he gave them what for in no uncertain terms. My listeners and I loved that and he came over as a real copper's copper. He was hard, straight-talking and inspired confidence.

Meanwhile Blair, just like his namesake Tony, would never answer with one word or sentence when there was an opportunity to prevaricate, spin and prove his PC credentials. The actor in him loves to dress up: how many more pictures do we need to see of him barefooted, with a turban on his head or a garland round his neck to prove he's connecting with the multicultural commuuuuuuuuuuuu-uuuunity of London?

Evidently he has two prints made by Nelson Mandela in his Spartan and minimalist office and a Sikh sword and Jewish prayer book in his display cabinet. I'm surprised that he hasn't followed the lead of his council chums and renamed Scotland Yard, Mandela Yard.

According to the *Guardian*, which no doubt he reads every day, Blair looks for tips, comparisons and ideas on how to run the Met from Mark Thompson and the BBC. God help us! Blair says that his old friend Thompson faces similar problems and they regularly compare notes. He describes both organisations as being 'iconic'. Chronic more like!

But I can see some similarities; they both get overpaid for running fat bloated organisations completely engulfed by political correctness, rammed full of middle managers who are hated and resented by the workers at the coalface and increasingly both organisations are irrelevant and out of touch with the people who pay their wages.

Unfortunately Ian Blair isn't alone and as far as I am concerned one of the most dangerous organisations in Britain is ACPO – the Association of Chief Police Officers. It is this collection of politically correct prats that are largely responsible for turning the British Police *Force* into a service and a laughing stock to boot. These self-publicists are always getting themselves into the news with their half-baked sociological ideas on crime rather than their initiatives of catching and locking up bad 'uns.

One of their leading members of course is Richard Brunstrom, Chief Constable of North Wales Police and the scourge of motorists. I'll talk about him more later in the book but this man isn't alone. There's the former Dyfed-Powys Chief Constable, Terry Grange, who thought it was a good idea to say that males aged up to thirty who had sex with post-pubescent girls should not be called paedophiles. The charity Kidscape said he was 'on very dicey ground'. I went further and said that this patronising plod was giving a green light to every pervert in the country to try and have sex with underage girls.

At this point let's just remind ourselves of what the law says, shall we? In England, Wales and Scotland, anyone who has sex with a boy or girl under the age of sixteen has committed an offence. The age in Northern Ireland is seventeen. If the child is thirteen or older and consenting, the offence is classed as 'unlawful sexual intercourse'. But if they are under thirteen the offence is rape.

'Strange' Grange was also on very thin ice when he talked about puberty, as girls are now having periods at eleven and twelve where quite clearly their emotional and intellectual development is not on the same level as their physical development. At this age they are still children and they need protecting both by parents and the police. What they don't need is chief constables suggesting that they are no longer 'jail bait'. By his definition Gary Glitter and Jonathan King should not be classed as paedophiles.

I'm sorry but I also don't buy the line that some girls look older when they're made up or dressed to the nines. Yes, some do, but it is the responsibility of the adult to verify the age before they commit the act. Anyone who doesn't agree with this is backing the old cliché that a woman who is wearing a miniskirt or hitchhiking is asking for it when they get raped.

Those perverts, both straight and gay, who want the age of consent to be lowered so that they can satisfy their perverted lust will also seize upon comments like Grange's. But what makes Grange's comments even more alarming is that he was the Association of Chief Police Officers' spokesman on child protection and managing sex offenders at the time!

Instead of making our children more available to these perverts and giving them in effect a new alibi, he and his colleagues should have been helping us to develop a Sarah's Law that would protect our children. He should have been putting the rights of our children above the rights of the nonce or pervert. The only good news is that a year or so later he was forced to resign after fiddling his expenses and shagging his secretary.

He resigned because he was being investigated for using his force credit card to wine, dine and pay for bed and board for his bit on the side. However, incredibly the CPS ruled out any criminal action and because Strange Grange has already resigned he will escape any disciplinary action but keep his massive pension.

The Independent Police Complaints Commissioner for Wales, Tom Davies, said, 'This is a sad end to a distinguished career.'

No it was not. It was another blatant example of one law for us and other for top establishment figures and proves without doubt that as well as shagging his mistress Grange had been screwing us all for years.

However Strange Grange isn't the only ACPO member with twisted ideas. Ken Jones, President of the Association of Chief Police Officers, famously said that he didn't recognise David Cameron's description of a 'broken society' after the Conservative leader talked about knife and gun crime.

This fool must have been holidaying on the planet Zanussi and missed the story of the ten-year-olds who stoned 67-year-old Ernie Newton to death while he was playing cricket with his son. Perhaps he was unaware about the kiddie-on-kiddie shootings and he probably didn't believe the fact that 3,000 crimes were being committed by under-tens during his and his politically correct mates' watches.

He of course needs to take his blinkers off, get out of his chauffeur-driven car and his heavily protected home and live in the real world. Either that or he should get a job with the idiots at the Children's Society who want to raise the age of criminal responsibility to fourteen and thus let even more teenage arsonists and sex attackers escape justice.

After going easy on paedophiles, gun crime and assorted villains the Association of Chief Police Officers then suggested giving junkies free smack on the NHS like they do in Switzerland. Women the length and breadth of this country are dying of breast cancer because they cant get Herceptin and oldies with Alzheimer's are being denied £2.50 drugs to slow down their deterioration. But Howard Roberts from ACPO suggested giving out free smack to cut out the link between addiction and crime. It seems to me that with that logic we should give muggers the mobile phone of their choice, rapists any woman they choose and child protection policy should be handed over to Ian Huntley.

This clown is the Assistant Chief Constable of Nottingham, the gun and murder capital of the UK. I would have thought he would have had his politically correct hands full with dealing with these gangsters rather than pontificating on policy. I repeat, a copper's job is to nick bad 'uns, not understand the reasons for their behaviour. Instead of capitulating and giving in on the war on drugs we should be redoubling our efforts. This man quotes what happens in Switzerland;

he should be quoting what happens in another country beginning with S – Singapore.

We've tried the softly-softly, junkies-are-victims policy and it's *failed*. We now need to treat these scumbags as *villains*. We haven't yet lost the war on drugs but we will if we let ACPO and the politically correct coppers who are members of it have their way.

When I spoke at the Police Federation Conference in Blackpool and Bournemouth I lost count of the number of ordinary coppers who told me that ACPO and the top coppers who are in it are completely out of touch with the reality of life on the streets. They are right but it's not only the police force, sorry *service*, that is infested with these liberal hand-wringers. The prison service, fire service and Westminster are stuffed full of these overpaid and pampered, out-of-touch quasi social workers who have no idea of what the reality is on Britain's mean streets.

We need more DCI Gene Hunts and less politically correct clowns running our police forces, and the reintroduction of a little fear might ingrain some respect for our boys in blue.

People are not laughing at Gene Hunt, they are laughing with him. He is popular because he is still able to say what most of us think but are too afraid to voice. I'm not saying I want a return to racism or overt sexism but the political eggshell-walking has to stop.

Simple question: who would you rather have patrolling our streets? Gene in his souped-up Cortina or Audi Quattro or Charlie Caroli of The Met Ian Blair and the over-educated ponces of ACPO?

My old man never rose above being a constable, I don't know whether that was because he was too rough or that he wouldn't suffer the fools above him. However, the fact remains that towards the end of his career I can still recall him saying, 'I can't wait to get out of this bloody job and if I had my time again I wouldn't join up.' You can disregard this as the sad mutterings of a disappointed man but let me tell you, copper after copper phones me or meets me at meetings and tells me exactly the same thing.

The simple blunt truth is that the job has changed and too many coppers have been removed from the job they joined. They are drowning in a sea of paperwork, diversity and understanding when what they want to be doing is getting out there and nicking people. When they do arrest someone or, heaven forbid, smack somebody with a baton or CS spray or a firearm there's weeks of inquiries and tribunals to make sure they acted in a measured way.

I'm not calling for a return to the bad old days of beating confessions out of people but surely the pendulum has swung too far the other way? Surely the public want our coppers to be more Gene Hunt than Ian Blair or, God help us, Brian Paddick. This is the politically correct prat who thought it was a good idea to decriminalise dope in Brixton and effectively turned this already depressing ghetto into a nirvana for all the drug scum of the UK.

When I was working on BBC London, black mum after black mum would phone me from Brixton in tears saying how their neighbourhood was getting worse and that they were fearful their kids were getting pulled into the drug culture. They would talk about seeing the dealers openly selling outside the Roxy or the KFC and they and I wondered that if they knew who the dealers were, why didn't the police, and why weren't they arresting them? Instead the Met – and of course the then Home Secretary David Blunkett, in a case of the blind leading the blind – continued with their social experiment and the streets deteriorated as the bodies of kids mounted up in the morgue.

Meanwhile ACPO keep chattering.

Back in November 2005, just after WPC Sharon Beshenivsky was brutally slain in a Bradford Street, Sir Ian Blair asked what kind of police service we wanted and I replied in my *Sun* column,

> After the brutal slaying of a female rookie cop in Bradford this week the answer is fairly clear. The Police should be called a force not a 'service', they need to be armed, fully supported by the public and Government and we need the death penalty restored.

However before Sharon Beshenivsky's body was even cold we had the political establishment bleating that if we arm the police then the criminals will only arm themselves and the whole thing will escalate. They make me sick.

Hello, the criminals have already got the guns and they are already using them, you morons. The use of guns in crimes of violence against other people is up by 31 per cent and it's been rising for the last five years. However the number of armed cops has actually decreased in the last ten years. Go figure.

How does every home secretary react to all this? That's right, they announce another bloody knife amnesty! God help us!

I can really see that striking fear into the hordes of leather-jacketed Eastern European gangsters who have flooded into Britain, bringing with them their guns, prostitution and tribal infighting. At this very moment Yardies, who are responsible for 80 per cent of gun crime, must be quaking in their two hundred quid trainers and deciding to ditch their gold chain and no brain culture for a degree in sociology at some former poly.

Mind you, just imagine if Sharon and her fellow officer had been armed and had shot one of these robbers. Would they have got the support of the chattering establishment classes? Would they hell! No, just like when any other looney or misfit waves a cigarette lighter in the shape of a gun or brandishes a chair leg in a bag these officers would have been suspended and dragged through inquiry after inquiry to satisfy the liberal left.

It's time for the decent people of this country to fight back and it's time for the police to be armed.

It's also time for life to mean life. But, most of all, it is time for Britain's top cops to start listening to their own rank and file and the British public and give us the kind of police force we want and the current state of Broken Britain demands.

19

First in the world and still the best: NHS in crisis

I'm immensely proud of the fact that we have a National Health Service with a founding principle of treatment free at the point of delivery in Great Britain. I also have nothing but admiration for those dedicated people who work on the frontline of what is still the best healthcare system in the world but we have to face facts: the NHS is in crisis and we need, in the words of Justice Heath Robinson, to cut out the waste.

The NHS is in financial meltdown with one in three Trusts effectively bankrupt and it's time for some drastic Sir Lancelot Spratt type surgery. We have to realise that the NHS was founded on a fundamental falsehood. There simply isn't and never will be enough cash in the pot to treat everyone free at the point of delivery.

However, it is not until you need the NHS, usually in a crisis, that you realise that despite everything and all its troubles just what a brilliant system we have and what utter dedication the staff possess.

I'll never forget when my old man had his first heart attack years ago. The doctors and nurses, even the paramedics, treated him with absolute respect and dedication. For an old cynic he was mightily impressed and they even convinced him to give up the fags. Likewise years later when my dad was in a coma, the staff at Woolwich were simply the best at caring for him and looking after us relatives as our dad's life ebbed away.

On a completely different and more routine level, as a type 2 diabetic my continuing treatment both at the local surgery and the hospital has been out of this world and of course all of my treatment and prescriptions are free. That's fair enough, I guess. I have paid into the pot and I deserve to be able, when in need, to take something back. But as a diabetic I have to question whether it is right that I should get all my prescriptions for free, regardless of whether they are in connection to my diabetes or not. In fact I would go as far as to say that I shouldn't.

I also think it is time to consider charging at least a tenner for missed appointments at doctors, hospitals and dentists. We should have a scheme where every person upon registering with a medical practitioner is forced to give his or her credit or debit card number. A missed appointment would result in a charge being levied; to me this seems perfectly fair and might lead to a reduction in the nine million missed appointments in GP surgeries alone every year. It's not just the financial cost of these missed appointments, it is also the knock-on effect of the difficulty of others getting an appointment as a result.

I'm not going to bang on about the cost of management and penpushers to the financial woe of the NHS but I would state that it is important that if we are going to have a truly national health service then the balance between administrators and health workers has to be redrawn. It's not an original thought I admit but the simplest and most cost-effective way of doing this is to return to matron and her sisters being in charge of all aspects of the ward and hospital, including the cleaners. I am a massive believer in the market but not when it comes to vital services like transporting our children to school on school buses or the cleanliness of our hospitals. These can never be left to a tendering process that will always favour the lowest bid, irrespective of standards.

If we are also to have a truly national service we have got to end the postcode lottery situation where treatments and pills are available in one area of the UK but not the other. The whole basis of our system is that we all pay in and therefore we should all be able to take out when most in need and the inequalities of people being refused £2.50 drugs for conditions such as Parkinson's and Alzheimer's has got to stop.

The National Institute for Health and Clinical Excellence (NICE) – now there's an unsuitable acronym if ever I heard one – are the people who decide what drugs you can have and they desperately need to need to get their house in order. They must stop stupid initiatives like the one where they offered drug addicts five-quid gift vouchers every time they tested negative and prizes if they stayed clean for any length of time.

Meanwhile if your dad needed a £2.50 Alzheimer's drug or your mum needed Herceptin they were of course entered into a different sort of competition. One called the National Health Postcode Lottery where they're guaranteed to lose while those who contribute little or nothing at all win the bloody jackpot again.

It's another case of treating junkies as victims rather than villains and another clear example of rewarding the reckless, feckless and long-term useless at the expense and sweat of the rest of us.

But before you get your blood pressure up about this and no doubt get refused medication on the grounds of cost by NICE, why not try and really break the pressure gauge by getting yourself down to the London Chest Hospital in Bethnal Green and check out the sign in the outpatients clinic which says, 'Patients needing trust interpreters will be given priority'?

No, don't bother checking your calendars, this isn't an April Fools joke, it's a fact, a very depressing fact and reality in inclusive twenty-first-century Britain.

Immigrants who can't even speak English *are* being given priority treatment in hospitals while English-speaking tax-paying Brits have to wait hours for treatment.

It's all down to cost, you see, because they don't want to keep highly paid translators on the premises all day so they push the foreign speakers to the front of the queue.

Don't kid yourself either that this is a one-off cost or just one leftie health authority wasting your hard-earned money, because last year alone we spent over £100 million on translators and so-called health tourism cost the British taxpayer a whopping £62 million.

Putting aside the question of how we have got ourselves into a situation in the first place where we are letting people settle in this country who can't and have no intention of learning our language, customs and history, can anyone explain to me how we are expected to continue paying this ridiculous amount of cash?

Clearly the clue should be in the title – it's meant to be a *National* Health Service not a world one so we must control both health tourism where people come here for free treatment and we must toughen up our border controls and entry requirements.

There just isn't enough dosh to treat the whole of the world off the blood, sweat and tears and of course tax and NI contributions of us Brits. That is why full medicals must be compulsory if someone wants to come and settle in this country. You wouldn't get into the States or Australia with certain known medical conditions without the proof that you can support yourself and pay for your medical care, so why the hell are we such a soft touch?

I'm sorry, but if you've got HIV/AIDS you ain't coming in because we simply can't afford the million pounds it will cost to treat you and that's not inhumane that just plain common sense. The politically correct buffoons won't like this but I am afraid there is a direct correlation between the rise in heterosexual HIV/AIDS in this country and lax border control that has allowed too many sub-Saharan Africans into the country. Similarly there has to be a link between the rise in TB, which was virtually eradicated in this country, and our open-door, no-medical policy. Again not racist, not polite dinner party conversation, but the truth.

If I see another news report or a BBC documentary talking about or asking if health tourism is on the increase in the UK, I think I will probably throw a brick at the TV because the answer is so blindingly obvious – of course it is.

Let's be honest: *our* NHS is being seen around the globe as a world health service, available to anyone who can get past our nonexistent border control. People are coming in to give birth, have abortions and every other treatment they can lay their hands on and it makes me sick.

Years ago, Lisa and I were on holiday in Florida while she was heavily pregnant with Rosie and we were messing about in the pool when she felt a sudden twinge. She was concerned that the baby might be in trouble so we rushed to the nearest hospital. As soon as we entered the examination room the first thing the American doctors examined was . . . our insurance documents!

Which is exactly how it should be in this country too. We were not American and of course they had to check if we had the means to pay for our treatment and that is how it should be here, and this by the way is one of the major reasons why I think a national ID card is so important in this country. No one should be able to use our system if they haven't or aren't willing or able to pay in. Why should our health service, which is paid for by our contributions, be available to all? The answer is it shouldn't be and can't be.

I saw a report on Sky News where a doctor who works at a hospital close to a major UK airport said that he'd lost count of the number of patients he had dealt with who had just got off planes with gunshot wounds or serious illnesses. He then went on to say that it was his job to treat these people and that their clinical needs should come before questions of their immigration status.

He actually said that, 'We are very fortunate that we were born here and are entitled to a good health care system, but that's purely through birthright rather than anything else.'

What a load of cobblers and what an insult to every single taxpayer in this country. There's no accident in the amount of tax and National Insurance I pay every month to have the NHS. It's certainly not an accident that Brits have to wait for operations or life-saving cancer drugs while illegals are given free glasses, dental treatment and even chiropody before they are sent home. And it's certainly not an accident of birth that we have a National Health Service. It was founded on the blood, sweat and tears of hard-working men and women like my dad.

When he collapsed at Heathrow he was transferred to Hillingdon Hospital. He was in their A&E Department for the best part of twelve hours because they didn't have a free intensive-care bed. The doctor apologised over and over again as she tried to find a bed anywhere in the country to take my 72-year-old dad who had paid in all his life. I don't think it is a coincidence that Hillingdon is the closest hospital to Heathrow.

It was five the next morning when they eventually found one, which turned out to be over 150 miles away from his home.

My dad didn't expect any more than anyone else, he didn't want to jump any queues, despite all the taxes and NI he had paid in his life, but surely the least he could expect was a bed somewhere in the UK in his hour, or as it turned out hours, of need.

Of course I'm not blaming foreign health tourists for my dad's plight but when the NHS is clearly in crisis, despite the politicians' boasts, then surely we need to make sure that we are only treating and caring for our own.

I am willing to pay for a National Health Service but *not* a world one.

20

Let Britain decide: why we need a referendum on capital punishment

Bringing back the death penalty would be uncivilised. So goes the hand-wringing argument, but please just tell me how civilised is it for two feral youths to stab to death a young lawyer and show no remorse?

How civilised is it for a young brother and sister to open the front door of their home to find their mother in a pool of her own blood after she has been bludgeoned to death? How civilised is it for Gary Newlove to be kicked to death in front of his twelve-year-old daughter? Finally, how civilised is it for a man to abduct a six-year-old girl from her bath, rape her and then abandon her in the street?

And that's just a few examples of so-called 'civilised' Britain.

That's why I agree with the *Sun* who says we are living in Broken Britain, but unlike the paper I believe one of the ways of mending our increasingly violent society is the restoration of the death penalty for such heinous crimes. Let's face it, we need the death penalty and we need it now.

In a recent poll in the *Sun* 99 per cent of readers wanted a return of capital punishment for such animals, and now that the public have spoken, and not just in that paper but also in poll after poll, the politicians must listen.

But will they listen? Will they hell!

In a country where Jack 'the man of' Straw tells courts not to send people to prison the metropolitan liberal ruling elite will still sneer down their noses at people like you and me who are demanding the restoration of the death penalty.

What planet do these fools live on?

If criminals actually thought that they were going to receive real sentences and that five years was going to mean five, ten, ten and life bloody life, then maybe they would think again.

That's why there should be no more free votes on the subject in the House of Commons where politicians can misrepresent and vote against the wishes of their constituents. Instead there should be a full and frank discussion about the pros and cons of the ultimate deterrent and the British public must be given a referendum to decide the issue. Politicians for too long have ignored the wishes of the masses and now we must all keep the pressure on to force a public vote.

I for one believe that the ultimate deterrent of the rope would surely make some of these madmen pause for thought.

But forget deterrent. When someone commits crimes as heinous as Steve Wright, the Suffolk strangler, Ian Huntley or the teenage thugs who took Gary Newlove's life then what's wrong with revenge as a motive? If a dog kills a toddler they are put down and can anyone really convince you or me that these two are more worthy of life than a rabid dog?

The only way to wipe the smirk off the faces of vicious killers like Donnel Carty and Delano Brown, who murdered solicitor Tom ap Rhys Price in broad daylight just a few steps away from his house, is the certain knowledge that if you take a life then the state will take yours.

I was moved to tears by the words of Tom's fiancée, Adele Eastman, who said his murder 'was a huge waste of life' for him and his killers. But the simple facts are that Tom's life is over yet these two scumbags could be back out on the streets before they are forty years old.

They could be free to offend again, just like evil child rapist Peter Voisey who, despite the fact that he had a previous conviction for molesting a twelve-year-old girl, was allowed the freedom to snatch another girl and rape her. This is the monster that in December 2005 sneaked into a house and abducted a six-year-old girl from her bath and sexually abused her several times as he drove around Tyneside.

Sentencing him at Newcastle Crown Court, Judge Hodson told him, 'I'm in no doubt whatsoever that you are a dangerous predatory man who poses a significant risk of causing serious harm. This is a most grave offence. This was a six-year-old girl being removed from her own bath in her own home and taken out into the cold night for the purposes of your sexual gratification.

'That more than justifies, in my opinion, a sentence of life.'

No it doesn't, it should have justified the Saddam shuffle. Instead Voisey stood in the court impassively and heard his sentence, safe in the knowledge that life doesn't mean life and that in ten years he could be considered for release.

The teenage killers of Gary Newlove smirked in court and Evil Levi Bellfield, who bludgeoned to death two young girls and is the prime suspect in the disappearance of Milly Dowler, was even allowed to stay in his prison cell rather than hear his sentence.

His barrister, William Boyce QC, told the judge at the Old Bailey that Bellfield had refused to attend his sentencing because of a 'welter of accusations' that he was behind other unsolved crimes including the disappearance of Milly Dowler. His brief went on to say, 'Overnight there has been what some consider to be a quite extraordinary explosion of bad publicity.'

In his absence he received a whole life sentence just as Steven Wright, the Suffolk strangler, had four days previously, but the point remains that he should have been dragged kicking and screaming by his nostril hairs in to the dock to hear his sentence for the brutal attacks on three innocent women.

Instead in softly-softly 'Criminals R Us' New Labour Britain, this thug was allowed to stick two fingers up to the British public and heap even further agony on to the relatives of the families that had lost their loved ones.

Now he's going to spend the rest of his life in a cushy prison, no doubt pumping up his steroid-filled body in between studying the human-rights laws so that he can screw even more out of the system. Just like Soham murderer Ian Huntley who is treated better than pensioners and lives in more salubrious accommodation than our squaddies, Bellfield and Wright will continue to haunt us from their cells.

However, he should have been forced to hear his sentence and then forced to watch as the judge placed the black cap on his head and then his next stop should not have been a cell with plasma TV but the gallows.

Similarly the feral thugs who kicked Gary Newlove to death now have the cheek and of course the legal aid to appeal against their sentences for his murder. The leader of the gang, Adam Swellings, who had only been let out on bail ten hours previously, reckons his sentence of seventeen years is 'excessive'. This is despite the fact that he handed Gary's widow, Helen, and her three children a life sentence when he chose along with his mates to kick Gary to death.

The former head of the Metropolitan Police, Lord Stevens, called for the death penalty to be reinstated for police killers after the death of WPC Sharon Beshenivsky. Writing in the *News of the World*, Stevens said: 'I genuinely never thought I'd say this, but I am now convinced that the monster who executed this young woman in cold blood should, in turn, be killed as punishment for his crime.'

But of course like the rest of us Lord Stevens was ignored by the cosy elite based in London who work in politics, the media, the BBC or in human-rights charities who believe their worldview is the only view. We are just the mob braying for blood and they know better. But what makes me really sick is that if politicians of all parties are so convinced of their arguments, why don't they try a novel idea and have a referendum on the subject and see whether we want to bring the death penalty back for such heinous crimes?

Of course this will never happen, and then they wonder why the vast majority of people in this country aren't interested in politics or don't bother to vote. I can even remember a week on *Question Time* when they were discussing whether Saddam Hussein should be executed or not and not one of the five on the panel agreed with the death penalty. Oh yeah, that's really representative of the country's view, isn't it?

Meanwhile a female lawyer representing the Yorkshire Ripper, again at our expense, claims that the man who butchered thirteen young women has had *his* human rights breached. Evidently he was never told how long his minimum tariff was going to be and under European law he has a right to know! Of course Sutcliffe will never be released but just like Soham murderer Ian Huntley he is using the hated Human Rights Act and legal aid to further wind up the general public and heap even more agony on his victim's families.

The only people who seem to benefit from the Human Rights Act are the scum of the earth, and of course the lawyers including the wife of the man who imposed this wretched act on us – Tony bloody Blair.

We need to forget about the civil liberties and human rights of these monsters and concentrate on the victims and their families if we truly want to build a safer Great Britain.

That's why I say: let them swing.

21

The long slow death of the British boozer

Four pubs a day are being closed down and the very future of the British boozer is under real threat. The fault lies with the big brewers, the pub estate companies, the smoking ban, overzealous health and safety idiots and the killjoys in the councils.

The Chief Executive of the British Beer and Pub Association, Rob Hayward, says, 'Britain's pubs are grappling with spiralling costs, sinking sales, fragile consumer confidence and the impact of the smoking ban.' He continues, 'These figures show the stark reality of the pub trade today, in contrast to the hype surrounding the myth of "24-hour drinking" and extended pub opening hours' and he warns that 'Pub closures at this rate are threatening an important hub of our social fabric and community history. We need to stop the decline and support is needed from Government and the general public.'

I agree with every single word he says and the time for action is now, we need to call last orders on the decline of the British boozer. Let's be clear, I am talking about the unique British pub where you go to drink alcohol not the gastro pub or pub chains with their poxy kids' activity centres, ballparks and even poxier kids' menus.

Just as a side issue, why does the title, 'kids' menu' in this country have to mean nuggets and chips, tomato spaghetti or a burger? Why can't pubs offer half-sized dishes off the main menu for our children and therefore healthier options?

I also really hate it when the big brewery chains come in and take over a village pub and turn it into a Hungry Horse or a Brewers Fayre and relegate the regulars to a small bar at the back which would be over-full if Jimmy Clitheroe and The Krankies even turned up for a beer.

But the pubs I am most concerned about are the real boozers, whether they are on our high streets or in villages and, dare I say it, a pub where a man can escape and actually enjoy male company. There's a great boozer in Coventry called the Royal Oak in Earlsdon that sums up what a pub should be and Lisa describes it as a typical man's boozer. That's not to say women are excluded but it is a place primarily for men to congregate.

Years ago this place was dying on its arse until an enterprising ex-advertising guy called Ray Evitts took it over. Instead of turning it into a gastro pub or a pale reflection of what some trendy London pubs are, Ray has made a success of this pub by going back to basics.

The first basic being the beer has to be well kept and he does an excellent job of this, offering a range of real ales and lagers.

Secondly he's resisted the temptation to offer food apart from crisps and nuts and therefore the atmosphere has remained authentic I'm a great believer that food and real pubs do not mix.

Thirdly he booted out all the lowlifes that used to drink in this pub and thus attracted a new clientele.

Fourthly there's no jukebox and no gaming machines or TV.

Fifthly he's employed attractive barmaids, usually from aboard, who not only serve behind the bar but offer waitress service at the table as well.

The place is doing well but even he is feeling the pinch due to a combination of the smoking ban, higher and higher rents and the Monopoly and Mergers Commission that was meant to save pubs like this but is effectively killing them.

As a direct reaction to the Commission breweries just split their operations into separate companies, one brewing the beer, the other owning and managing the estates. This resulted in the creation of several large chains that own vast estates of boozers across the country and effectively act as estate landlords.

Back in 2004 a Trade and Industry Select Committee made five recommendations about how these massive pub estate owners should act or treat their tenants of their pubs. One of the most important recommendations was that the pub owner should be more open with their tenants on how they calculated the rent and that it shouldn't always be put up.

Most landlords including a new campaigning group of pub managers called the Fair Pint Campaign believe that the companies have simply ignored the select committee and are now calling for another inquiry to stop the decline of the traditional British boozer.

Now I know that running a pub or club is bloody hard work because I have done it and learned the hard way; it may be everyone's dream to hold a licence but for many, far too many, it turns into a nightmare.

It's practically impossible to get a freehold house so most people lease off one of these big companies who shall remain nameless for the sake of the sleep of my publishers and the bank balances of us all. But the bottom line is this: the latest mug arrives, agrees to pay a substantial amount for goodwill and fixtures and fittings and then signs a full repairing lease for the premises. This lease and its tight terms will also include a drinks tie which I will explain in a minute but is often the thing that financially knackers the new landlords.

Full repair means they are responsible for all the repairs at their cost. I had a mate who went into a country pub under this arrangement and had to pay for new windows and the resurfacing of the car park. When he went bust, several months later, the pub chain got another mug to pay the lump sum for goodwill – why, I don't know, because there were hardly any customers let alone goodwill, and of course before you know it the roof needs repairing and the fiasco continues. Successive landlords go bust while the estate company's asset appreciates in value due partly to the repairs.

As for the drinks tie, these self-employed landlords are then in a position where they have to buy the beer and bottles from the pub chain, often at prices higher than they can get them in the local cash and carry. Then you wonder why so many pubs are closing down quicker than Lewis Hamilton does in a Formula 1 rival's wing mirror.

If despite these problems the landlord actually manages to turn the pub around and start selling more beer, eventually the rental will be renegotiated and the landlord rewarded for his success by receiving a hefty rent rise.

Meanwhile the taxes on alcohol served in pubs is at an all-time high and the traditional drinker has been tempted away with the lure of cheap booze from a supermarket and the fact that he can still, for the time being, at least smoke at home. That's why Government must play its part and reduce the tax on sales in pubs to encourage more trade and at the same time encourage light-handed rather than heavy-handed regulation from local authorities.

A classic example of this being the threat of prosecution by Stroud District Council of licensee Graham Jones. Jones wanted to offer free taxi rides home to his customers. The pen pushers in the council, in between counting paper clips, said that he had to have a taxi licence to carry out such a scheme, otherwise he would be fined. This was a self-employed man who was just trying to make his venue more attractive and he was stopped at the first hurdle by a bureaucrat.

One also can't underestimate the impact the smoking ban has had on trade as well. Now let me nail my flag to the post first, I was against the smoking ban when it was first suggested and I thought it was an affront to democracy. As far as I was concerned, if there was a demand for non-smoking bars and clubs then the market would have provided it.

I used to have furious rows with Lisa over this, as she would constantly remind me of how I would come home from running my clubs stinking of nicotine even though I have been a non-smoker all my life. She would force me into the shower and of course even next morning I have to admit I could still smell the smoke on my skin, disgusting! However I still believed that the unique nature of the pub would be lost if smoking was banned. I also didn't fancy the conversation or the craic being interrupted by my smoking mates having to leave the bar for a crafty drag.

Then our local village pub, which for the sake of anonymity we will call the Slaughterman's Arms in the Village of the Damned, went smoke-free eight months before the law actually came in. There were the inevitable protests and walkouts by regulars who vowed they would never drink in the place again and for the first few weeks the atmosphere definitely changed. Then one by one the regulars returned and I've got to say that the place is now more comfortable and for a non-smoker it's great to come home not smelling of fags. There's even a chance that Lisa won't realise I've popped in for a swift one on the way home! Plus you can't get away from the simple basic fact that smoking kills and it is best for everyone if you can kick the filthy habit.

However, I still wonder if the ban is a prime example of the nanny state going too far and if a better option would have been clearly defined smoking and non-smoking bars and rooms. It's OK for analysts to suggest that pubs should try and attract a new customer base with things like coffee during the day, free wifi and newspapers etc, but do you really want your local to change that much because I know that I don't. Surely one of the pleasures of British boozers is that you never know what you are going to find behind those doors as you escape the street and if everyone became uniform wouldn't we be in danger of returning to a health and safety politically correct version of the dreaded and not missed Watney's Red Revolution of the Seventies?

However, I can see that it has affected sales. As my mate Ray the licensee in Coventry says, it's not because smokers are meant to feel unwelcome, it's just that if it is a lifelong habit and you are forced by law to move outside each time you want a fag it will affect your judgement as to whether you can be bothered to go and watch the game in the pub or even meet your mates there. Couple that with the easy availability and cost of supermarket beer and the pub is bound to take a hit and they have.

So in conclusion I hope that you agree with me and realise it is not an exaggeration to say that the British pub is in danger of extinction and should it disappear a large part of our indigenous culture will go with it.

So there's your excuse – get down the local and get drinking, cheers!

22

Bravest of the brave: honouring the Gurkhas

What do you know about Gurkhas? Probably about as much as me. They're little blokes from Nepal who are as brave as hell and if they ever pull out their big knife (the Kukri) they have to draw blood with it! Most of our knowledge probably comes from old editions of *Blue Peter*, which always seemed to feature them in the Sixties, or old comics like *Victor* or those little *Commando* mags.

However, did you know that being a Gurkha is so highly prized that over 28,000 Nepalese youths apply for only 200 places each year? The selection process is the toughest in the world and as part of it the young hopefuls have to run uphill for forty minutes carrying a wicker basket in their back with 70lb of rocks in it. Once selected they will be based at Shorncliffe, near Folkestone but they can, and have, served with the British Army all over the world.

But the most important fact you need to know about Gurkhas at the moment is the shameful way they are being treated by this British Government. Lousy Labour are willing to pay out over £18 billion of our taxes on sickness and invalidity benefits every year but then are sick enough themselves to refuse to give all Gurkhas equal pensions and the right to live in our green and pleasant land.

I've lost count of the number of Gurkha ill-treatment stories I have covered on my radio show and *Sun* column in the last three years but every time another one hits the headlines it sickens me as much as my readers and listeners.

What is it with New Labour? Are they all trying to join the Heather Mills Appreciation Society? How else can you explain them consistently shooting themselves in the foot on this issue?

Most of the Cabinet's experience of the armed forces is limited to a visit to the army surplus store to buy a flak jacket when they were shouting, 'Maggie, Maggie, Maggie, *out, out, out*' in between drinking themselves senseless in the student union bar.

This bunch of failed barristers and former polytechnic lecturers make me sick and are as about in touch with the general public as Vanessa Feltz is a stranger to the all you can eat buffet.

It's clear that these brave men are the very foreigners that we the British public want to invite and embrace and allow into our country rather than the illegals and criminals who haven't paid a penny, don't want to lift a finger and only want to exploit our easy-going benefit system.

I don't know about you but I would rather pay for Gurkhas than shirkers.

It's another example of the feral, the feckless, the freeloaders and the long-term useless getting rewarded while those who are willing to serve this country are put to the bottom of the heap and refused help or respect.

The first brave Gurkha to hit the headlines was 84-year-old Tul Bahadur Pun who won the Victoria Cross during the Second World War when he single-handedly took out some Japanese machine-gun nests in Burma. His citation from the *London Gazette* of 1944 illustrates this man's courage;

Firing from the hip with a Bren Gun he charged towards the enemy on his own while they put him under a shattering concentration of automatic fire, directed straight at him. With the dawn coming up behind him, he presented a perfect target to the Japanese. He had to move for thirty yards over open ground, ankle deep in mud, through shell holes and over fallen trees. Despite these overwhelming odds, he reached the Red House and closed with the Japanese occupants. He killed three and put five more to flight and captured two light machine-guns with the remainder of his platoon which enabled them to reach their objective.

Mr Pun is now suffering from a heart condition, poor eyesight, diabetes and asthma and had been living in near poverty on a hillside in Nepal.

He quite rightly wanted to live out his last years in Britain but some pen-pushing prat in the Home Office told him, 'You have failed to demonstrate that you have strong ties with the UK.'

How much stronger do your bloody ties have to be than being awarded the highest military decoration for being willing to lay down your life for this great country?

My phone lines lit up with angry Brits who again and again made the point that if Mr Pun had arrived at Watford Gap in the back of a lorry he would have been treated with more respect and by now would have been tucked up in a nice warm house with hot and cold running benefits.

Eventually after much lobbying and a petition on the Number 10 website Mr Pun was allowed to stay and receive the medical care his brave dedicated service deserved.

However, the real tragedy is that there are still thousands of Gurkhas who are being denied the right to live in the UK and thousands more who are being denied equal pension rights.

Clearly this is an example of *Rubbish* Britain not Great Britain.

Let's just take a moment to consider the history of these men and be absolutely clear what Britain owes them. They have been part of the British Army for 200 years. Following the partition of India in 1947, an agreement between Nepal, India and Britain meant four Gurkha regiments from the Indian army were transferred to the British Army, eventually becoming the Gurkha Brigade. Since then, the Gurkhas have loyally fought for the British all over the world, receiving thirteen Victoria Crosses between them.

They serve in a variety of roles, mainly in the infantry but with significant numbers of engineers, logisticians and signals specialists.

More than 200,000 fought in the two world wars and in the past 50 years, they have served in Hong Kong, Malaysia, Borneo, Cyprus, the Falklands and Kosovo and now in Iraq and Afghanistan.

Finally during the two world wars 43,000 young Gurkhas gave their lives for this country and our Government are now refusing them equal treatment with other soldiers. Makes you proud to be British, doesn't it?

The facts are that Gurkhas who retired from the British Army after 1997 can automatically stay in the UK, but those who retired earlier must apply, and many have been refused and face deportation. This ridiculous rule was only created in 2004 and at last after such a massive public outcry from the British public is now being attacked by MPs from all parties.

Mr Madam Gurung, a retired Gurkha who left the Army before the 1997 cut-off date, is one of the men who now faces deportation. His application to stay in the UK has been declined even though he served 24 years in the British Army and left with an *exemplary* record. At the moment while awaiting news of his appeal he is being forced to live on charitable handouts in a one-room bedsit in Tonbridge, Kent.

A land fit for heroes – my arse! To make matters worse he is not allowed to work by UK law. Even though he wants to work as a bus driver or security guard.

He is treated like a common criminal and worse than a bogus asylum seeker, all because he wants to live in the very country that he was prepared to die for. Meanwhile anyone who manages to jump out of the back of a lorry at Watford Gap appears to be allowed to stay as long as they want.

The police have even been told not to arrest them but give them instructions, in every language under the sun, on how to find 'Lunatic House' in Croydon so they can start to leech off the rest of us. To add insult to injury even paedophile Raymond Horne was allowed to begin a new life in Blighty despite the fact that this 61-year-old pervert was deported from Australia following a long line of sex offences against children.

British-born Horne emigrated as a child but never took Australian citizenship, meaning the UK was powerless to stop his return and return he did.

According to Labour MP Kate Hoey, who is backing the rights of Gurkhas, around 2,000 immigrants every day are given National Insurance numbers, which allow them to live and work in the UK.

While this row was brewing leading Labour Cabinet member, Alan Johnson, was even calling for an amnesty for the 500,000 illegals that were in the country!

To add insult to injury, pension rights for years served by Gurkhas before 1997 count at only around a quarter of the level of years served after that time. This is ludicrous and patently unfair. As far as I'm concerned if you are willing to lay down your life for this country then you deserve the same pensions, medical care and rights as any other British squaddie.

Despite a demonstration by 4,000 brave Gurkhas who marched on Westminster in March 2008, where fifty of the bravest gave back their campaign medals to Lib Dem leader Nick Clegg, the Labour Government are still refusing to right this wrong.

Fair dues to Nick Clegg and the Liberal Democrat Party – they have been at the forefront of the campaign and Clegg is right when he remarks that,

> It is a national disgrace that Gurkhas who have loyally served Britain are being denied the right to live here in retirement. These men have been a credit to the country. To deny them the right to live here and gain British citizenship after years of service and distinguished conduct is nothing short of scandalous. If someone is prepared to die for our country they should have the right to live in our country.

What a savage indictment of the country that Labour has created. Not content with letting pensioners go to prison for refusing to pay escalating council tax bills and treating our own soldiers with contempt by not issuing them with the right gear and making them live in squalid conditions, New Labour are now insulting the bravest of the brave.

There is a petition on the Number 10 website (petitions.pm.gov. uk/Gurkha-soldiers/) which is demanding that, 'We the undersigned petition the Prime Minister to give all Ex Gurkha soldiers and their families who have served our country British citizenship on leaving the service.'

So far there are 23,371 signatures, which is nowhere near enough, so why don't you add yours and show your support for these brave little men whose motto is, 'It is better to die than live a coward.'

23

Lock them up but *don't* throw away the key

USA JAIL – SOME INTERESTING READING TO THOSE OF YOU NOT
FAMILIAR WITH JOE ARPAIO, HE IS THE MARICOPA COUNTY
SHERIFF (ARIZONA) AND HE KEEPS GETTING ELECTED OVER
AND OVER AGAIN.

These are some of the reasons why:

Sheriff Joe Arpaio created the 'tent city jail' to
save Arizona from spending tens of millions of dollars
on another expensive prison complex.

He has jail meals down to 20 cents a serving and
charges the inmates for them.

He banned smoking and pornographic magazines in the
jails, and took away their weightlifting equipment
and cut off all but 'G' movies. He says: 'They're in
jail to pay a debt to society not to build muscles so
they can assault innocent people when they leave.'

He started chain gangs to use the inmates to do free
work on county and city projects and save taxpayer's
money.

Then he started chain gangs for women so he wouldn't get sued for discrimination.

He took away cable TV until he found out there was a federal court order that required cable TV for jails. So he hooked up the cable TV again but only allows the Disney channel and the weather channel.

When asked why the weather channel, he replied: 'so these morons will know how hot it's gonna be while they are working on my chain gangs.'

He cut off coffee because it has zero nutritional value and is therefore a waste of taxpayer money. When the inmates complained, he told them, 'This isn't the Ritz/Carlton. If you don't like it, don't come back.'

With temperatures being even hotter than usual in Phoenix (116 degrees just set a new record for June 2nd 2007), the Associated Press reported: About 2,000 inmates living in a barbed wire surrounded tent encampment at the Maricopa County Jail have been given permission to strip down to their government-issued pink boxer shorts.

On the Wednesday, hundreds of men wearing pink boxer shorts were overheard chatting in the tents, where temperatures reached 128 degrees.

'This is hell. It feels like we live in a furnace,' said Ernesto Gonzales, an inmate for 2 years with 10 more to go. 'It's inhumane.'

Joe Arpaio, who makes his prisoners wear pink, and eat bologna sandwiches, is not one bit sympathetic. 'Criminals should be punished for their crimes – not live in luxury until it's time for parole, only to go out and commit more crimes so they can come back in to live on taxpayers' money and enjoy things many taxpayers can't afford to have for themselves.'

The same day he told all the inmates who were complaining of the heat in the tents: 'It's between 120 to 130 degrees in Iraq and our soldiers are living in tents too, and they have to walk all day in the sun, wearing full battle gear and get shot at, and they have not committed any crimes, so shut your damned mouths!'

Way to go, Sheriff! If all prisons were like yours there would be a lot less crime and we would not be in the current position of running out of prison spaces.

If you agree, pass this on.
If not, just delete it.

Sheriff Joe was just re-elected as Sheriff in Maricopa County, Arizona.

No doubt you've had this email in your inbox just like me – well, to be truthful I've had it sent to me more times than adverts for Viagra and offers of millions from Nigerian fraudsters. But the very fact that this email is doing the rounds and is so popular in Great Britain speaks volumes about how fed up people are about our Mothercare style of prisons.

Now before we get started let me reiterate I am not a bread and water merchant and I do not believe in locking them up and throwing away the key. As you are aware, I am in favour of capital punishment for heinous crimes like serial rape, murder and predatory paedophiles, but when it comes to other crimes I believe of course in punishment but I also believe there is a drastic need for rehabilitation and above all else education.

I actually agree with the bleeding-heart liberals who say prison doesn't work. *It doesn't*. Well at least our style of prison doesn't at the moment. There is no point in banging up criminals three in a cell for twenty-three hours a day because the prisons are overcrowded and understaffed. There's no way on God's earth that will do any good for either rehabilitation or punishment and again I agree with the liberals that it will only result in even more hardened criminals returning to our streets and our prisons will just become universities of crime.

However – and it is a very big however – the answer to the present prison crisis of over 84,000 prisoners is not to start releasing these criminals early or to instruct the courts not to send people to prison. The answer is blindingly simple, *build more prisons* and *give them longer sentences*.

Labour should have started a massive prison-building programme years ago and for a government that has introduced over 3,000 new laws since it came to power it has been woefully neglectful in its provision of prison places. To those who say we already lock up more people than any other country in Western Europe, maybe the answer is that we simply have more criminals. I am not interested in other countries, I only care about Britain and the protection of the decent silent majority of this country and that should be the first responsibility of any government. It is astonishing and quite frankly outrageous that when he was Home Secretary Straw started an early release programme for prisoners that has now resulted in these criminals committing further crimes including rape.

If there were more prison places and criminals were actually given longer sentences, then there would be more space and time for them to confront their offending behaviour, be educated and hopefully rehabilitated and of course punished. There also has to be a massive investment in prison resources and education classes but prisoners should also spend time paying back their debt to society by being engaged in real productive work, rather than playing with their Playstations.

Prison officers need to be better rewarded for their work and it was a savage indictment of a government that promised to be tough on crime and tough on the causes of crime when officers decided that they had had enough and went on wildcat strikes for more pay and better conditions. We need our officers to be better educated but also we need them to be more like Officer Mackay than Mr Barrowclough in *Porridge*.

Fletcher would be spinning and laughing in his grave over the stories of prison officers being told to wear slippers on the landing to avoid waking prisoners, or being instructed to address them by their Christian names or as Mr and Mrs rather than 'Fletcher, you horrible little man'. He would have laughed his smelly socks off at the thought of people like the Consumer Council being worried and concerned about how much prisoners are having to pay for phone calls. As for junkie prisoners being able to sue the Home Office for an infringement of their human rights because they were allowed to go cold turkey, he would believe that he was on drugs as well.

Slade Prison may have been effectively run by the gangster Grout (played by brilliant British character actor, Peter Vaughan, also brilliant in *Citizen Smith*) but many prisons now appear to be run by governors who are more limp-wrested than Christopher Biggins's character, Lukewarm.

Prison should be primarily about punishment and when a freed prisoner hears the clang of the prison door behind him he should never, ever, want to return there again. However in Britain it would appear that our prisons have revolving doors where the usual suspects keep re-entering.

My listeners and readers are sick to the back teeth of hearing stories about prisoners playing computer games or having better TVs, for which incidentally they don't pay a licence fee, than pensioners in the UK. We are also sick of hearing about the human rights of these men and women who appear to have no regard for the human rights of the decent silent majority whom they choose to rob, mug, stab and murder almost with impunity.

As far as I am concerned, a man loses his human rights once he enters my house through the kitchen window to nick my DVD player and he shouldn't get those rights back until he has served his time and made his amends to society. I don't agree with what Tony Martin did, as he lay in wait and used an illegal gun, but I do believe that an Englishman should have a right to protect his family and home and the presumption of guilt should be on the toerag burglar not the houseowner. Likewise five years must mean five and ten must mean ten. Good behaviour inside should lead to release at the end of the term, not a shortening of a sentence.

Although I would remove many of the privileges in prison and make it a harsher regime, I am not in favour of a breaking-rocks-in-the-hot-sun kind of regime favoured by Sheriff Joe, though I would like to see community sentences being toughened up and used less. Of course these criminals should wear high-visibility jackets with the word 'criminal' on the back and they should feel humiliated while they pay back their debt to society and they should be involved in high-profile clean-ups of motorway verges and inner-city graffiti. There should also be tough, very tough penalties for those who fail to turn up and on time for such community punishments, which will have to include immediate, with no appeal, sending to custody.

Of course to really get on top of crime, law and order and punishment in this country and truly make the streets of Britain safer, we have to tackle the major cause of crime and antisocial behaviour and that is the scourge of Class A drugs. There has to be a complete sea change in our approach to drug dealers and drug users. We need to stop treating the users as victims and start treating them as the villains they really are and we need really tough draconian sentences handed down to the dealers.

It is ridiculous that up to 17,000 junkies and alcoholics can use their pathetic addictions as a valid reason for picking up an extra seventy quid a week in Disability Living Allowance. Being a junkie or alkie I am afraid is not a disability, it's a weakness, an illness at best but in most cases definitely a self-inflicted wound. That's why I believe the Tories were right when they declared in an election manifesto that they would create 20,000 more residential drug rehabilitation centres and give addicts the choice between treatment and prison. This idea needs to be adopted immediately as you will never cure an addict if you allow them to live within their community. I don't know about you but it sickens me to sit in a chemist waiting for a prescription with my children and have to witness druggies approaching the counter to swig their methadone heroin substitute.

Just tell me, you liberal berks, how that is meant to be a civilised modern Britain? All it does is just maintain them in their drugged stupor, their subsidised lifestyle. Yes, yes I know you can't force someone to give up drugs unless they want to, but you can create an enforced environment where they are given time and a real chance of getting clean. Of course some, perhaps many, would come back out of rehab centres and get back on the gear but if this happens we will have to have a three strikes and you're out rule and their long-term incarceration will have to be the only answer.

For those who say you can't punish their kids by removing them for treatment can you please get a life and tell me what kind of life a toddler has with a smacked-up mum or a crack-using dad? We need to intervene earlier and get these vulnerable children out of these pathetic and dangerous and chaotic lifestyles and offer them some hope, otherwise the pattern will repeat itself.

The dealers must be treated much more harshly than they are with life sentences for dealing in large quantities of class A drugs and prison governors have to stop turning a blind eye to drug use inside. If that means compulsory and daily cell searches, including full strip searches, then so be it. For those who say you need the drugs inside the pressure cooker of overcrowded prisons to keep the lid on, the answer is again simple: build more prisons, have more prison places and relieve the temperature and tension that way rather than through the illicit use of drugs.

As a former user of speed and coke, I know how easy it would have been to fall into an addictive lifestyle, and the acceptance of it within the showbiz, pop music and celebrity world is something to crack down on too. For once I agree with the Charlie Caroli of the Constabulary, Sir Ian Blair, when he said he wanted to crack down on the casual dinner-party use of cocaine in the middle classes. Likewise the light-handed way the police and courts deal with junkie celebs like Pete Doherty, Amy Winehouse, and with the allegations against Kate Moss, needs to stop. Newspapers and so-called comics and TV shows need to drop the jokes about coke and other drug use and we need to start telling our kids that there are other ways to get those highs.

I'm neither a puritan nor a moralist and I know what I am talking about as I have been there and got the T-shirt. Of course some drug use will always remain a rite of passage for young people but we need to clearly draw a line (sorry) when it comes to addiction and the criminal acts that go with that, which include the recent spate of gun and knife crime that is blighting broken Britain.

Until we as a nation get tough on both the pushers and the users of hard drugs and prisons become centres of punishment, education and rehabilitation we will never put the Great back into Rubbish Britain.

24

National service and why we should bring it back

Instead of everyone who feels like it taking everything out of this country it is time for everyone to start putting something in and that should start with the reintroduction of national service.

I don't necessarily mean a return to the Tony Selby and *Get Some In* (what a great TV show that was?) style of national service with square bashing but I have long held the view that every sixteen-year-old should be forced to give one year of their life to serving their country.

National service formally ended in Britain on 31 December 1960 and it's clear that the military don't want a return to conscription but we have to face the unpleasant fact that we do have an increasingly broken Britain and urgent action needs to be taken.

There are over 200,000 so-called NEETS on the streets. These young people who are not in education, employment or training are obviously a drain on our resources and a potential source of crime.

If we had a new form of national service then every kid at sixteen would be forced to get involved before moving on to A levels and then university and the world of work. This would have a twofold effect of making them more mature when they reach college and more aware of the world around them. It's the old Kennedy line, isn't it, 'Ask not what your country can do for you, ask what you can do for your country.'

The work could be everything from community work such as making their own environments cleaner, safer and tidier through work with the elderly and disabled.

This should be interspersed with sport and outward bound courses that would teach leadership and teamwork and these sections should be run by ex-military personnel who would know how to instil the necessary discipline, fitness and pride in the youngsters.

Obviously if some kids wanted to spend their year in the forces, this should be encouraged as well, but the most important aspect of my proposal is that every kid, regardless of race, religion, colour, class or creed, must be forced to do this year's service. There must be no exceptions and no exclusions.

My old man used to say that his two years' national service was both pointless and also the greatest learning curve of his life. He met people from different backgrounds and cultures and they were forced to get along even if many of the tasks were a waste of time.

Perhaps this last point is one of the most important aspects of national service: it forces people to learn from others' experiences. I remember watching a documentary presented by the ex-political editor of the BBC, who was talking to a bunch of factory workers up north. They were discussing youth crime, both the perception and the reality, and one of them made the point that nowadays the generations hardly mix, which leads to distrust and apprehension, perhaps even fear on both sides of the age divide.

The workers made the point that it was different when everyone, whatever age, was either working in a factory or down a pit. The younger lads might have gone out of a weekend and got up to no good but on Monday when they recounted the story they would be firmly, either verbally or physically, put back in their place by one of the older men. I agree with this sentiment and have long argued that it is the root cause of many of our problems today.

When you're walking down the street and you see a bunch of lads you are tempted to cross the road and avoid them, even turn a blind eye if they are misbehaving, but – and I don't think this is romanticised – in the old days you would probably know one of the boys from work or at least know his brother or uncle or dad. With the demise of heavy industry and the subsequent movement of labour or, in the case of NEETS, the inability to move out of their stinking pits, there has been a growth in the fractionalisation of society which we need to address.

Meanwhile in the home many children, especially young boys, are being brought up without a significant male role model. We used to call them dads before the age of political correctness, and therefore the introduction of ex-military personnel into schools could be a way of plugging this gap.

If we employed ex-military types as a form of classroom assistant, perhaps they could instil some much-needed self-respect and discipline, even fitness into these youths. It's the old adage of going on an outward bound course, isn't it, and letting the bully abseil in the full knowledge that it is the weakling, his victim, that is holding the rope at the top. This tends to focus the mind of the bully and the bullied and make them realise that life is all about teamwork and as my old PE teacher would say, a team is only as strong as its weakest link. The truth is, though, so many kids are never challenged like this so they never realise both their own capabilities and the strengths and weaknesses of their peers.

I don't believe that kids are intrinsically evil. I firmly believe they are the products of their environment so it's that environment that we need to alter.

It sounds pathetic to even write this but surely programmes like *Bad Lads' Army* have kind of proved this. This was a fascinating reality programme (or is that an oxymoron?), originally entitled simply *Lads' Army*, where young lads underwent two weeks of 1950s-style basic army training to see if the modern youth could cope. The success of the first series led to three other series where the title changed to *Bad Lads' Army* and where the idea transformed into taking petty criminals and seeing if the army routine could actually alter their outlook on life and their behaviour. The basic proposition was to see if the reintroduction of national service could be a way of solving youth crime.

The results have been mixed, with some kids walking out and preferring to take their punishment, which roughly translated probably means a slap on the wrist, from the courts whereas others have claimed it really helped them and several have actually signed up to become professional soldiers.

Of course it was only a TV series and of course the lads were all from one section of society rather than the real genuine social mix of the Fifties, but I still find the results fascinating and I know for a fact that many of my readers and listeners believe this could be the way forward.

It's interesting to note that both Brown and Cameron are now suggesting some form of voluntary community service for all sixteen-year-olds and the reintroduction of cadet forces into schools.

I've also found that in places like Cyprus, where of course they still have national service, young lads do genuinely seem to have a stake in their society. However, I am a firm believer that for national service to have any real effect it must be compulsory *for all* and not just used as a controlling mechanism for the working class.

Interestingly in Switzerland, where conscription and the ownership of guns by conscript soldiers are mandatory, the level of gun and gun-associated crime is very low.

Of course it is always dangerous to compare different countries as there are vast differences in culture and the influence of family and religion in different societies to take into consideration, but it seems to me that the restoration of some form of national service is long overdue.

25

Tolerance: one of the greatest British traits

One of the greatest British traits is tolerance. I truly believe that we are probably the most tolerant nation on the planet so it really winds me up when people either accuse us of being racist or abuse our tolerance.

Recently I was asked to appear on BBC2's *Newsnight* to discuss whether the white working class had been ignored and marginalised in British society. I told the researcher, 'That's not a discussion, that is a statement of fact.'

Let's face it, for ages it's almost become a crime to be white, heterosexual, married and British in Great Britain.

In typical BBC style they wheeled out the swivel-eyed, knuckle-dragging leader of the BNP, Nick Griffin. I told them in no uncertain terms that this man and his bunch of neo-Nazis doesn't and never will represent the white working class and they should be ashamed of themselves for suggesting that he might.

So for the benefit of the Biased Broadcasting Corporation and the record let me state clearly that you can be a patriot and not a racist. You can be a patriot and celebrate our glorious history, traditions and culture without hating people for the colour of their skin. You can want to control immigration and protect our borders and not be racist. Finally you can wrap yourself in our flag without resorting to racism.

However over these past few years it would appear that New Labour have wanted to celebrate every culture and tradition that immigrants have brought into the country but somehow rejected – even despised – the indigenous population's heritage.

It is New Labour's immigration free for all and obsession with multiculturalism that has created this increasingly divided nation. They have been too swift to accept or even turn a blind eye to injustice, sexism, homophobia and racial hatred if the perpetrator is a Muslim for fear of being called racist.

Practices that would be condemned by the 'PC thought police' if the majority population carried them out have been accepted under the guise of being inclusive and multicultural.

It is Labour that allows misguided Muslim women to think it's OK for them to wear a veil at school or even more ludicrously in a court of law. It is Labour's fault that some young British Muslim men think it's acceptable to call women slags if they dance at nightclubs. It is Labour's fault that mad Muslim clerics can call for gays to be thrown off cliffs or stoned. It's Labour's fault that a woman can be murdered, by her father, for kissing her boyfriend in the street. It is Labour's fault that extremists can hurl insults at our injured troops in hospital because they are wearing the Queen's uniform. It's Labour's fault that hotheads thought they could preach murder and celebrate 9/11 and 7/7 on the streets of London with little fear of being arrested until we in the press kicked up a storm.

We are a tolerant nation but how much more of this nonsense do we have to take before the establishment classes understand that they are creating the problems by not laying down strict guidelines for how to behave if you want to live in this country?

If I were to visit or live in a Muslim country like Saudi Arabia, I would fit in. The girls and Lisa would dress modestly and Lisa would not drive – which would be a Godsend or Allah-send! But the point is we would conform. So why can't these Muslim extremists do the same?

This is still a Christian country with the last available census clearly showing that 72 per cent of us would classify ourselves as Christian. However, most Brits haven't got a problem with people celebrating their own culture, traditions and religions and they don't care whether someone goes to the mosque on a Friday or the temple and synagogue on a Saturday, it's a case of live and let live. Where people have a real problem, however, is when these religious groups try to impose their belief structure and religion on the rest of us and I am afraid the Muslim community are the worst offenders at this.

So let's be clear and state that there is no place in modern twenty-first-century Britain for the veil. Let's stop the rows over whether Luton schoolgirls can wear the full *burka* or not and the even more ludicrous arguments about doctors dressing like this and just ban the bloody thing altogether. According to my Muslim callers and readers, nowhere in the Koran does it state that the wearing of the veil is a religious obligation, so why are we allowing a small subsection of a religion or community to dictate terms to the rest of us? Clearly the veil is a sign of repression and oppression that has no place in a modern twenty-first-century liberal society that believes in equal rights. Therefore it must be banned.

Instead the Government have shown the backbone of a blancmange and we have had to endure endless debates about whether we should remove all religious symbols from schools and the workplace. Why? This is a smokescreen. There is nothing wrong with wearing a crucifix, a skull cap or the *hijab*. It is the full-face covering that has no place in modern Britain.

Tolerance has to be a two-way street and I am afraid it is clear that some Muslims are not doing enough, or being made to do enough, to fit in with the majority way of life and illustrate their loyalty to and love of this great country.

Other groups like the Jews, Sikhs and Hindus have fitted in while retaining their own deeply held beliefs and customs and despite massive provocation Brits of all religious and ethnic backgrounds have shown remarkable patience and restraint since 7/7.

However, judging by my mailbag and the phone calls to talk-SPORT this patience is now wearing thin and politicians, but more importantly the Muslim community and its leaders, need to do more to show that this is a United Kingdom not a collection of different religious and ethnic ghettos. David Davis from the Tories was right when he warned Muslim leaders that they were 'creating apartheid by shutting themselves off'.

Meanwhile a recent poll in the *Daily Telegraph* showed clearly that 57 per cent of voters want Muslims to do more to fit in. Also let's not pussyfoot around: the Muslim community must do still more, much more, to weed out this cancer within them. I also want to stop hearing the appeasers of terrorism on the left blaming all these outrages on our foreign policy and our occupation of so-called Muslim lands and I do not want to hear a Muslim leader condemning these latest attacks and then saying but . . .

There is no time for ifs and buts. We are at war. The enemy has brought the war to our front yard and it is time for us Brits of whatever race, religion or sex to stand firm and defeat these medieval madmen.

Gordon Brown needs to listen less to the bleating of Liberty's Shami Chakrabarti – remember, she only represents 9,000 people – and start listening to the majority of Brits who want to live without fear and want these sickos washed off our streets. That's why we must have the 42-day detention rule brought in immediately and even consider internment for those that we feel may be a threat.

So can we forget all this bull about the battle for hearts and minds and just start standing up for our way of life, our values and our great democracy, and if that requires force let's just get on with it.

But still the Muslim leaders don't seem to get it, do they?

Inayat Bunglawala of the Muslim Council of Great Britain believes that 'No group in Britain has been as systematically vilified in recent years in the media as British Muslims.'

Oh Inayat, please put a sock in it will you, mate? Look, no group in Britain has been such a pain in the *burka* as some of the Muslims in recent years and no group has contained elements that wanted to blow the wider community up. The problem lies with your community and their failure to integrate, not with the majority population. The sooner you realise that and cease celebrating your victimhood and stop bleating about Islamophobia the better for all of us.

Instead of blaming the media for Muslim problems, Inayat and his mate Dr Bari with the dodgy Ted Rogers wig should make sure first that they actually represent the community they claim to speak for. If they're so keen on fair play why don't they hold open and free elections to elect themselves to their positions of responsibility? In fact, let's go one step further: why do we need a separatist council? Why can't local MPs represent all sections of communities and even Inayat can stand for election to a real council or parliament.

Once they've done that they and the rest of the community need to do more to weed out the terrorist cancer in their midst and persuade the one in ten members of their community who say they sympathised with the 7/7 bombers that they are wrong.

It is clear to me that New Labour has turned tolerant Britain into a powder keg of racial and religious mistrust through their misguided and ill-thought-out policy of multiculturalism.

Multiculturalism is meant to celebrate differences but I don't see much to celebrate in today's Britain. What I actually see is clowns like Sir Ian Blair pussyfooting around the sensibilities of a minority while the rest of us have been silenced for fear of being called a racist.

Since the 7/7 bombings this Government has bent over backwards to win support from the Muslim community. There's been £40 million spent on Muslim road shows, laws against forced marriages have been dropped and prominent so-called community leaders have been knighted and promoted.

The latest bonehead initiative to spend another £12 million diverting Muslim youth from terror is another classic example of too much carrot and not enough stick. It's the equivalent of giving rioting inner-city yobbos another brand-new youth club to burn down as a response to their criminal activity.

The Home Secretary Jacqui Smith should stop acting as a social worker and start behaving like a home secretary. Doesn't she realise that Osama Bin Laden must be laughing in his cave and Abu Hamza would be sticking up two fingers, if he had any, at her policy of appeasement.

I'm sorry, there is an enemy within and no amount of road shows, hand-wringing and stupid initiatives like this will stop it. We need to fight fire with fire whereas Spliff intends to turn a blind eye to youths who are just on the fringes of terrorist activity.

According to the secret services there are at least 2,000 terrorist sympathisers in this country. Well, I'm sorry, I for one do not want to wait until another atrocity takes place. So if we know who these alleged 2,000 sympathisers are, we should lock the bastards up, interrogate them and divert them or re-educate them until we know that they are safe to release back into the community.

Because, pray tell me, what's been the result of all this appeasement and eggshell treading so far?

There's been an increased level of victimhood, demonstrations and outrage at the slightest criticism of the Muslim religion and culture. Well, enough is enough. Forget lifting veils, Labour should remove the kid gloves and treat Muslims the same as every other British citizen. They should send out a clear message: Fit in or fuck off.

26

Different but equal: the modern British bloke

While the Government and British society in general seems to be rushing to accept all kinds of relationships and families it appears to me that those of us who opted to go down the traditional route and actually marry someone of the opposite sex before having children are increasingly being marginalised in twenty-first-century Britain.

I'm forty-seven, married with two daughters, and I appear to be facing a crisis. It's not the typical mid-life crisis that seems to affect forty-something blokes that culminates in them sleeping with the secretary, wearing denim and killing themselves on a Harley Davidson. It's more fundamental than that: it's a crisis about being a man and about what a man, a husband and a dad's role should be in modern Britain.

The latest attack on British men, our masculinity and me is the invention of the so-called metrosexual.

Not content with turning women into anorexics and their models into cocaine-snorting stick insects, the fashion and cosmetic industries have now turned their attention to men. If you believe the hype, the average British male is spending £600 a year on cosmetics.

But who the hell are these 'men' that are spending this ridiculous sum? In a houseful of women I hardly have enough time in the bathroom in the morning to expectorate let alone exfoliate. So do these guys really exist? Is the British man changing and is masculinity being redefined as I am left behind, smelling of last year's aftershave? Or is this just another example of the 'gayification' of Britain where every bloke has to be in touch with his feminine side and every male pop wannabe has to sing like a castrato with a lisp!

I can understand why gay men follow a beauty regime – after all, they are trying to attract other blokes, and to be honest, straight as I am, I will admit that most men are turned on by the visual rather than the intellectual. As John Dowie, the comic, once said, 'I might be the new man but show me a porno mag and I'll show you an erection.'

However, do straight men want to try that hard? Please tell me, do women expect anything more from their men than clean teeth, no body odour and definitely no hint of a combover?

One thing's for sure, I certainly don't want to be regroomed, restyled or reprogrammed by the makers of programmes like *Queer Eye for the Straight Guy*. I'm not interested if my hair colour or complexion favours 'autumn hues'. I just want my clothes to be comfortable. But does the failure to moisturise blackball me from the modern masculinity club? I hope so. Because I don't want to be defined by that icon of new manhood, David Beckham. When I think about him shaving as well as bending his balls I feel slightly queasy and it's put me off kiwi fruit for life. Does this make me a caveman? Am I stuck in Victorian or Fifties Britain?

Thirty years on from the beginning of the Women's Movement, it seems to me that women and indeed more recently gay men, by and large, can have it all. Or at least they have choices of the role they want to play in British society, but straight men have been ridiculed, marginalised, confused and even emasculated and it's time for us to fight back. I'm not suggesting the formation of some 'Iron John' type men's movement where men burn their razors, grow bushy beards and run naked into the woods to discover their inner selves, but we do need to stand up for ourselves and the vital role we play in family life.

In the rush and desire for equality between the sexes, we have forgotten that men and women can be equal but different. This ranges from trivial observations like, 'I've never met a straight man that could ever sit through the *Bridget Jones* film' and 'I don't know any bloke who actually likes females commentating on male sport!' to the more important truths such as seeing my role as being the breadwinner, the provider and my wife, Lisa, as the main nurturer in the family. Nearly every bloke I've ever met feels likes this, but most are afraid to voice these opinions in mixed company. They feel open to ridicule, being seen as uncool or just plain old-fashioned and, perhaps worst of all, they don't want to appear as if they are the same as their dads!

I used to look at my dad over the Christmas table or at other family occasions and wonder if it was easier for his generation. Was it easier to be a bloke in Britain when there were clearly defined roles in a marriage and society. He worked and provided and my mum was the homemaker and nurturer.

One Christmas meal and the generations nearly collided when Dad, commenting on my wife's desire to go back to work after her degree, said, 'Yes, love, it would be nice to have a bit of "pin money".' He was lucky – I was carving and holding on to the knife! It was an easy mistake for him to make as Lisa and I fulfil what, on the surface, look like the traditional roles but the difference between Dad's marriage and mine was vast. This is what those who sneer at stay-at-home mums and relationships based on traditional values and roles miss when they denigrate the importance of marriage and the family. Marriage has changed in the last thirty years but it's still the bedrock of any family and should be the cornerstone of British society.

The emotional and physical effort I put into the family would have seemed radical, even revolutionary, to my dad thirty years ago. I know that surveys always point out that even when both partners are in full-time employment, women do more of the domestic chores but the fact remains that men, like me and my mates, would be seen as aliens to my dad's generation. I can vividly remember my dad and us boys watching *Grandstand* with Frank Bough and our only contribution to the domestic chores was to lift our feet up on to the settee so that Mum could Hoover under them. Now we wash, cook, iron, clean and soon we'll even master wiping a work surface down like a woman!

Like most men of my generation I also want to be emotionally involved in the rearing of my children, and being at their birth was the greatest moment of my life, but I recognise primarily that my wife is the chief nurturer. I know it's almost sacrilegious to say but I actually think that women are better than men at this. Why does the pursuit of equality mean that we have to pretend otherwise? What purpose does it serve? I can't stand these new dads who wear those baby slings and act as if they secretly want to breast-feed their child. The new mums practically have to rip the baby, à la Lady Macbeth, from their bosom to feed. What are these men trying to prove with their play-acting? Don't most women resent this too and aren't most suspicious of such antics?

This doesn't mean that I want to be a 'wait till your father gets home' kind of dad, but it does mean that I recognise our strengths and weaknesses. I was on the dole when Rosie was born and for the first few months of her life I was at home twenty-four hours a day and though this intimacy has led to a tight bond between me and my eldest daughter, if I'm honest it was still Lisa who did most of the nappy-changing and caring. Was that because I was lazy? Frightened? Not as good as Lisa? Or did Lisa see it as her role as mother? It was probably a combination of all four but if I'm honest I have to admit that when I did get a job it was a relief to leave the domestics behind for the safety and stress of the workplace. It felt right to go out and work and earn, to provide and why should men have to feel ashamed of this, embarrassed by it?

British blokes don't seem to be able to win. If we desert our children and our responsibilities then the Government chase us through the CSA. If we want to work and our wives stay at home, what tax breaks do we get? Since the collapse of John Major's family values campaign all those years ago amongst a deluge of sleaze and sex it seems as if it has become commonplace to think that all marriages and families are based on insecure and hypocritical foundations. They are not and us men who are providing for our families have a right to be recognised for our contribution.

When I was just writing for the *Sun* and not doing the daily grind of an early-morning radio show I used to do the school run and nothing could have prepared me for the rollercoaster of emotions that charged the car each morning.

Don't get me wrong: I enjoyed taking the girls to school but if I'm really honest I found that I was severely lacking in the listening and counselling department. I don't know whether this happens to other dads but I often find when I'm talking to Rosie who is nearly fifteen and Beth who is thirteen that I am constantly glancing over their heads for Lisa's approval that I'm hitting the right note. Recent discoveries are that you don't point out spots and you never comment on levels of make-up!

Do I want to be more sensitive to my daughters' emotional needs and moods? Yes I do. Do I want to be as tuned in as Lisa? The honest and direct answer is no! I'll be there for them if they are in trouble, danger, I'll be the rock, the protector, but I don't know if I am equipped to be the emotional lightning conductor, the empathiser, the emotional sponge. I don't know whether this is a case of nature or nurture but what I do know is that from my observations most men are like this. I love my family to bits but I actually like the sound of the front door as it closes behind me as I leave for work. I've lost count of the number of guys who tell me at Christmas that they enjoy the family time but by the day after Boxing Day they are always looking forward to getting back to work. Does that make them and me bad dads or just honest?

I accept that our domestic relationship is both odd and strange to many families who would cite economic necessity for Mum returning to work, but is it too outrageous, sexist, or reactionary to suggest that it is better for the kids if Mum stays at home?

The reaction we receive when asked what Lisa does and she replies, 'Look after the children' would make one think she is a Stepford wife, chained to the kitchen sink. I still can't quite work out how our traditional domestic relationship has appeared to become a novelty rather than the norm and although I am not advocating a return to women only earning pin money, I do wonder why active motherhood has lost all its status?

Interestingly it appears that more and more women are coming to a similar conclusion with a survey suggesting that over 50 per cent of British women want to stay at home with their young children and only have a part-time job rather than work full time. Of course it is an acknowledged fact that women's equality and ability to earn, to stand alone, has also meant that women have been able to escape and leave unhappy marriages. However, is it unpalatable, unjust, even unfair to suggest that this economic independence has also led to women and men giving up too early on marriage and family life? I know it's easy for me to say, as I'm not the one who gets pregnant and therefore has to make these choices, but I still think that Lisa made the best decision for her, the children and yes for me!

Then I look at my two daughters who are doing so well at school and I think of their ambitions and opportunities. I think of their long-dead grandma, my mum, and the vast difference in expectation, ambition, desire and achievement that is possible for these two. Of course then I have to face the contradiction of my argument: am I willing for them to be disadvantaged by their sex? Am I willing for them to be the homemaker while their children are pre-school? Will I be happy if they put their careers on hold to look after their children while their husband climbs the greasy pole and provides for them?

The honest answer is . . . yes. Because in modern Britain we are different but equal.

27

Gold chains, no brains

Fifteen-year-old Billy Cox was shot dead on his doorstep in Clapham on Wednesday, 15 February 2007.

Just over a year later Shakilus Townsend was stabbed to death in the street.

What connects these two young boys isn't just the fact that they are both just another depressing statistic of Broken Britain but also the fact that within moments of their death, online tribute sites were set up describing them both as brave 'soldiers'.

It soon became clear that both Cox and Townsend, far from being innocent mummy's boys, were actually gun- and knife-toting examples of the filth that is plaguing this country. I guess, however, now that both have ended up in the morgue that's two less hoodlums the police have to round up.

Obviously not all the victims of knife crime are members of gangs but I am afraid the depressing facts are that many are and they are not afraid to brag about it, as proved by the pictures of Cox and Townsend on social network sites brandishing weapons or posing as teenage boys in the hood.

Their violent deaths and the online tributes and pictures to them paint a terrifying picture of modern inner-city Britain.

As far as I am concerned, if you live by the gun or knife then you deserve all you get and I don't buy the excuses from the parents that they didn't know how their sons were behaving. They should have known, it is their responsibility – they were their children.

Cox's dad, Tommy, urged the community 'to get behind the police 100 per cent'. However it's a pity that Tommy and his wife didn't both get behind their drug-dealing son '100 per cent' and the police years ago and then maybe Billy wouldn't have ended lying on the morgue's slab.

I know the families are probably still grieving but I am afraid this is not the time for pussyfooting round their feelings and sensitivities – there's a war going on out there and some harsh truths and judgements have to be said and made before there are more angels with dirty faces, another angelic upstart lying in the morgue.

The majority of us are bringing up kids the right way and teaching them right from wrong. But unfortunately there is a growing underclass that couldn't spell right from wrong let alone recognise it. This is the 'gold chains, no brains' culture that revels in ignorance, misogyny and celebrates gun violence and gang warfare.

It is these people who need to stop being rewarded for their useless, often criminal lives and it is time for the political classes to stop ignoring these people and refusing to be judgemental about their chaotic criminal lives and start intervening and challenging their wayward behaviour.

And they could start by criticising Billy's mum and dad because it seems to me Billy's home life was not full of love. If it was, his mum and dad would have diverted him from his life of crime. They could have started by coming down hard on him when they realised he was spraying his 'tag' like a stray cat over all the walls and buildings in the neighbourhood. Are we really meant to swallow the line that he just fell in with a bad crowd and they didn't know he was running with a gang? How many times have we heard that?

Cox was wearing an electronic tag when he was gunned down. He had the tag because he had been found guilty of burglary. If that's the case why wasn't he actually locked up and if he was free, where was the supervision from the probation service? Clearly the electronic tag, which he was still wearing when he was lying on the mortuary slab, didn't stop him and no doubt thousands of other toe-rags from escalating their criminal behaviour from burglary to crack dealing.

There needed to be greater tough love and intervention in Billy's life years ago both by his family and the authorities.

Likewise the morons who turned up outside his home dressed in hoodies and sunglasses putting down their pathetic floral tributes and barely legible misspelled tributes to their 'fallen soldier' need to be cleaned off the streets and cleaned up.

But there's fat chance of that happening in politically correct non-judgemental Britain.

Labour hasn't got a clue how to deal with this problem. First Home Secretary Jacquie Spliff proposes making knife-carrying thugs visit hospitals and meet victims of knife crime. When she is told this idea is half-baked she performs a U-turn quicker than a Clarkson handbrake turn on *Top Gear*. This is the political equivalent of putting an Elastoplast on a severed jugular and would have done nothing to stem the bleeding or the shooting.

My solution is simple: if you're caught with a knife it's five years – and five must mean five. If you use that knife it's life – and life means life. When it comes to guns, if you're caught with one, even if you haven't used it, you're going to prison for a ten-year stretch – and ten years must mean ten not four or five. And it should be ten hard years not the custodial equivalent of a youth club or holiday camp where in between drug-taking sessions these hoodlums can keep their trigger fingers active and in training by playing on Nintendos or channel hopping on Sky.

If you use a gun despite the consequences it should result in the death penalty but I guess I would compromise on a life sentence, but again life must mean life.

Meanwhile politicians need to attack the root causes of this problem, which are drugs and the breakdown of family.

Let's stop treating druggies, junkies and pushers as victims and start treating them as the lowlife scum they are. We've tried the softly-softly approach including the insane idea of reclassifying cannabis and the potty Paddick experiment of turning a blind eye to so-called soft drug dealing in Lambeth. And kids – some, unlike Billy, wholly innocent – are now lying in the morgue.

We need to go down the harsher route and fight fire with fire.

Likewise when it comes to family we must make sure that family, the traditional family – and yes that means a mum and a dad – need to be put at the centre of all policy. Families and men and women who put their children first should be rewarded both by the tax and benefit system.

We could make a start by immediately restoring the married man's tax allowance and encouraging, financially and socially, mums to stay at home until the kids reach the age of five.

We need to cut the financial umbilical cord between young teenage slappers getting pregnant and being rewarded with a council flat. Perhaps allowing one mistake but intervening if the young lady continues acting as if her feet are pen pals by having a succession of babeeeees with a selection of feckless fathers.

Similarly the men who think that their responsibility to their offspring finishes as they roll off the dozy bird and light up the fag need to be chased down and made to pay for the upkeep of their children.

We also need to stop calling children young people. A child is a child until they are bringing in a wage packet and we need to support adults and parents who are willing to lead by example and discipline and inspire children in equal measure. It is not the role of a parent to be their child's best friend. It is your role to be their guardian, their mentor and sometimes their disciplinarian.

And I don't buy the line that this violence is all about poverty, depravation or racism and that it would all be solved if the Government set up a task force and opened a few youth clubs and training centres. This attitude is both dangerous and patronising to those families who don't descend into this gutter of criminality and squalor.

Hard work, graft, loyalty and discipline need to be rewarded and praised and at the same time we need to punish financially and socially the misfits, criminal and plain irresponsible.

28

If Britain is so good why are so many Brits leaving?

It's a fair question and one that I get asked all the time. I think I have highlighted some of the main reasons why up to 250,000 Brits are leaving every year. I've even bought a bolthole myself in Cyprus because I love their laid-back approach to life coupled with the sunshine and their real belief in family values. I was also thinking of buying a shop in downtown Islamabad and only selling union flags and effigies of Blair and Bush as I reckon I would make a small fortune.

But the serious question is: could I actually contemplate leaving Blighty for good and, do you know what, I don't think I could and I don't think you or I should.

Despite this second section of the book, where I've amply described what is wrong with our country, I do think that we true Brits should stay and fight for our country. I don't think it's too late to save Great Britain. I just think we have got to force the self-serving pigs in Westminster and the skinny-latte metropolitan elite who run the media to start listening to us. And I actually believe that this is beginning to happen.

People are angry in this country; angry about immigration, knife and gun crime and spiralling inflation, and politicians are having to listen and act on these complaints and that's why I think radio programmes and columns like mine have some real influence. Of course when people say to me, 'Gaunty, why don't you stand for

Parliament?' I always reply, 'I can't afford the pay cut.' However the truth is I actually believe that I can do more on the outside by criticising those in power and throwing up alternative views on how we should run our country than actually joining them at the trough!

People often say, 'Eh, Gaunty, you say what we're thinking or what we're afraid to say' and the truth is, they are right. Whatever limited success or influence I have got is a direct result of the fact that I've always been a bolshy opinionated sod who isn't scared of anyone or anything. I just try to say it how I see it and if you like it, good, if not, tough titty. I just know if you become an MP with our stupid whips system there is no way you can be like that and I wouldn't want to be part of that system.

However, I also firmly believe that some politicians are now listening to what I say but, more importantly, what my listeners say on talkSPORT, which is why so many top politicians and coppers are actually ringing me now, rather than the other way round, to come on the show. This is progress and this is a way ordinary people can make their voice heard.

talkSPORT is pure uncensored opinion and is probably unique in the British broadcasting world in that it is the only place where you will hear real people talking about real lives. Similarly with the *Sun*, some weeks I receive incredible emails or letters that in just a few words succinctly sum up all that is wrong in society and hit the nail harder on the head than I can ever do.

Politicians should listen to these people more often and then perhaps they wouldn't have voted to keep their dodgy expenses in direct contradiction of what the British public wanted. It is this arrogance of power, this disconnection with voters, that makes me so damn angry with the modern British politician and it is this that needs to be changed. So if in my own small way either via a TV appearance, a column in the *Sun* or a radio phone-in on talkSPORT I can prick an MP's pomposity, arrogance or smugness then maybe we can begin to rebuild Great Britain.

That said, just take a look in the next section of the book at what this small nation and its people have achieved and realise why this country is worth staying in and fighting for. Yes, some days it does feel like Rubbish Britain but, by God, despite everything this is still Great Britain.

PART III
The Very Best of British

29

'Oooh *Matron*': best British comedy catchphrases

We British love a catchphrase and it is the uttering of these in the playground, the workplace or in casual conversation that links us together and binds us. You only have to hear the phrase 'Don't tell them your name, Pike,' and immediately you see the *Dad's Army* crew and the German U-boat skipper played by a young Philip Madoc.

Every catchphrase, never mind how short, brings back a collective and a personal memory of a well-loved show or comedian. Almost all of the following catchphrases would provoke a titter, 'Oooh matron' (Thank you, Kenneth) of recognition in a bar full of Brits but would be incomprehensible to a foreigner and that's 'Magic, our Maurice' (Selwyn Froggit) or 'Super, Smashing, Great', isn't it, Jim Bowen? Know what I mean, Harry?

1. Morecambe & Wise/Eddie Braben

- 'What do you think of it so far?' '*Rubbish!*'
- 'Short, fat, hairy legs'
- 'You can't see the join!'
- 'The play what I wrote'
- 'Arsenal!'
- 'He's not wrong, you know!'
- 'You said that without moving your lips'

- 'Look at me when I'm talking to you!'
- 'This boy's a fool!'

Just reading those catchphrases, you can't help but see Eric slapping Ernie's cheeks or Eric dressed as a Roman centurion with Luton on his banner, or the pair of them humiliating one of their guests in one of the plays what Ernie wrote. The scripts were brilliant, of course, courtesy of Liverpudlian writer, Eddie Braben; the set-pieces, both the plays and the big musical parodies, are part of every Brit's childhood and certainly every one of our Christmases; and Eric and Ernie are quite simply the greatest double act Britain has ever produced. This was the Golden Age of British Comedy and the BBC, where millions would tune in and as a result every conversation at work or school the next day would be about Eric and Ernie.

The greatest tribute to these comedy geniuses and their writers is that the shows are as fresh and funny today as they ever were and new generations like my children enjoy them and recite the catchphrases and delight in the visual gags just like I did years ago.

2. *Only Fools and Horses*

- 'Rodney You Plonker'
- 'This time next year we'll be millionaires'
- 'Luvverly Jubberly'
- 'Cushty'

This brilliant series, written by one of Britain's greatest scriptwriters, John Sullivan, has more catchphrases in it than Del Boy has scams. I have chosen four but there's plenty more, some of which like Plonker have actually now become official words in the English dictionary. It ran for seven series on BBC1 from 1981 until 1991 with Christmas specials up until 2003. It's fair to say it wasn't an overnight success but the BBC persevered with it and it became one of the most successful sitcoms of all time.

Only Fools and Horses was voted best British sitcom ever and rightly so as the show, especially the Christmas specials and the characters, are an intrinsic part of British culture.

3. 'I don't *believe it!*' – Victor Meldrew in *One Foot in the Grave*

This was another classic from the BBC and ran for six series from 1990 until 2000. It was written by David Renwick and wasn't an instant audience success. However by the third series – something that would never be allowed to happen in today's TV world of demands for instant ratings – it was getting an audience of millions and an incredible 20 million of us watched the Christmas special in 2003.

Victor Meldrew made Scottish TV-actor Richard Wilson into a household name and one of Britain's best-loved comedy actors. In each episode Victor's ever-simmering temper at the unfairness of life boils over into a vitriolic rant, occasionally preceded by his immortal catchphrase, 'I don't *believe* it!'

Many viewers, myself included, identified with his rages at the irritants of modern life: litter, junk mail, traffic, rudeness, streetlamps and car mechanics. And to some, Victor Meldrew was a champion of the people, albeit a very grumpy one. The character was so popular that the term 'Victor Meldrew' is now a British cultural reference for any grumpy old bastard.

Quick trivia: David Renwick's writing career started on the *Luton News* which was where I first started writing newspaper columns . . . 'I don't *believe* it!'

4. Bruce Forsyth – *The Generation Game* and every other show he has ever appeared in

- 'Nice to see you, to see you . . . nice'
- 'Didn't he do well?'
- 'Give us a twirl'
- 'Scores on the Doors'
- 'Good game, good game'

What true Brit can forget the opening bars of *The Generation Game*'s theme music, 'Life is the Name of the Game', which coincidentally Bruce wrote, and then the image of Brucie in silhouette in that Rodin pose as The Thinker? Then he turned and gave us the immortal catchphrase that was part of all our childhoods in the Seventies – 'Nice to see you, to see you . . . nice.'

Of course Bruce had already become a household name in 1958 when he took over *Sunday Night at The London Palladium* but it was his six years (1971–1977) hosting British TV's greatest-ever Saturday night family show that made Brucie the star and the British cultural icon he is today. And the catchphrases rolled out quicker than the tacky prizes on the conveyor belt.

Bruce is the archetypal song-and-dance man and although his act is clearly influenced by his hero, Sammy Davis Junior, there is no doubt that Bruce is one of the last great British variety acts still treading the boards and gracing our screens. As I have said in other parts of this book, he must be knighted.

5. 'You *Dirty* Old Man' – *Steptoe & Son*

This groundbreaking comedy by Ray Galton and Alan Simpson, the men behind *Hancock's Half Hour*, is one of my all-time favourite British sitcoms. I've got to be honest, I never really got *Hancock's Half Hour*. Maybe I was too young but even the blood donor scene doesn't really make me laugh, whereas *Steptoe & Son* still makes me roar to this day. Its basic theme of the clash of the generations is as relevant now as it was back in 1962 when it broke the mould of British situation comedies.

Out of the window went slapstick, gags and trouser-dropping farce to be replaced with gritty realism. Just as the British theatre and then British film was being dramatically transformed with plays like *Look Back in Anger* and movies like *This Sporting Life*, now it was TV's turn to be dragged into the class and generational conflict of the Sixties.

The comedy was aided and abetted by the fact that the characters of Albert and his son 'Harold', another catchphrase, were played by straight actors, Wilfred Brambell and Harry H Corbett, rather than comedians. I loved the way they used realistic language and tackled, as much as you could in the Sixties, real themes and subject matter such as sex.

Harold wanted to better himself and had ideas above his station; he thought he knew about literature, classical music and fancied himself as an actor, primarily of course to attract a posh bird which his dad would then both salivate over and try to ruin any budding romance for fear of losing his son from the family rag-and-bone business.

Who can forget the classic episodes where Albert teaches Harold the wrong ballroom dancing steps or where in desperation and wanting to escape the 'Dirty Old Man', Harold splits the living room in half, including a line down the centre of the TV? Harold thinks he has won this battle of the generations because the control knobs are on his side of the divide; the only problem is the plug is on his dad's side and a wheezing Albert cackles as he pulls it out.

These episodes are absolute classics in any language but for us Brits they absolutely capture the intergenerational conflict of the Sixties and Seventies that was also evident in British pop music and the subcultures of mods and rockers through to punks and Goths. This was our working-class life portrayed on TV for perhaps the very first time and the bonus was it was bloody funny as well.

In *Steptoe* I think we see the foundation stones for such British classics as *The Liver Birds* or Carla Lane's other brilliant working-class series *Bread*, set in the depressed but ever hopeful and enterprising Liverpool of the Eighties and Nineties. Clearly there are also parallels between the relationship of Harold and Albert and Del Boy and his younger brother Rodney and then their Granddad and later Uncle Albert.

Although it was social realism, the use of catchphrases and stock characters were still part of the unique winning formula which would mean that this programme would run from 1962 to 1965 in black and white, returning in colour for four more series from 1970.

Obviously I was too young to see the first series – I was only born in 1961 – but when it came back in colour in 1970 my old man, much to the disappointment of my mum, would allow me and my brother to watch it with him if we had behaved ourselves. It was the same rule with *Monty Python* and *Till Death Us Do Part*, and actually I think it was this liberal approach to TV in a pretty illiberal police house that first got me into the idea of wanting to be an actor or write for a living. Thanks Dad. But most of all thanks to Galton and Simpson – you are absolute stars.

Don't forget that along with *Till Death Us Do Part*, this is one of the only British sitcoms that had a successful adaptation for the US market when it was launched over there as *Sanford & Son*. The two film spin-offs are also well worth buying when you buy the DVD box set of both series.

6. 'You silly moo' – Alf Garnet in *Till Death Us Do Part*

This is another brilliant British sitcom that was and only could be a product of the social and political upheaval that was happening in

Britain in the early Sixties. Again it was a generational comedy and centred on the unbelievable bigotry of its central character Alf and his relationship with his younger daughter Rita, played by Una Stubbs, and her 'lazy Scouse git' of a boyfriend Mike, played by Tony Booth (Cherie Blair's real-life dad).

Alf represented the old guard, he was conservative, a royalist and a supporter of Enoch Powell, and his battles with his left-wing son-in-law were not just ideological but also generational and cultural. Rita and Mike represented the younger generation who had a more relaxed attitude to race, religion, sexual morals and fashion which of course Alf hated and had no hesitation in shouting down with rants that seemed to always begin with 'It stands too reason . . .' and ended up with him calling Mike a 'lazy Scouse git'. Should his wife, Dandy Nicholls, interject with a reasonable comment, she would be shouted down with the catchphrase, 'You silly moo'. Originally this was 'silly cow' but was softened by the head of BBC Comedy at the time, Frank Muir.

The term groundbreaking is too casually used to describe TV series these days but this programme truly deserves the title because Johnny Speight's character and Warren Mitchell's portrayal of Alf was a true working-class grotesque that even to this day makes you question whether you are laughing with Alf and his bigotry or at him. It puts you in the opposite of the comfort zone, just as Ricky Gervais does in *The Office* where you really are challenged as to what you stand for and will stand up against.

I don't want to get all Open University on you but this is what made the series, which with a couple of breaks ran from 1966 until 1974, so absolutely astonishing for British TV. Clearly some people didn't get the joke and sided with the bigot that was Alf but I think we could do with the so-called radical comedians and writers having the same bravery and vision now to write a series that tackled the problems Rubbish Britain is facing today. But could you imagine that happening in today's politically correct world of TV? No chance.

The programme was softened up and adapted for the US market where it was renamed *All in the Family* and was amazingly successful, running between 1971 and 1979.

7. 'I'm free' – John Inman as Mr Humphries in *Are You Being Served?*

If *Steptoe & Son* and Alf Garnet were social realism dressed up as comedy then *Are You Being Served?* was pantomime at its best, set in an aging department store full of British stock comedy characters and shelves full of innuendo. I and millions of other Brits loved it for over a decade from when it started in 1972 as a single play through to its closing-down sale in 1985.

Written by Jeremy Lloyd and David Croft, two of the three comedy writers, the other being Jimmy Perry, who would dominate Seventies and Eighties British TV comedy, this was a juggernaut of a success. Remember Croft, Perry and Lloyd between them and in different combinations are responsible for *It Ain't Half Hot Mum*, *You Rang My Lord*, *Dad's Army*, *Hi Di Hi* and *'Allo 'Allo*.

Of course John Inman's character of Mr Humphreys with his camp, innuendo-laden catchphrase, 'I'm free', was imitated in playgrounds up and down the country but equally popular were tales of 'Mrs Slocombe's pussy' and chants of Young Mr Grace's 'You're all doing very well' as the old-timer was escorted out of the building by dolly birds in nurse uniforms. The comedy was broad with the subtlety of a sledgehammer and reminiscent of saucy seaside postcards and pantomime and at first glance would have seemed to be only intelligible to a British audience. However, the truth is *Are You Being Served* became a cult classic and still is in the States.

8. 'Stay out of the black and into the red, nothing in this game for two in a bed' – Jim Bowen in *Bull's Eye*

This series, based on a game of darts (they don't make them like they used to, thank God!) ran from 1981 until 1995 and should have been a complete flop with its gaudy sets, crap concept, thick contestants and amateur but charming bumbling host Jim Bowen, but it was compelling viewing. I loved it.

It had no pretensions and even if it did I doubt whether former schoolteacher, Jim, would be able to spell it but that wasn't the point. It was candyfloss TV for the Sunday evening tea-on-the-lap 15 million of us who watched it. Quintessentially British, like a pair of slippers, a pint and a fag, we let the programme wash over us and revelled in Jim's catchphrases and as we all know, 'You can't beat a bit of bully.'

9. 'Just like that' – Tommy Cooper

One of Britain's best loved and funniest comedians who could even make you laugh before he appeared on stage just by messing around and laughing into the microphone behind the curtains. Tommy was a brilliant magician who made a fortune and a nation laugh by deliberately messing up tricks while muttering the immortal line, 'spoon, jar, jar, spoon' and of course the classic, 'Just like that'.

I love the story – I don't know if it's true or an urban myth – where Tommy gets out of the cab and puts something in the lapel pocket of the cabbie and says, 'Here cabby, have a drink on me' and strides off into the sunset, the cabbie reaches into the pocket and pulls out . . . a teabag!

Tommy will always be remembered unfortunately for dying on stage on TV on 15 April 1984 on ITV's variety show *Live From Her Majesty's* in front of millions, many of whom believed it was part of the act, but I would prefer to remember him by some of his immortal lines:

- 'I slept like a log last night; I woke up in the fireplace.'
- 'Man walks into a bar. Didn't half hurt. It was an iron bar.'
- 'I had a ploughman's lunch the other day; he wasn't half mad.'
- 'My dog took a big bite out of my knee the other day and a friend of mine said, "Did you put anything on it?" I said, "No, he liked it as it was."'
- 'I backed a horse today at 20 to 1. It came in at 20 past 4.'
- 'You know, somebody actually complimented me on my driving today. They left a little note on the windscreen; it said "Parking Fine". So that was nice.'
- 'I bought some HP sauce the other day. It's costing me 6p a month for the next two years.'
- 'Police arrested two kids yesterday. One was drinking battery acid, the other was eating fireworks. They charged one and let the other one off.'
- 'So I rang up my local swimming baths. I said, "Is that the local swimming baths?" He said, "It depends where you're calling from."'
- 'I went to the doctor's the other day and I said, "Have you got anything for wind?" – so he gave me a kite.'

- 'I was in the attic the other day with the wife. Damp and dusty . . . but she's great with the kids!'
- 'So I rang up a local building firm, I said, "I want a skip outside my house." He said, "I'm not stopping you."'

10. 'Settle down now' – Ken Goodwin

If Tommy Cooper is gone but not forgotten then poor old Ken is just forgotten, but in the Seventies after his appearance on *Opportunity Knocks* and then *The Comedians* Ken never seemed to be off the box with his stuttering style and his catchphrase of 'Settle down now, settle down.'

Ken was one of the stars of *The Comedians*, a brilliant and hugely successful TV show made by Granada TV in the Seventies, which took the stars of the northern clubs and put them on mainstream TV. It made household names of Bernard Manning, Frank Carson, Mike Reid and Charlie Williams amongst others. It ran for fifty episodes and of course spawned *The Wheel Tappers and Shunters Social Club*, with Colin Compton as the compere and club secretary, that tried to recreate the atmosphere of a genuine working man's club.

I loved both of these shows but they were definitely products of their age. When Granada Plus repeated *The Comedians* they faced a barrage of complaints about the so-called offensive material in the show. In reply they said that if they removed all the homophobic and racist content, they would only be left with the opening and closing credits. I'm not sure if that is true but I do think both programmes are perhaps comedy's versions of our guilty pleasures.

11. Frank Carson

- 'It's a cracker!'
- 'It's the way I tell 'em!'

Frank is a Great Briton and a national treasure. The man is a natural who of course rose to stardom through *The Comedians* after winning *Opportunity Knocks* three times in a row. Born in Belfast in 1926, Frank, like most Brits, is a mongrel, his granny being of Sicilian descent. No doubt Frank would have a joke about that but I just point it out as a bit of trivia.

I love Frank and had the great pleasure of working with him on *The Alan Titchmarsh Show*. I'll never forget the moment when I walked into the make-up room which was already rocking with laughter as Frank was in full flight, cracking jokes as they tried to apply make-up to his permanently grinning face. I went up to introduce myself and he told me in no uncertain terms that he knew who I was and read my articles every week. I was simultaneously flattered and taken aback – Frank knew me? Until the inevitable punch line came: 'Yes, I never miss Littlejohn's columns!' He was joking, I think, but for the next half-hour before we went on screen he had me in stitches.

Once on set Alan tried to hold a debate with Frank and me, which was like trying to juggle with a jelly as Frank took over, won over the audience and left us two struggling to get a word in edgeways. It was the easiest and funniest fifteen minutes of TV I have ever appeared on.

I had actually been in the same room – well, actually the smallest room, the toilet – with Frank a few years previously. I was invited to a screening of *An Audience with Al Murray* and Frank was at the urinal as I and a mate entered the toilets at the TV studios. The toilets were packed so I went into a cubicle while my mate Michael stood next to Frank at the urinal. As usual Frank was cracking jokes and I was laughing behind the door. He came to the end of a joke and Michael interrupted and did Frank's catchphrase, 'It's the way I tell 'em.' Behind the door I heard the pause and then the witty response from Frank . . . 'FUCK OFF! Get your own catchphrase!' . . . which had the whole room rolling with laughter and my hairy-arsed builder mate dying of embarrassment and pissing on his shoes.

To this day I only have to say 'it's the way I tell 'em' to Michael in any situation, serious, tragic or funny, and we both dissolve into fits of laughter. That's what great comedians can do, they make you share the moment, they give you the memory and they have the craic. Frank is one in a million and a gag-teller of the old school. I love him and millions of Brits feel the same way too.

12. 'Mr Grimsdale' – Norman Wisdom

Norman is a national treasure and was deservedly knighted in 2000. He was born in London in 1912 but his showbusiness career didn't start until the relatively mature age of 31 when he became the straight man to another of my childhood heroes, the magician, David Nixon.

With his trademark too-tight suit and flat cap he quickly became a star, making his West End and TV debut within two years and was soon to be hailed by Charlie Chaplin as his favourite British clown.

The catchphrase of course comes from all those low-budget films he made for Rank in the Fifties and Sixties starting with *Trouble in Store* in 1953. The plots in most of these films were pretty similar with Wisdom playing the helpless fool being bossed around by an unreasonable gaffer, which gave plenty of room for Wisdom to use his slapstick routine to the full. What kid hasn't pulled his tie askew, put his school cap on sideways and walked pigeon-toed screaming, 'Mr Grimsdale'? Let's face it, Lee Evans has made a fortune out of it! That's a little unfair because Lee actually brought Norman back into the limelight in the early Nineties when he clearly cited him as an influence on his style.

I also love the fact that Norman was a national hero in Albania as his were the only films allowed to be shown under the communist dictator, Enver Hoxha. In later years of course he also starred in *Last of the Summer Wine* and he only retired from performing in 2005 at the age of 90. He was a massive part of my childhood and it is so sad to hear that Sir Norman can't even recognise himself in his own films now. However one thing is for certain: he will always be remembered as one of our greatest clowns and not just by Charlie Chaplin but the whole nation – another great Brit.

13. Windsor Davies – *It Ain't Half Hot Mum*

- 'Oh dear. How sad. Never mind'
- 'Mr La-di-da Gunner Graham'
- 'Lovely boy'
- 'Chest out, shoulders back, show them off, lovely boys'
- 'You is a bunch of puffs'

This was a fantastic series and was written as a follow-up to *Dad's Army* by David Croft and Jimmy Perry and it's the kind of programme that will never be made again, especially by the BBC. This programme was gloriously politically incorrect, gloriously British and bloody funny. It had everything that nowadays would make the froth on a TV commissioner's skinny latte go flat; a blacked-up lead character, Rangi Ram, who speaks strangled pidgin English and thinks he's a Brit, played by Michael Bates (later in *Last of the Summer Wine*), an effeminate drag artist (Melvyn Hayes) who is called 'Gloria' by his concert-party mates and 'a raving poofta' by a moustachioed, manic-eyed and macho sergeant major played by Windsor Davies.

The programme ran for seven years from 1974 to 1981 and its creators went on to make the equally politically incorrect *Hi Di Hi*. I don't think *It Ain't Half Hot Mum* was racist, sexist or even homophobic. It just used stock characters and stock situations to make people laugh, just as comedy has done since time immemorial and I see no reason why the BBC shouldn't repeat this classic British comedy from Episode 1 with no censorship or abridgement. For God's sake, there is no cruel intent in the programmes and the only intention was to make us laugh.

14. 'Shut that door' – Larry Grayson in *The Generation Game*

Let's be honest, Larry didn't have much talent, but what little he did possess he made the most of and after a lifetime of touring the clubs with his anecdotal and observational style of comedy he hit pay dirt when he took over from Brucie as the host of *The Generation Game* in 1978. Before this he had his own comedy show on ATV called *Shut That Door* which I found moderately amusing, with his cast of characters like Apricot Lil and Slack Alice. If I'm brutally honest, even though he was a local lad coming from up the road in Nuneaton, my mates and me just laughed at him rather than with him as 'that puff off the telly'.

In hindsight and with maturity and less of a bigoted outlook I can now see that actually Larry was groundbreaking as he was really the first comedian on British TV who openly suggested that he led a gay lifestyle. I suppose he opened the doors for those that would follow like Lily Savage, Graham Norton and Dale Winton. What a pity though that he didn't Slam that Door on the gloriously unfunny Julian Clary. It's also true to note that, aided and abetted by Isla St Clair, he actually made *The Generation Game* even more popular with an audience of over 18 million.

15. 'May your God go with you' – Dave Allen

Of course Dave wasn't British but I have included him in this book because his show was made here and because of his enormous influence over our culture and present comedians. Dave Allen died in 2005 but by God do we need a comedian like him on the box now more than ever. I used to love his gentle style and delivery and his complete debunking of religion and in these times of religious extremism, wouldn't it be great if there was a comedian brave enough to do such an act and a TV company with the balls to transmit it?

All religions should be strong enough in their faith to be able to laugh at themselves but unfortunately, as we know to our cost, that is no longer the case and the world is a sadder, less safe place as a result.

One final note: I don't recall effigies and flags being burned in the street when Dave portrayed the Pope as a gangster and used *The Sweeney* theme to poke fun at him in his sketches.

Well, that's my fifteen favourites and it was hard to choose them because one thing is for sure: us Brits have produced some of the best comedians, catchphrases and TV comedy shows in the world. I have deliberately left out *Little Britain* because I think it is gratuitous and unfunny. Maybe I'm getting old. And I didn't use *The Fast Show* as that was full of catchphrases but they didn't seem to spring from the plot or the characters although I'll grant you some were funny, maybe 'brilliant'. TalkSPORT listeners couldn't stop sending me their favourites so here's a few more that didn't make the Top 15 but will surely bring back a memory or two:

- 'All in the best possible taste' – Cupid Stunt, *The Kenny Everett Show*
- 'Calm down, calm down' – The Scousers in *Harry Enfield's Television Programme*
- 'Loadsamoney' – Harry Enfield in *Saturday Night Live*
- 'Ding Dong' – Leslie Phillips in *Carry On Nurse* and for the rest of his brilliant career
- 'Ere, stop messing about' – Kenneth Williams in *Round the Horne* and for the rest of his brilliant career
- 'I didn't get where I am today . . .' – CJ in *The Fall and Rise of Reginald Perrin*
- 'I shall say this only once' – Michelle in *'Allo 'Allo*
- 'My arse' – Jim Royle in *The Royle Family*
- 'Nudge nudge, wink wink' – Eric Idle in *Monty Python's Flying Circus*
- 'Oooooo Matron' – Kenneth Williams in *Carry on Matron*

- 'Stupid boy' – Captain Mainwaring in *Dad's Army*
- 'They don't like it up them' – Corporal Jones in *Dad's Army*
- 'Titter ye not', 'Nay, nay and thrice nay' – Frankie Howerd
- 'Goodnight Vienna' – Rigsby in *Rising Damp*

30

Best of the bard, or If all the world's a stage then Shakespeare's everywhere!

For those of you who say Shakespeare isn't relevant to the modern world, take a gander through these everyday phrases and please start to understand just how much influence this man had and how important he is to our British culture. The simple bottom line is that if Shakespeare hadn't been born, we would have had to invent him.

As You Like It

- 'All the world's a stage, and all the men and women merely players. They have their exits and their entrances; And one man in his time plays many parts.'
- 'Can one desire too much of a good thing?'
- 'We have seen better days.'
- 'For ever and a day.'

Hamlet

- 'Brevity is the soul of wit.'
- 'In my mind's eye.'
- 'The lady doth protest too much.'
- 'Neither a borrower nor a lender be.'

- 'To thine own self be true.'
- 'Though this be madness, yet there is method in it.'
- 'What a piece of work is man!'
- 'Ay, there's the rub.'

Julius Caesar

- 'A dish fit for the gods.'
- 'The dogs of war.'
- 'It was Greek to me.'

King Lear

- 'Nothing can come of nothing.'

Macbeth

- 'A charmed life.'
- 'The milk of human kindness.'
- 'What's done is done.'

The Merchant of Venice

- 'All that glistens is not gold.'
- 'If you prick us, do we not bleed? If you tickle us, do we not laugh? If you poison us, do we not die? And if you wrong us, shall we not revenge?'

A Midsummer Night's Dream

- 'The course of true love never did run smooth.'

Much Ado About Nothing

- 'Are you good men and true?'

Othello

- 'It is the green-eyed monster which doth mock.'
- ''Tis neither here nor there.'
- 'Wear my heart upon my sleeve.'
- 'A foregone conclusion.'

Romeo and Juliet

- 'Good night, good night! Parting is such sweet sorrow.'
- 'What's in a name? That which we call a rose by any other name would smell as sweet.'
- 'A fool's paradise.'

Twelfth Night

- 'If music be the food of love, play on.'

31

Chips with everything: best British chippie

Yeah, yeah, I know we all like a curry and some surveys reckon that Chicken Tikka Masala is our favourite meal but the bottom line is for true Brits you still can't beat traditional fish and chips.

In 1999, fish fryers served up more than 283 million meals, making it the most popular takeaway among the British population. There are over 8,600 fish and chip shops in the UK who dished out around 49,200 tonnes of fish last year. Cod and haddock account for around 45 per cent of all fish consumed in Britain.

The record for the most portions of fish and chips served up in one day by a fish and chip shop is over 4,000!

1. The late great Parson's Nose in Coventry

Affectionately known to thousands of drunken kids as the Parson's Arse. The food wasn't particularly great but after a skinful and in the days before kebabs, Chinese and fast food, no night was complete without a trip to Mama Louis.

The place was run by a couple of Greek Cypriot brothers but the main honcho was big Maria. She was a huge mountain of a woman with black hair and the biggest mole or beauty spot depending on your view on her cheek. She was famously rude to the customers, especially girls, but served up the best faggots, peas and chips in the universe.

The Parson's Nose was demolished years ago to make way for an office building and more bland uniform food chains but the memory lingers on. Coventry City Council, where's the blue plaque?

2. The Anstruther Fish Bar and Restaurant, Anstruther, Scotland

No visit to the Kingdom of Fife would be complete without grabbing some fish, chips and mushy peas and eating them on the harbour front of this real Scottish fishing village. Voted chippie of the year three times in a row (or should that be roe?), the latest being in 2006–07. The queues at lunchtime seem to back up the place's reputation (or should that be plaice?). You can queue for up to an hour and a half but let me tell you it's well worth it. You can go posh and sit inside the 52-seater restaurant but as far as I'm concerned seaside fish and chips have to be eaten outside.

While you're in town make sure you visit the fascinating Scottish Fisheries Museum next door or sample a few of the many boozers that can be found in the pretty cobbled streets.

When we were living in Livingstone Lisa and I had many happy weekends over in the Kingdom of Fife and loved the place. It's like Cornwall without the crowds and is a great place to holiday with kids. You've also got the attractions of St Andrews, including the great Sea Life Centre up the road.

42–44 Shore Street (*next to Scottish Fisheries Museum*)
Anstruther, Fife KY10 3AQ
tel: 01333 310518
email: info@anstrutherfishbar.co.uk

3. Squires Fish and Chip Restaurant, Braunton, North Devon

This is a great chippie and well worth the car trip from the surfing beaches of Croyde for the best fish and chips in Devon. You can either sit inside, and even have a beer instead of the traditional cup of tea as the place is fully licensed, or you can get them wrapped double and get back to your caravan site at Croyde and eat them in the fresh air.

I love this part of North Devon and the beaches at Croyde have got to be some of the best surfing beaches in the country, whether you want to stand up or just bodyboard. I love squeezing into the wet suit, obviously keeping out a keen eye for Japanese whaling ships, and then getting into the surf with the kids.

We have stayed at both the caravans and the more luxurious lodges at Ruda Holiday Park and I heartily recommend them if you are looking for the traditional family holiday.

Back to the chippie, make sure you check out the picture of Denis and Margaret Thatcher eating at Squires.

Exeter Road, Braunton
Nr Barnstaple, EX33 2JL
tel: 01271 815533

4. L'Alba D'Oro, Edinburgh

Fish and chips in Edinburgh is called a fish supper and is traditionally served with salt and sauce instead of vinegar. There are many superb traditional chippies in the Athens of the North but my favourite is L'Alba D'Oro at the bottom of Dundas Street and just round the corner from one of Edinburgh's finest pubs, Clark's Bar.

The place is run by a short fat Danny DeVito lookalike called Filippo Crolla and his fish and chips are out of this world. You must try his deep-fried haggis and chips, all of course smothered in the obligatory salt and sauce.

We found this place when we first started promoting at the Edinburgh Festival Fringe and over the fifteen years we worked there we kept going back for more and more. Don't ask for pizza though because I seem to recall that went into the fryer as well!

5–7 Henderson Row
New Town
Edinburgh, EH3 5DH
tel: 0131 557 2580
email: info@lalbadoro.com
web: www.lalbadoro.com

5. Bob Carver's Fish and Chips, Hull

After being in care, I lived in Hull for a year with my Auntie Rosemary and one of my fondest memories was shopping in the town centre of a Saturday and then having lunch at Bob Carver's. In those days the chippie was in a tent just by Trinity House in the heart of the old city. The tents have long gone but I was delighted to be able to take Lisa to Hull when I was doing book signings for *Undaunted* and realise that Carver's was still alive and kicking even if they had moved indoors.

The chips were still brilliant and the fish was as fresh as ever and I even pushed the boat out, sat inside, ordered bread and butter – white of course – and lashings of tea. The food still smelled the same and tasted even better. They've got two restaurants now and you can either take away or eat in.

9 Trinity House Lane
Hull HU1 2JA
tel: 01482 226660

3 Chapel Street
Hull HU1 3PA
tel: 01482 228814
Both closed on a Sunday

32

'You hum it, son, I'll play it': best British TV ads

I'm a firm believer that Britain has created some of the best TV programmes in the world but it has to be said that some of our commercials have put some of the turgid rubbish that has been churned out over the years to shame. So I thought it would be good to wallow in a bit of TV nostalgia and remember the ads that as kids we could all recite parrot-fashion.

1. The PG Tips adverts with the chimpanzees

These adverts started in 1955 and were the second TV advert ever aired; the first was for Gibbs SR toothpaste. They ran for over forty years and they are in *The Guinness Book of Records* as the longest-running ad campaign ever. They were removed, probably by the politically correct Thought Police, in 2002 and the chimps now live at Twycross Zoo in Staffordshire, which, by the way, is a great day out for the family.

The voiceover on the first advert was British comedy genius Peter Sellers and ever since then a literal Who's Who of British talent have acted as the narrator including amongst others: Bruce Forsyth, Arthur Lowe, Stanley Baxter, Kenneth Williams, David Jason and of course Irene Handl in my all-time favourite advert, Mr Shifter ('You hum it, son, I'll play it').

These classic ads were replaced by the Typhoo T birds, which were crap, and then by the unfunny revival of Johnny Vegas and his knitted monkey. I say bring back the chimps.

2. Tetley tea folk

The Tetley tea folk have been the public image of Tetley tea since 1983. I really liked these cartoon characters when they were led by Gaffer and the voice of one of Britain's greatest character actors, and no mean wrestler too, the late great Brian Glover, who played the deluded Bobby Charlton-obsessed PE teacher in *Kes*.

As well as Gaffer, there were six other Tetley tea folk – Tina, Archie, Clarence, Gordon, Maurice and Sydney. And who can forget the classic pay-off line, 'Tetley make Teabags make Tea.'

3. Smash

'For Mash get Smash' is one of the most instantly recognised British TV advert jingles of all time and, when combined with the antics of the Smash Martians, has got to be one of our best-loved TV adverts.

For the record I hated this Cadbury's product and it brings back memories of free school meals, spam fritters and pink custard, but I adore the adverts, which started in 1974 and were voted as TV ad of the century by *Campaign Magazine*.

Don't you just love that bit where the Martian says, 'Earth people peel their own potatoes, boil them for twenty of their minutes, then smash them all to bits. They are clearly a primitive people' and then they all fall about laughing.

To summarise: brilliant ad, crap product.

4. Watch out, watch out there's a Humphrey about

Do you remember this campaign from Unigate milk back in 1970?

It was absolutely simple in concept – just a procession of red and white straws nicking and drinking your milk. Do you remember the one with that classic British comedy actor Arthur Mullard in it? Then there was all the memorabilia you could pester your mum to get for you off the milkman, like mugs, T-shirts, badges and even aprons.

I'm a great believer in the very British tradition of doorstep deliveries and even to this day at Gaunty Towers we still have a milkman. I know it costs more and I know it no longer comes in bottles – by the way, did your dad have loads of them and Corona bottles full of oil and turps in the garage as well? But there is something great about waking up in the morning, opening the front door and picking up a pint – or is it a bloody litre nowadays?

There was also nothing better as a kid than coming in from playing football on the common, having a quick glance round to check Mum wasn't in the kitchen and then opening a bottle of milk and necking it straight out of the bottle. Pure bliss.

5.The classic Cinzano ad with Joan Collins and the late great Leonard Rossiter

On a plane, drink and ice down the ample cleavage of Miss Collins, 'suffused with herbs and spices from four continents'. Do I need to say any more?

Fantastic spoof adverts which started in 1978 taking the mickey out of rival drink Martini's ads. The only problem is the campaign was so funny it actually led to an increase in sales of Martini as people were laughing so much they forgot which product it was promoting.

Other adverts that could have been in the running:
● The Milk Tray Man
● The traditional Oxo family – with Katie (Mark I) or Lynda Bellingham (Mark II)
● Aah Bisto
● Imperial Leather on that train in Russia
● Any Flake advert
● Flash with that Scottish woman – not Karl Howman
● Nudge, nudge, wink, wink, suggestive digestive. A great advert for a biscuit which I think was called Breakaway?
● The Milky Bar Kid
● Guinness – just so many brilliant adverts over the years
● Barclaycard with Rowan Atkinson as toffee-nosed English diplomat

One of the greatest things about the Internet is that there are loads and loads of sites where you can now watch these old adverts and wallow in pure nostalgia.

33

Never say heavy: the best British boozers

1. Clark's Bar, 142 Dundas Street, Edinburgh

I discovered this bar 26 years ago when I first went to the Edinburgh Fringe and I am delighted to say it hasn't changed one bit in all that time. It's a traditional drinking boozer, which doesn't mess around with food and serves some of the best real ale in Scotland. I love the way the old guys behind the bar wear traditional cream jackets and it's a great pub for watching football, with at least three screens if my memory serves me right.

2. The Diggers, 1–3 Angle Park Terrace, Edinburgh

Don't go looking for a pub called the Diggers, as there isn't one! This pub's real name is the Athletic Arms. It's only called the Diggers because it is opposite the graveyard and legend has it that the gravediggers use the place after digging!

This is simply a spit and sawdust at its most unreconstructed best. Cracked lino, bare walls apart from some football pictures, no jukebox, a few old-fashioned one-armed bandits and the best beer in Scotland if not the world, and I am not exaggerating.

However – and this is a big *however* – whatever you do, make sure you don't identify yourself as a newcomer or first-timer when you order a pint of the smooth and creamy McEwan's Heavy. You do not,

I repeat *do not*, walk up to the bar and order, instead as you push through the doors from the street you just hold up your fingers to instruct the eagle-eyed barman how many pints you want. By the time you have fought your way through to the bar the nectar will be waiting. Do not ask for lager, alcopops or other such rubbish. There are sixteen beer pumps in the Diggers, one for lager, one for Guinness and the other fourteen for Heavy.

However you should never say the word 'Heavy'. Just remember on subsequent visits to the bar – simply stick your fingers up. I can't really explain just how special this place is, but make sure you visit before what is probably the greatest bar in the world disappears under corporate rebranding. Get there before some wet-behind-the-ears brewery executive closes it down, refurbs it and tries to recreate the atmosphere of a traditional Scottish bar, as they have so miserably failed to do with ever-growing chains of 'real Oirish' pubs!

3. The King's Arms, Main Street, Farthingstone, Northamptonshire

This is a great little boozer dating back to the eighteenth century. Fantastic real ales, traditional Northamptonshire skittles and no jukebox or fruit machines. Not only does the landlord, Paul, serve a great pint of real ale he also specialises in selling, for consumption both on and off the premises, great English cheeses and specialist fine foods from around the British Isles.

4. The White Hart, Northampton Road, Grafton Regis, near Towcester, Northamptonshire

The kids, Lisa and I love this place. Superb IPA and other real ales and a great wine list with probably the best steaks anywhere in the county. There's a restaurant if you want to go a little upmarket or enjoy almost the same grub in the bar. Make sure you check out Alan's home-made soups but the speciality of the house has got to be the steaks and the fish. Andy and Alan who run the place have become great friends and we have used the place so often. Well worth a detour off the M1 at Junction 15.

5. The Royal Oak, Lime Avenue, Eydon, Northamptonshire

This is a beautiful seventeenth-century Ironstone Inn which serves great food in the heart of Northamptonshire.

It's a gastro pub without the attitude and ridiculous prices. Again a favourite of the whole family and run by a husband-and-wife team from South Africa, who prove without a doubt that *Spitting Image* was wrong and you *can* meet a nice South African, in fact two in this quiet corner of England. Landlady Bronnie and her staff never fail to make you feel welcome and the beer and the food is fantastic.

6. The Town Wall Tavern, Bond Street, Coventry

This is a great traditional little old boozer right in the heart of the city just behind the Belgrade Theatre. It has been the location of much of my misspent youth and as well as serving great beer and food it has always been the unofficial green room for the actors and backstage staff at the theatre. It also has one of the smallest rooms in a pub in Britain, The Donkey Box. This small bar has only enough room for about four drinkers and it necessitates drinkers to sup in a synchronised fashion.

Years ago when I was a member of the Belgrade Youth Theatre myself and Clive Owen would spend many a long afternoon or evening drinking – with me always buying, I hasten to add – in this pub that has survived the Blitz and several attempts by the council to demolish it.

It now stands defiantly among all the new developments and still serves great beer. Over the years it has had many characters running it, but probably its most famous (infamous?) landlord was Ray Hoare. In my late teenage years and into my twenties Ray and his wife Jo ran this pub with a rod of iron. Ray could be a right miserable bastard to strangers but once accepted into his customer base he was a loyal if somewhat cantankerous mate.

Jo worked in a kitchen the size of a wardrobe and conjured up some of the best food I have ever eaten, not just in a pub but in a restaurant too. Every day she would produce just one pie in a pot and they ranged from steak and ale, through rabbit to steak and Stilton. Combined with a pint of cask-conditioned Brew XI or a pint of Bass there was no better lunch available in Coventry, as testified by the place being packed with actors, journalists from the local paper, and businessmen. At night the only food available was doorstep sandwiches or cold sausage with home-made pickle.

During this period this was my home from home, and straight after university when I was working backstage at the panto I was always in the place. Ray prided himself on beer and woe betide any students who entered the place who would be greeted by mine host with the immortal line '*out*'. An even more heinous crime was to ask for Ray's beer to be adulterated by lemonade.

'Can I have a bitter top please?' one stranger asked, to be greeted by an ice-cold stare above his glasses from Ray and a witty riposte.

'This isn't a fucking cocktail bar. *Out!*'

In Ray's worldview, customers came for his beer when in truth, although no one would ever tell him, they came for the pies, even though he kept a decent pint as well.

Years later when Ray was running another pub in the city his famous grumpy nature and bizarre customer relations got him into the national press when he decided to start charging 50 pence for a glass of tap water! His excuse was that he still had to pay all the costs of washing the glasses and staffing the boozer for these people who were also of course taking up real drinkers' boozing space!

That said we had some cracking nights in there over the years and there was no need for a jukebox or fruit machine as the entertainment was provided by the oddballs who frequented the place.

One winter's night, the door of the bar flung open and a very wet German couple walked in. Ray eyed them with his usual welcoming grimace and the old fella approached the bar.

'Excuse me, can you tell me the vay to the cathedral?'

The accent recognised immediately by all the drinkers meant that we were suddenly in a scene from *An American Werewolf in London*; the whole bar went quiet waiting for Ray's riposte.

But another regular, insurance salesman and cider drinker Tom McLaughlin beat him to the post from the end of the bar:

'Fuck off, you found it alright in 1940!'

The place erupted with laughter, the Germans retreated into the cold wet night and Ray bought Tommy another half of cider.

7. The Dirty Duck, Waterside, Stratford upon Avon

This boozer is world-famous in theatre circles and is located directly opposite the Royal Shakespeare Theatre and just down the road from the new Courtyard Theatre. It's a fifteenth-century building and its walls are full of photos of famous actors who have performed both in the theatre and probably in the boozer too.

It is now the official St George's Day venue for talkSPORT after this year's fantastic outside broadcast from the bar. It serves great real ale including Flowers and IPA and has a very good menu. It's an ideal venue for a bite to eat before watching a play by Britain's greatest playwright or even for a night out with the stars of today and tomorrow. Check out some of the tables, which have autographs on them from some of the stars that have appeared with the RSC.

8. The King's Arms, Roupal Street, London W1

I shouldn't really tell you this but this is talkSPORT's second home. It's just round the corner from talkSPORT Towers and this is a real old-fashioned London boozer. The sort of pub that is fast facing extinction in the capital as the big chains with their apron-clad bar staff, bowls of bloody olives and sandwiches called *paninis* take over the traditional pub.

This gaff serves great real ale, has a lively bar but then round the back in what must have been the stables or a garage is a fantastic Thai restaurant selling great oriental food at down-to-earth prices. No pretensions, no poncing about, just a proper pub. Use it before you lose it.

This book is about my likes and dislikes about our great country but when it came to the best boozers I threw the phone and text lines open to the talkSPORT listeners to recommend their favourites. The criteria were simple: the pubs had to be real boozers and if they sold food it had to be home-made and no pub chains were allowed. I can't vouch for all the recommendations as I haven't visited them all . . . yet! But one thing's for sure: I am going to have a damn good try at sussing out these establishments in the near future. *Cheers!*

- **The King Ethelbert, Reculver, Kent**
  Just by the cliffs and Reculver Fort. Great food and local ales (*Dan in Herts*)
- **The Old Crown, Digbeth, Birmingham**
  The oldest pub in Brum, 1368. Authentic-type furniture and great beer (*Ian, Brum*)
- Whilst you're in Birmingham I would also suggest trying the **Fighting Cocks** and the **Prince of Wales, Moseley**, two great

pubs, and also don't miss out on a trip to **The Bear, Bearwood**, home of great local music and the birthplace of bands like Dexys (*JG*)

- **Birch Hall Inn, Beck Hole near Whitby**
  One of the smallest in the UK, traditional, maintained as original, great beer, stunning location! (*Dave, York*)

- Of course whilst you're in Whitby you have got to grab yourself some traditional fish and chips, I love the place (*JG*)

- **The Black Bull, Mottram St Andrew, Cheshire**
  A proper English country pub. Fantastic (*Scott, Perth*)

- **Anchor Bar, Newcastle, County Down**
  11 different beers, 2 dartboards, 3 pool tables and 7 TVs [*not sure about that! (JG)*], live acoustic music on a Friday night [*that's better!*] Best home-made burger you have ever tasted (*Ryan*)

- **Scarborough Taps, Leeds**
  Open since the 1700s. CAMRA pub of the year on numerous occasions due to the copious amounts of real and great food to top it off. If you're ever in Leeds, get yoursen down for a jar! (*Rob*)

- **The Bull's Head, Barston**
  A real British pub with good ales (*Malcolm, Solihull*)

- **The Baker's Arms, Waddesdon, near Aylesbury, Bucks**
  The best pub I have been in. A great village pub that could have gone downhill after the smoking ban but due to the gorgeous landlady Sarah it's still kicking (*Seb*)

- **The Crown, under the Railway Viaduct, Stockport**
  Best pub in Stockport, 16 real ales, no TV, live music most nights and great food including a cheese night on Mondays. Most of all, a friendly pub with real people to talk to (*Geoff Foster*)

- **The Cheshire Cheese, Fleet Street, London**
  Old-fashioned traditional pub (*Keith, Knutsford*)

- **Beacon Hotel, Sedgley**
  Loads of home-brewed real ales and pub of the year (*Simon, Wolverhampton*)

- **The British Oak, Rothwell**
  Best pub in Leeds. Not only has it got a great name but also a comedy landlord, pool table and darts board. You can buy a pork pie in there with Brown sauce and that's as far as the food goes. A proper pub (*Andy*)

NEVER SAY HEAVY: THE BEST BRITISH BOOZERS

- **The White Lion, Braunton**
  A proper pub; friendly, lively free live music upstairs on a weekend and a curry kitchen in the bar (*Garry, Devon*)
- **The Penlan, Pwllheli, North Wales**
  A real old quaint boozer (*Gary, the Wirral*)
- **The Five Crosses, Coedpoeth, near Wrexham**
  Top pub in Wales. In the daytime it is like walking into the 1950s, with ticking wall clocks, quiet and old-fashioned, great ale and good company (*Rod, Wrexham*)
- **The Prince of Wales, Kenfig, near Bridgend, South Wales**
  Proper food and real ale (*Rob*)
- **The Red Lion, Penderyn, near Aberdare**
  Best pub in Wales. All real cask ales (you can see the wooden barrels), open log fire, stone floor, warm atmosphere and a fab location. Johnny Depp discovered it a couple of years ago and befriended the staff and whenever he is in the UK heads straight to the Red Lion. Numero uno. Class (*Simon, South Wales*)
- **The Butcher's, Cardiff**
  A traditional back-street working man's pub where you can get a great pint of Brains' Dark. This is the same pub that the Coventry City chairman stopped off in for a pint after a Coventry v Cardiff FA Cup game and gave the barmaid a lift home in his chauffeur-driven car (*Tony, Edinburgh*)

Finally this email from Andy Healey summed up the battle for Britain's boozers

```
The new breed of 'bars', not pubs, in Britain make me
sick. They have hiked up the price of a pint to over
three quid, which was unheard of two years ago. The
answer is simple, do as me and my mates do and boycott
them and their samey corporate-owned glass and steel
décor, Fajita wraps and jumped-up poncey barmen. Seek
out real pubs and go there instead, have a pint and a
pie and be REAL MEN.
```

Couldn't have put it better myself mate!

34

We can be heroes: top ten British sporting superstars

One thing is for certain: us Brits love our sport and when I say sport I know that as a nation we are football obsessed; however, we should and increasingly are having plenty of time for other sports which sometimes don't get the media attention they deserve.

I was a great fan of speedway when I was a kid, following both the Coventry Bees and the Hull Vikings when I lived up north, and it's been great as a dad to rekindle that love of the shale with my eldest daughter Rosie.

With me it was the unique smell of the fuel and the idea that these nutters reach speeds of up to 70 miles an hour without brakes but perhaps for Rosie it's the young lads in leather, whatever? However, what I do know is that the two of us have loved our nights together at Brandon.

That's what's so good about sport. Sport can bring together the generations and the nation. I mean, who would have thought that millions of Brits would stay up to watch Redgrave and co. win the rowing or that we would be discussing the finer points of curling when the Scottish ladies did so well a few years back? But that is exactly what sport can do and that's why we love our sporting heroes and why perhaps all of us, especially in the media, should remember and make time to follow more than just our football teams.

I've picked out just a few British sporting heroes, some have already made it, some are still to achieve greatness, but they are all household names who make us feel proud to be British when they represent us.

1. Bobby Moore

Simply the greatest football captain of all time. An inspiration to generations of footballers and a role model that all future England captains should be based on.

2. Martin Johnson

The record speaks for itself. This is the man who lifted the World Cup for England in 2003 and continues to lead by example as England's rugby union manager.

I spent a weekend in Cannes with Jonno two years ago and he is a giant in all respects. He was courteous and always had time to talk, sign autographs and have his photo taken with the fans, no matter what time of day or night. I hate it when footballers barge past kids at training grounds without signing their programmes or books. Why do they have to behave like that and are they so thick that they can't make the link between that kid's adulation, their ticket fee and their massive wages?

Walking round Cannes with Martin we looked liked Schwarzenegger and Danny DeVito in that movie, *Twins*, and it took a week for me to get the crick out of my neck from permanently looking up at him.

I love his no-nonsense approach both to the game and discipline and it's clear from his press conference in July after selecting his elite squad that he will stand for no messing about on or off the field. These words are inspirational and should be the mantra of every British team in any sport:

Attitude is everything. What occurs off the field is so important to what happens on it. The culture of a squad defines its resilience. Squad discipline is at the top of my agenda and, when we gather as a squad for the first time next month, one of the first issues we will address is the code of conduct. The last few weeks should have ensured that all the players in British rugby have learned the lessons of all this: if they haven't, they never will. Certain things in the code will be non-negotiable, other measures I want the players to come up with themselves because it is their team. When I was a player, I never had to read a code: it was something that was understood and, if we cannot trust our international players, we have problems.

3. George Best

The Belfast boy and the world's greatest ever footballer needs no more words, except, at the risk of upsetting the Northern Irish, what a shame he didn't get to grace the world's greatest international tournaments.

4. Amir Kahn

OK, Amir is not technically a sporting superstar yet even though he won silver in the Olympics and hopes one day to be a world champion, and perhaps he will be. I have put him in this category because of the man he already is.

I love the way he symbolises modern Britain just by wearing those shorts. With the Pakistan flag on one side and the Union flag on the other, here is a young man who is British and a Muslim but is also fiercely proud of where his mum and dad come from. His dad is a true patriot too and both are great examples of integration – real integration – working.

5. Sir Henry Cooper

Quite simply Our 'Enry is the most popular boxer we have ever had and who can forget his fights with Cassius Clay, as he was then, especially the knockdown in the first bout which, if it wasn't for the bell, would have made Henry the winner.

I've interviewed Henry a few times and the first thing you notice is those hands – they are the size of a digger bucket. He's a great man, a marvellous ambassador for the sport and the country and a truly great Brit.

6. Sir Freddie Trueman

As Ronnie Irani mentions in the section on cricket, Fiery Fred quite simply was our best ever bowler and of course the first man to take

300 Test wickets. He would have taken many, many more if the snobs in charge of the game hadn't resented him so much.

He was a blunt, no-nonsense Yorkshireman who took no prisoners on the field or in the commentary box in his second career as a match summariser. I love this attitude and the arrogance is vital in elite sportsmen but the snobs in charge of cricket resented his character and clearly Freddie knew this:

> Irrespective of the fact I was at the top of my game for Yorkshire and frequently topped the county bowling averages, I was often overlooked for England. To my mind the reason for this was personal. Quite simply, some of the selection committee did not like my forthright attitude, which they misinterpreted as being 'bolshy'. Rather than pick the best eleven players for the job, the selection committee would often choose someone because he was, in their eyes, a gentleman and a decent chap. Such attributes often took precedence over someone's ability to play international cricket.

Superb Freddie, they don't like it up 'em!

As a kid I used to also love him on the TV show, *Indoor League*, that was an absolute corker of a programme. It was basically televised pub games like arm wrestling, darts, shove ha'penny, bar billiards and pool and it was always on at teatime.

And finally, lest we forget, back in the 1950s Freddie was the face who modelled that quintessentially British product – Brylcreem.

7. Sir Jackie Stewart

Jackie and of course Graham Hill were heroes of mine when I was growing up and Jackie is arguably our greatest ever Formula 1 driver with three world championships to his name and 27 victories out of 99 starts.

He had a late start in motor sport because after his racing driver brother Jimmy was seriously hurt in a crash at Le Mans his parents, who owned a Jaguar dealership, discouraged him from going into racing. As a result Jackie actually took up shooting and narrowly missed out on a chance of representing Britain at the 1960 Olympics. But the lure of the cars was too much and by 1961 he was testing and then progressing on to racing, eventually signing a contract with Graham Hill at BRM in 1965. He's also the man who made safety a number one concern for the sport after he had a terrible crash at Spa in Belgium in 1966. He was trapped in his car with petrol pouring over him and which with one spark could have killed him. At this stage in his career the chances of a Formula 1 driver who raced for five years being killed in a crash were two out of three.

> I realized that if this was the best we had there was something sadly wrong: things wrong with the race track, the cars, the medical side, the fire-fighting, and the emergency crews. There were also grass banks that were launch pads, things you went straight into, trees that were unprotected and so on. Young people today just wouldn't understand it. It was ridiculous. If I have any legacy to leave the sport I hope it will be seen to be an area of safety because when I arrived in Grand Prix racing so-called precautions and safety measures were diabolical.

It was Jackie who was responsible for the removable steering wheel and fuel cut-off switches in F1 cars and a host of other safety initiatives that have now become commonplace. That said, with his distinctive tartan livery and his accent he soon became every boy's hero. He's the kind of name that even now when I get the chance to interview him, my heart beats a little quicker at the thought of being so close to a living British legend.

8. Alex Higgins

Yes, yes, I know he's thrown it all away but The Hurricane is, was and always will be a flawed genius, and I and the British public still love him.

It was Alex who single-handedly made snooker a household sport – and who can forget him winning the World Championships in 1972 at the age of 22 on his first attempt? Of course we all have that memory of him crying, holding his little girl, with his ex-wife at the Crucible when he repeated the feat in 1982 burned into our collective subconscious.

Even Steve Davis has acknowledged, 'Alex was the one true genius that snooker has produced.'

Yes there have been players better, more consistent and more successful than him, including Davis and Hendry, but no one, not even Ronnie or Jimmy, had or has the swagger and the crowd-pulling and pleasing ability of The Hurricane.

Try to forget what he is now and rejoice in what he was. The original flawed *genius*.

9. Andy Murray

Murray really wound me up when he said that he would wear a Paraguay top and wanted anyone but England to win the World Cup but I've mellowed to him because I have begun to realise that the boy is a true Brit who has shown true grit to get to where he is today.

A survivor of the Dunblane massacre, Andy is the perfect antidote to that middle-class 'Tiger' Tim Henman and is a player who I really feel we can get behind.

I love the way he shouts at himself and works the crowd and I'm just hoping that his tenacity and God-given talent will be enough for him to become our next hero.

Mind you, after his thrashing by Muscle Man Nadal he's still got some way to go, but hey – we can dream – after all we put our faith in the Tiger, or was it Pussy, for all those years!

10. Lewis Hamilton

I adore this lad and there's no doubt in my mind that he will be world champion sooner rather than later. The only thing that winds me up about his story is the fact that every news bulletin and newspaper feature about this British hero goes on and on about him being a real role model and hero to black youths. I'm sorry, but he's mixed race. If I were to say he was a real role model to whites I would be up on a charge. It's all PC nonsense. Lewis is as much white as black and most importantly he's just British.

He's a bloody role model to *all* kids.

35

Ten Brits who can do no wrong

1. Barbara Windsor

Why on earth hasn't she been made a dame yet? She is Britain.

2. Sir Cliff Richard

Much as it pains me to say it, Sir Cliff is a national treasure. Now don't get me wrong, I loved *Summer Holiday* and I'll never forget his TV programme in the Seventies with Una Stubbs and his slightly risqué road sign sketches, but let's face it, Grannies' Cliff hasn't released a decent record since 'Devil Woman'. And who can forget that stripy jacket in the video?

I can't wait until they get that bloody roof on Wimbledon. In fact I'm almost tempted to pay for it myself if it stops Cliff singing in the rain!

But clearly I'm in a minority as there seem to be millions of middle-aged women who are willing to camp out for days to get a ticket to see the 'Peter Pan of Pop'.

I will also give Cliff credit: whenever I've done the annual Let's Bash Cliff's Christmas Record routine on the radio, he's always been a good sport and been willing to give an interview and have the craic with me.

3. Joanna Lumley

A true British icon from Purdey to Patsy and everything in between, including being stranded on a desert island. We love her.

4. Henry Cooper

Of course us Brits love Henry and it's not just because he should have beaten Cassius Clay all those years ago. It's also because he has become a national institution with his charity work and those classic Brut adverts from the Seventies. Who can forget Henry telling us to 'splash it all over'?

5. Bruce Forsyth

We've all loved him since *Sunday Night at the London Palladium* through *The Generation Game*. We even stuck by him during *Play Your Cards Right* and of course we love him on *Strictly Come Dancing*. And yes, he *should* be knighted.

6. Sir Richard Branson

People love this classic British entrepreneur and self-publicist. Branson is the brand Virgin and the story of how he went from running a student magazine to becoming one of Britain's most successful businessmen is or should be every Brit's dream.

I know he came from a wealthy middle-class background but he had a dream, a vision if you like, and he went for it. In a country where many, especially the Bloated Broadcasting Corporation, see profit as a dirty word nearly on a par with the C word it is important that entrepreneurs and job creators are more recognised by society in general.

It might just be me but I hate the way certain BBC presenters sneer when they have to do a business story and spit out words like 'obscene profit'. What's obscene about making money? And I wouldn't mind it so much if just a few of these so-called journalists and presenters had ever actually worked in the real business world themselves, but just like most modern politicians they come straight from the student union bar to the Beeb and haven't got a clue about turning a dollar. I'm sorry, but without business and without profit there is no economic basis to build our great country on.

Branson also might have got rich by looking after the pennies because he still owes my brother-in-law fifty pence from years ago. Mike was in a band called King back in the early Eighties and they were recording at Branson's studio in Oxfordshire. Mike was just trying to get some Coke (that's Coca-Cola!) out of the vending machine when a bloke behind him asked him if he had a spare fifty pence. He turned round to be confronted by the Bearded One.

In shock he handed over his only fifty pence, Richard bought the drink, said, 'Thanks, I'll sort you out later,' and waltzed off. Twenty-five years later, Richard, we are still waiting and the interest is clocking up, Big Boy!

7. Lorraine Kelly

The Queen of daytime TV and a national institution.

8. Sir Alan Sugar

If Richard Branson is the public schoolboy made good then Sir Alan is the original working-class boy who pulled himself up by his boot straps to become one of Britain's most successful businessmen.

Born in a council flat in Hackney in 1947, Alan left school at the age of sixteen and started selling car aerials and electrical accessories out of the back of a van. However, he was no Del Boy and certainly not a plonker as he has become one of Britain's richest men with an estimated fortune of over £800 million.

Of course much of this fortune was based on that blasted Amstrad PCW 8256 home computer with the green screen that I used to bang out piss-poor scripts for *Emmerdale Farm* on!

He's now most famous for his performances in *The Apprentice* and his catchphrase, 'You're fired!' With this programme he has proved, rather ironically on the BBC, that people are interested in business or at least the business failures of his candidates.

It's superb and probably the best reality TV show on screen, although I must admit I am always left with the feeling after watching the programme, 'Christ, if that's the cream of young British business talent, no wonder we are fast turning into a nation of burger flippers.'

9. Rolf Harris

Yes, yes, I know he's an Aussie but, as Lisa said when she suggested him, that's still part of the Commonwealth and he is a massive part of all of our childhoods.

Rolf's the one who taught us to paint, play the didgeridoo and sang three of the best children's records of all time, 'Tie Me Kangaroo Down, Sport', 'Jake the Peg' and 'Two Little Boys'. This was in the days when musicians actually bothered to write songs just for kids and we had those great dedicated children's programmes like *Children's Hour* with Uncle Mac and then *Junior Choice* with Ed 'Stewpot' Stewart.

Of course, we all loved him in the learn-to-swim adverts too and in later years his art programmes have opened up the art world and the secret of the great artists to millions. I also adore his portrait of Her Majesty the Queen.

All of which means I can almost forgive him for recording a version of those wrinkly rockers Led Zeppelin's 'Stairway to Heaven' and perhaps planting (pardon the pun) the idea of a reunion in their minds. Just in case you are not aware, I hate the Zep and everything they and their music stands for and the recent concerts and the sight of denim-clad old men like Clarkson reviving, reliving and celebrating their youth was sickening.

Just what was the point of punk if Zeppelin and even worse Pink Floyd can make comebacks?

10. Her Majesty the Queen

No words can adequately sum up the debt of gratitude we owe this hard-working woman.

36

By appointment to the British people: classic tastes for true Brits only

1. Worcester Sauce

Foreigners only understand this if it's in a Bloody Mary but there are loads of other uses for this sauce, which was first manufactured in 1838. This is a 'must have' in every kitchen store cupboard. Try it on cheese on toast or use it to pep up any casserole, stew or chilli con carne. Or alternatively join our colonial cousins and pour a large vodka over ice, add tomato juice, two dashes of the magic and enjoy!

2. Marmite

I'm in a minority in my house because Lisa and the girls love the stuff. So much so that jars of Marmite have travelled the world with us, as it's so difficult to get abroad. However whether you like it or hate it you have to admit that this product is pure Britain and even the jar is a British icon. Made of course from yeast extract, Marmite's origins are in the Bass Brewery in Burton on Trent, which is why it's very surprising that I don't like the taste when I consider the gallons of Bass I've thrown down my neck over the years.

3. Lemon Curd

As a kid I loved it on toast, then I got more sophisticated and had it on scones, but for my money you can't beat a lemon curd tart.

4. Marmalade

Sorry, it's got to have pieces in it and if it's not home-made, usually bought from a fat old bird at a church fete, then it has got to be Robinson's Golden Shred and I'm afraid I want the Golly back too. I still can't believe the furore over the Golly but as a kid I loved collecting the tokens, didn't you? Evidently marmalade can be traced back to 1480 and although it chokes me to say it, it was a French invention – but of course we Brits refined it.

5. HP Sauce

The best thing to come out of Birmingham, apart from the Aston Expressway or City fans after an all too seldom win at nearby 'Scum' Park. Of course this classic British sauce was made in Aston from 1899 until Heinz took over the company and transferred production to the Netherlands in 2007. There was a massive campaign to save this sauce with its iconic image of the Houses of Parliament on its label. Even the local Labour MP, Khalid Mahmood, brandished a bottle of the sauce in the Commons in a heated debate while reminding fellow MPs that it was former Prime Minister Harold Wilson's favourite condiment. It was all to no avail and over 125 jobs were lost and the factory and its landmark chimney were pulled down in 2007.

6. Lion's Midget Gems

As a kid these were my mum's and my favourite sweets but they had to be Lion Midget Gems and Mum would accept no alternative. She was probably spinning in her grave when Maynard's bought out Lion and started to change the sweet in 2005. Their first act of sacrilege was to turn the black sweet from being liquorice flavour to blackcurrant. That upset thousands of fans and the company were besieged with emails and petitions. As one protester remarked, 'There goes another part of my childhood!'

7. Pork Scratchings

I don't know about foreigners not getting our food but there are a lot of southerners who don't appreciate this Black Country delicacy that has been a traditional accompaniment to a pint of mild or bitter for nearly two centuries. I love them. Who cares if they're unhealthy and where they come from. As long as you don't do what my mate did and put his finger in a pack and pull out what looked distinctly like a pig's ring piece, what have you got to worry about?

8. Banks' Mild

One of the best, if not the best, pint of mild in the world and certainly the biggest selling mild in the universe. To really appreciate it you have to be drinking it in a back-street spit-and-sawdust boozer in some God-forgotten place like Tipton or Dudley. But one sip and you will be transported to Nirvana and in all likelihood end up in A&E having your stomach pumped after a night on the lash. Be warned – one sip and you will be hooked.

9. Branston Pickle

In production since 1922 and selling over 28 million jars a year, this is Britain's pickle. You can't beat it with a ploughman's or simply on a doorstep of a cheese sarnie with a real pickled onion on the side and a pint in your hand.

10. Black Pudding

Don't buy it without the fat lumps, you tart! You can't have a full English without it and have you tried it uncooked? Bloody beautiful.

11. Curry Sauce on Chips

I don't know who started this, but let's face it, when you're about eighteen and you've had a skinful, what better way of soaking up the bevvy than a plastic tray full of chips, cooked in dripping obviously, with a dollop of curry sauce on top.

12. Jellied Eels

Not to my taste but those cockneys love them.

13. Vimto or Dandelion and Burdock

Have you ever tried drinking any of these two after the age of consent? They have loads of happy memories of sun-filled afternoons playing football on Radford Common or long bike rides with my brothers and mates with Shippham fish paste sarnies for lunch. But by God as you get older you just can't drink the stuff. It's similar to how you fantasise about having a baby as an excuse to eat Farley's Rusks, but again the harsh reality is that they just don't taste right with the mature palate. You can't even have proper burping competitions with Burdock like you did when you were a kid.

14. Porridge

I love the stuff and it's great that it's now become trendy and healthy to eat it, but let's be straight – it's got to be made with milk and you've got to have heavily buttered hot toast with it so that you can dip each slice into like a nan bread with balti. *Delicious*.

15. Pork Pies

Of course they must be Melton Mowbray, served at room temperature with a massive dollop of Branston or Taylor's English Mustard on the side.

16. Haggis

Lisa and I are massive fans of haggis. Served simply and traditionally with neeps and tatties it has to be one of the best British meals ever. I even like it deep-fried with chips from one of Edinburgh's finest fish and chip shops. To ponces who turn up their noses and worry about what it's made of, I say get a life and get out of mine.

17. Taylor's English Mustard

In our family this is called the 'secret recipe'. It's simply the best English Mustard in the world and is made in Newport Pagnell near Milton Keynes. It's the supreme English mustard and should come as no surprise that it's manufactured in the birthplace of one of our greatest British cars, the Aston Martin. The reason why it's called the secret recipe is basically because I refuse to travel without it. I've put this mustard on steaks in the Seychelles, the States and all over the Caribbean. Wherever we are Lisa is 'instructed' to carry it in her handbag and quite simply failure to deliver on this essential service would result in the divorce courts.

Seriously if you have never tried this, get some. Then get down to a traditional butcher and buy some well-hung steak, show the steak the frying pan for a second or two, make sure the cow is almost still mooing, whack it on to a preheated plate with a mountain of hand-cut real chips and a spoonful of peas and a fried tomato. Wait a second or two until the blood seeps into the chips, dip the steak into the mustard and tell me, is there any finer meal in the world? Answer, no!

18. Arbroath Smokies

I once had the privilege of eating these almost direct from the smoke house on a holiday in Scotland and it was one of the nicest breakfasts I have ever had. Essentially this is haddock that has been gutted, beheaded and tied in a pair and then smoked all night over chippings of oak and beech in little shacks in the town of Arbroath. It's delicious hot or cold and the trip north is worth it alone for this brilliant British delicacy.

19. Hull Curd Cheesecakes

When I was a kid we used to have to go to Hull two or three times a year to visit my mum and dad's relatives and the highlight, apart from the new jumpers from Auntie Jean, was buying and eating real Hull cheesecake. As an adult I took Lisa back up to Hull primarily so that she could taste it. She didn't like it, good! That meant all the more for me, but seriously this tart is delicious. It's an open tart with currants in it and I have never been able to find it outside of Yorkshire. There is a variation of it in Northamptonshire called the Towcester Tart but I am afraid it's not a patch on the real thing from Hull.

20. Beer and Cheese

I could write pages on traditional British beer and cheese but would rather leave that to an expert rather than a self-confessed addict. Suffice to say, I find it bizarre that British people will walk into a bar serving real ale and ask for a pint of fizzy mass-produced weak-as-piss lager. These are the same people who will pontificate and spend lifetimes in Threshers discussing what wine goes with which food but show absolutely no respect for our brewing culture, skill or heritage. I don't want people to grow beards, wear sweaty beer-stained real ale festival T-shirts and join the bores of CAMRA, but for God's sake, give traditional real British beer a chance. By the same token I believe there should be massive tax breaks for brewers of real ale and other producers of traditional British foods such as independent cheesemakers.

There were nearly divorce proceedings the other week when I noticed that Lisa had bought some cheese so mild it made a Liberal Democrat look like he had a backbone.

'What's this?' I bellowed.

'Oh, the kids don't like the strong stuff you buy.'

'Well, they'll have to get used to it because I don't want this manufactured X Factor, Simon Cowell crap in my larder.'

I was only half joking but I truly believe if you feed your children bland rubbish, that is all they will ever know and want. The palate needs educating and there are so many wonderful British cheeses out there just waiting to be tried.

Of course not everyone is going to like every style of cheese but again the supermarkets are trying to homogenise our taste with their domination of the market. That's why I am a champion of the traditional retail and food markets and welcome the emergence of the farmers' markets and farm shops where the real taste of this country can still be found and discovered. It may cost a few pennies more to have a real British taste, but buy it please because quite simply it's a case of us Brits having to use it or lose these foods for good.

In praise of British food

It's true to say that until Delia, Rhodes, Worrall Thompson, Oliver and the ubiquitous (is that a swear word?) Ramsay came on the scene most British restaurant food was crap. However and with the exception of Fanny Craddock (quick diversion – did Johnny really say, 'I hope that your doughnuts turn out like Fanny's' or was it an urban myth?) British food has now come out of the dark ages of Angus steakhouses, Bernis and the old-fashioned Wimpy. Thank God!

However we Brits will still retain a love for our distinctly British food whether the rest of the world gets it or not and so I'll be pleased if you nodded in agreement with some of the above, even tasted them in your mouth as you read them or simply scrunched up your nose and grimaced at the thought of eating some of that muck again.

Whatever your reaction they are our nation's grub and long may they be found in the back of the British store cupboard just next to last Christmas's jar of piccalilli and those old packets of Angel Delight!

Enjoy!

37

Top ten singles about UK life as only we can possibly know it

1. 'Ghost Town' – The Specials, 1981

This record was bang on the money because in 1981 Britain was in crisis with mass unemployment and massive factory closures, which would culminate, as 'Ghost Town' hit Number One in the charts, with rioting on the country's major cities' streets. It was as if The Specials had predicted all this, when in effect all they were doing was just commenting on what they had witnessed as they toured the country. The single and the accompanying video with the band squeezed into an old car was equally memorable and was a fitting ending to a brilliant live band who managed to combine politics and social comment with some of the best dance tunes ever.

2. 'Up the Junction' – Squeeze, 1979

I love this song because it can only be about London and could only have been written by this band. The song is clearly influenced by the book of the same title by Nell Dunn and later one of my favourite social-realism British movies of the Sixties starring great British actors Dennis Waterman, Maureen Lipman, Suzy Kendall and the incredibly sexy Adrienne Posta. I had the privilege of meeting Tilbrook and

Difford, the main songwriters of Squeeze, when they performed live in my talkSPORT studio in 2007 and I love the quirky social realism in their lyrics. They are truly great British songwriters and deserve much more success and critical acclaim.

3. 'Down in the Tube Station at Midnight' – The Jam, 1978

I love this song but I could have picked any number of Jam songs that would fit in this category, including 'Eton Rifles', 'A Town Called Malice', 'That's Entertainment' or 'Going Underground'. Paul Weller is a superb chronicler of British urban youth and the lives they led or lead; this, combined with the music and the sheer brilliance and energy of a Jam live gig, made them one of Britain's best-ever bands. I love the opening sound of the tube train on this record and of course it's an anti-racism record about a mugging by fascist bully boys down the tube. A sign of the times was the comment by Radio 1 DJ Tony Blackburn who allegedly complained: 'It's disgusting the way punks sing about violence. Why can't they sing about trees and flowers?'

4. 'Waterloo Sunset' – The Kinks, 1967

If you don't know this song you cannot possibly call yourself British. This is London. This is Great Britain. End of.

5. 'One in Ten' – UB40, 1981

Even though they're from Birmingham I have always loved UB40. When I was at university I saw them play loads of times in small venues and then at a huge open-air gig at the Cannon Hill Park in Edgbaston and it was clear they were destined for great things. OK, they went off into cover versions and with it they became massive worldwide but the early stuff was fantastic social comment, even their very name is a political statement. I still have their first album with the cover being a dole card. I also love the way that these eight guys were on the dole, taught themselves to play and through sheer hard work, commitment and drive became one of the biggest-selling bands in the world.

6. 'We'll Live and Die in These Towns' – The Enemy, 2007

Yes of course this Coventry punk trio are heavily influenced by The Jam, Oasis and of course Coventry's finest, The Specials, but the fact remains that they are a brilliant new band singing what will soon be stadium anthems for a new young generation.

7. 'Anarchy in the UK'– The Sex Pistols, 1976

I've picked 'Anarchy' but it could have been 'God Save the Queen' or anything off the *Never Mind the Bollocks* album. The Pistols could have only come from Britain. Yes, The New York Dolls and The Ramones influenced them but the sound was, and definitely the attitude and clothes were, determinedly British. Punk didn't just change music, it changed fashion and youth subcultures for ever. I know I'm biased but it was a great time to be a British teenager.

8. 'London's Burning' – The Clash, 1977

I can still vividly remember the follow spots flashing over the pogoing crowd that was going wild in Tiffany's nightclub in Coventry as The Clash powered through the tracks from their first album on the White Riot tour. I was there and this was the music I had been waiting all my life for. If I remember that night correctly they were supported by The Splits and Subway Sect and The Clash were like no other band I had ever seen and in truth they were probably the best punk band live. As the band developed and got more left wing you could argue that they could have come from a country other than Britain but in the first three albums this was without doubt the sound of the times, and it was bloody exciting.

9. 'New England' – Billy Bragg, 1979

I love this song, which isn't about England of course but is actually a love song. A cover version by Kirsty McColl, for which Billy actually wrote another couple of verses, was a big hit in 1985. I had the absolute pleasure of booking Kirsty a few times at my venues in Coventry and Edinburgh, and her early and tragic death robbed us all of another great British talent. Politically Billy and myself are opposites but I love his music as it's from such a traditional English folk tradition. I also love the fact that Billy is helping to reclaim the flag from the far right bullyboys and he's a true patriot.

10. 'Good Morning Britain' – Roddy Frame, 1990

I have always loved Roddy and Aztec Camera from his first releases on Postcard Records along with stablemate Edwyn Collins and Orange Juice. This song was a duet with one of his heroes and mine, Mick Jones of The Clash, and it's a corker. Back in 1990 I had the great pleasure of having Roddy and Edwyn doing a double-header show for a week at one of my Edinburgh venues and the night that Tom Robinson and the violinist Nigel Kennedy came along and jammed with the pair was one of the greatest of my life. Roddy and his love songs should have been much bigger than they have been as he is one of our greatest songwriters. If you don't own any of his albums get out there and buy them or get your kids to download them.

38

Leather on willow: best five British cricketers

I am indebted to my talkSPORT colleague and former England international Ronnie 'Chicken Biryani' Irani for his selection of Britain's best-ever cricketers.

1. Fred Trueman

A colossus of a man who stood for no nonsense. 'Our Fred' was a big man in build but a pure athlete, charging into the crease when he bowled. He psyched out many a batsman before they even got to the wicket!

2. Ian Botham

Comfortably the best all-rounder England will ever see. He used to take the Aussies on single-handedly. His batting would change a game, just like the Headingley Test Match in 1981, and his bowling was capable of getting the best batsmen in the world out at any one time. He also changed the style in which slip fielders caught by standing closer than others, having a sharp eye and great hands.

3. Graham Gooch

England's greatest batsman to date! When Gooch was at the crease for Essex or England his side was winning, he was that good. A powerful batsman who took on the best in the world and usually came out on top.

4. Marcus Trescothick

Since Gooch retired, Tres was the closest cricketer to him there has been. A brilliant eye and he read the length of any bowler early. He wasn't afraid of being aggressive against spin – just like the Gooch mould.

5. Darren Gough

Could bowl well in any conditions and was the pioneer of taking reverse swing for fast bowlers in England to another level. The Dazzler was the modern game's Trueman.

39

Fifteen frames per second . . . *and British*: my personal favourites

Over the years I've nearly done as many phone-ins on the subject of the best films as I have on immigration or law and order. So I reckon that I have earned the right to compile my own list. However by their very nature these lists are subjective so the following is *my* list – not based on box office income, critics or any other form of scientific evidence but purely on my prejudice, likes and dislikes . . . oh and a few of Lisa's as well! So in no particular order . . .

1. *This Sporting Life*

This brilliant film, made in 1963, written by David Storey and based on his novel, was directed by Lindsay Anderson, who also directed another of my favourites, *If*, with Malcolm McDowell.

The film stars Richard Harris (what an actor!), Rachel Roberts and Alan Badel. It won loads of awards including an Oscar nomination for Harris. Incidentally Rachel Roberts was also the star in another classic and favourite British movie of mine, *Saturday Night and Sunday Morning*.

It's a kitchen-sink drama about the love between rugby player Frank Machin (Richard Harris) and widow Mrs Hammond (Rachel

Roberts). Frank is a bitter coalminer who gets into a scrap at a nightclub with a professional rugby league player and ends up getting a kicking off the whole rugby team. Without giving too much away he then gets signed up by the team and becomes a real local sporting star.

Meanwhile off the field he falls in love with his landlady (Roberts). She's a passionless widow, who eventually has a physical relationship with him but refuses any emotional involvement.

Frank, like many working-class blokes and not just sports stars, finds it hard to cope with his 'fame', his love, life and the money. There's a great scene in a restaurant where the waiter is being snobby to him and he comes out with the immortal line, 'Is my money not good enough?' It's a line that Lisa and I often mutter to each other when we end up in a situation that is either alien or intimidating. The moment when this particular boy from the backstreets of Coventry is in a position of feeling like a fish out of water, just like Frank.

However the film was a flop when it first opened and the critics panned it. But what do they know! I think it is brilliant and still as relevant today as it was years ago.

Look out for William Hartnell, the original Doctor Who, playing a supporting role.

2. *The Long Good Friday*

Probably the best of the modern British gangster movies and although firmly set in the early Eighties the story is still gripping today. It stars Bob Hoskins and Helen Mirrren and has a host of great British actors in it that went on to find fame in their own right including Felix Dexter (*Press Gang*), Pierce Brosnan (*James Bond*, this was his first film role) Karl Howman (*Brush Strokes*), Gillian Taylforth of *EastEnders* and sausage fame, and Derek Thompson, who later became everyone's favourite male nurse as Charlie in *Casualty*.

Paul Freeman, who would later go on to play the main villain in *Raiders of the Lost Ark*, is also in the movie. I remember seeing him at Warwick Arts Centre in a play called *Cloud Nine* when I was in the sixth form and years later, after college, when I was doing bit parts on the TV, I had a very small part in an ITV series called *Yesterday's Dreams* in which he starred. I spent about a week in a posh hotel in Buxton during the miners' strike filming this programme with him, but unfortunately my scenes ended up on the cutting-room floor!

It was a bizarre experience all round because we were sharing the hotel with the breakaway/scab, depending on your politics, miners' union, the newly formed UDM, who were holding their first conference in the conference hall. Paul was a real pro and gentleman and he also introduced me to the delights of Laphroig whisky!

Back to the film – it was written by a playwright called Barry Keefe whose plays I used to watch as a kid at the Belgrade Theatre studio. One of these was called *Barbarians*. It was about football and it was loud and aggressive and if I'm really honest it was this play that influenced my own playwrighting style and certainly my own most successful play, *Hooligans*, years later. So in a bizarre way I kind of feel connected to this movie.

Plus, my beautiful wife, Lisa, has always been obsessed by the scene where Hoskins takes a shower! Women, you can't live with them, you can't live without them!

Whereas I'm old enough to remember Bob before he found real fame and he was in that TV show called *On the Move*, which was designed to promote adult literacy. Whatever happened to the other bloke in the lorry?

The plot? What, you don't know the plot? Have you been in a coma for the past twenty years? Get it out on DVD now and watch it for yourselves.

Just one thing – they are planning on doing a remake to be made in Miami! The question is why? You can't improve on the original and I'm sorry but this is a British story that can only be set in London.

3. *The Italian Job*

Every true Brit reckons they can do an impression of Tommy Cooper, just like that! And of course Michael Caine's famous line, 'You're only supposed to blow the bloody doors off!' from this brilliant 1969 crime caper written by Troy Kennedy Martin. By the way, Troy was also the co-creator of *Z-Cars* and wrote the brilliant Bob Peck TV serial, *Edge of Darkness*.

This is a classic British movie with great British stars like Caine, Noël Coward and even Benny Hill and of course with great British icons like the Mini almost sharing the limelight with the actors.

As a Coventry kid, it's great to be able to brag that the famous car chase through the sewer tunnels was not filmed in Turin but in my home town. 'Not a lot of people know that!'

I'm not going to detail the plot as we all know what happens but I love this movie because it is such a celebration of Swinging Sixties Britain. Yeah I know it's a romantic rose-tinted version of the underworld but, hey, aren't movies sometimes meant to be about escapism? Anyhow Caine went on to make the brutally realistic *Get Carter* with Alf Roberts out of Corrie as a balance to this jolly romp. By the way, that's another brilliant British movie too.

There was a remake of this movie in 2003 set in LA (naturally!) and although it's OK it shouldn't be confused with the real thing.

4. *Quadrophenia*

In 1979 as Two Tone was ripping up the country this film was released that, although based on The Who's double album of the same name and set in 1964, seemed perfectly to catch the atmosphere of the end of the Seventies too.

Not only that but it starred Phil Daniels and didn't every boy want to be him? And of course there's that scene with Leslie Ash. A blistering soundtrack, fights on the beaches and the late great Michael Elphick playing Phil Daniels's dad. What else could you want? Even Sting puts in a reasonable performance as leader of the Mods who ends up as a bellboy and of course everyone's favourite Brit villain Philip Davis is his usual menacing self.

The ending – later ripped off by *Thelma and Louise* (good movie too, by the way, but not British, although directed by Brit Ridley Scott) is just perfect and sums up every teenager's feelings of isolation and despair at the end of their youth. I love the way the movie's ending is ambiguous and that we as the viewer are left to decide whether Jimmy is dead or alive.

It's a cult classic and Daniels's performance is spellbinding. It's a film that could only ever be set in England and it's a movie that revels in our teenage subcultures and fashions.

The film was the directorial debut of Brit Frank Roddam (original creator of *Auf Wiedersehen Pet*) and was panned by the critics for its large amounts of sex, violence, profanity and drug use but teenagers like me couldn't get enough of it. It was our lives at last being portrayed on the screen and I feel it had a real resonance with teenagers like me who were just becoming men.

Make sure if you are getting this out on DVD you double up and get Ray Winstone starring in *Scum* too. British subculture and British movies at their best.

5. *This is England*

This is a relatively modern film, written and directed by Shane Meadows in 2006. If you haven't seen it, put down this book and get down the DVD shop now.

Filmed in and around Nottingham it is set in the skinhead culture of the early Eighties and stars a young lad who had never acted before, Thomas Turgoose. His character, Shaun, is a mixed-up lad who after being bullied at school and losing his dad in the Falklands War falls in with a group of older skinheads. This gang eventually splits into two separate groups. One a 'white power' knuckle-dragging racist gang and the others who are non-racist. The soundtrack is absolutely blinding with loads of Ska, soul and reggae in it.

Again, just like *Quadrophenia*, it captures that moment in time of British history, post-Falklands with industry in decline and shows the brutal reality of living in poor council estates through the eyes and experience of the young lad. I think it is a masterpiece and deserves a bigger airing. Unfortunately it was given an 18 certificate, which has meant that the very youths who should be watching this movie are not allowed to view it. This is crazy because it is one of the most damning indictments of why racism is so utterly stupid that I have ever seen. It should be part of the bloody National Curriculum.

6. *The Dam Busters, Reach for the Sky, Sink the Bismarck!, The Battle of Britain,* and *Bridge on the River Kwai*

I've grouped these films together and I could mention loads more great British war movies but this selection seems to sum up a time when we weren't afraid to talk about our military past. A time when we could commemorate and celebrate the brave men and women from around the Commonwealth who fought to make this a land fit for heroes instead of council bureaucrats (watch what you're putting in that bin!) over-zealous traffic cops, self-serving pigs in Westminster and the health and safety Nazis who have succeeded in curtailing our freedoms where Hitler failed.

They also bring back fond memories of lazy, usually wet, Sunday afternoons with nothing to do but watch the telly with my brothers in Coventry.

By the way, I wanted to mention *The Great Escape* but of course that was an American movie based on a book by an Australian writer and former POW, Paul Brickhill. It's also interesting to note that both *Reach for the Sky* and *The Dambusters* were also based on his books.

The Dam Busters

Made in 1955 and based on the true story of the RAF's 617 Squadron and the development of the bouncing bomb which was created to attack the Ruhr dams in an operation called Chastise. Michael Redgrave stars as the bomb's developer Barnes Wallis and Richard Todd (God, he's in nearly every British war movie, isn't he?) as Wing Commander Guy Gibson.

Before we go any further, if like me you're a child of the Sixties, can you remember turning your hands inside out to make the shape of goggles and then charging around the playground singing the theme tune to this brilliant movie?

The film's theme tune which is rather 'imaginatively' called, 'The Dam Busters' March', was written by Eric Coates and as well as being a staple of every playground in Britain also became a brass band classic and of course is still sung by our 'Army' of supporters when England play football, especially against the Germans! The plot's straightforward as it follows Barnes Wallis and his attempts to build a bomb capable of destroying the dams on the Ruhr and thus crippling Germany's heavy industry in the valley. He knows that the bombers will have to fly at an incredibly low altitude of only 150 feet for the bombs to actually bounce and at first the Ministry of Defence is reluctant to sanction such an attack. Eventually he meets and convinces Bomber Harris and the project gets the green light.

A special squadron of Lancasters is formed commanded by Wing Commander Guy Gibson and they start to practise over Derwentwater. Some of these scenes are probably the best ever in any war movie. However, in the story and in real life the bombs start to explode when they hit the water so Barnes Wallis decides that the planes have to fly even lower, sixty feet, to deliver their payload.

The bombers eventually attack and destroy two dams but in the process several Lancasters and their crew are lost. This produces the last dramatic and poignant scene that accurately summarises the true bloody nature of war – the heroes know their mission has been a success but their elation is tempered by the knowledge that many have died in delivering it. This is what makes the film one of the greatest war movies of all time because it does not gloss over the deaths of the aircrew or indeed the collateral damage of the Germans who would have died in the valleys below the dams.

Here's the bad news . . . Universal Pictures are planning a remake, why? Stephen Fry is writing it and Peter *Lord of the Rings* Jackson is going to direct it in New Zealand.

Movies like this do not need to be remade. They just need to be remastered as this one was in 2007. Then they need to be re-released and become part of the National Curriculum so that every child in the country can be aware of the sacrifice their ancestors made so that this country could enjoy free speech, and so that fanatics like Abu Hamza can spew their hatred of us on to the streets.

Of course all that *does* happen in politically correct Britain is that there is a row about whether Guy's dog can still be called 'Nigger' as it was in the original movie and in real life. In recent years the dog's name has been either bleeped when the movie has been shown on TV or redubbed so that his name becomes Tigger. As someone whose name escapes me said, you couldn't make it up!

Quick bit of film trivia, which you may well know, is that the final attack on the dams sequence was lovingly ripped off by George Lucas in the climax of the film *Star Wars IV: A New Hope*. Hey, there's nowt wrong with a quick bit of plagiarism or borrowing – even Shakespeare nicked a plot or two!

Reach for the Sky

Made in 1956 and winner of a BAFTA for best British film of that year the film is based on the book of the same name by Paul Brickhill and tells the true life story of Douglas Bader, played by the brilliant Kenneth More.

The plot is simple, telling the true story of how Bader, a brilliant sportsman, loses both his legs in a flying accident in 1931 but still manages to convince the RAF to let him rejoin at the start of the Second World War and then let him fight in the Battle of Britain. After bailing out over France in 1941 he gets taken to Colditz Castle

until his release in 1945 when Bader then leads a flypast commemor-
ating the end of the war.

Of course we all know this movie so well because it was on nearly
every Sunday afternoon, or at least it felt like it. When I was growing
up it was as big a part of Sundays as church bells, roast dinners and
saying, 'Mum, I'm bored.'

'Come and do the washing up then?'

'No, not that kind of bored!'

But then you would sink into the film and I loved his pig-stubborn
arrogance and refusal to give in either to the doctors when they said
he would never walk again or to the Nazis whom he forced to
confiscate his legs to stop him trying to escape.

Bader's real life story should be an inspiration to both able-bodied
and those with a disability and I couldn't see him swinging the lead
and trying to claim some extra dosh on benefits like those with the
new backache of stress and depression in twenty-first-century Britain!

I'm really pleased that this was made by Brits because can you
imagine how sickeningly sweet the Yanks would have made the story?
As per usual the plot would have been altered so that they would have
won the war for us and made Douglas walk again, probably on water!

However Lewis Gilbert's direction had none of this and it was very
understated and reserved. This was no surprise really from the man
who went on to direct other British classics like *Carve Her Name with
Pride*, *Sink the Bismarck*, *Alfie*, three James Bond movies, and later in
life *Educating Rita* and *Shirley Valentine*.

A brilliant and inspiring movie and surprisingly Mike Myers's
favourite movie as well.

Sink the Bismarck!

Made in 1969 and another classic from director Lewis Gilbert and
again starring Kenneth More, this time as Captain Jonathan Shepard
who is tasked with seeking out and destroying Germany's most
powerful and largest battleship. Based on a true story with large
dollops of fiction thrown in, including a suggested romance between
Shepard and his glamorous Wren, Anne Davies played by Dana
Wynter.

This is one of the last of the generation of classic British war films
to be made after the Second World War and as with many of them it

shouldn't be viewed as a purely factual account of history; however, that doesn't mean it and many others aren't brilliant movies.

The film opens with actual Nazi footage of the *Bismarck* being launched in 1939 juxtaposed with Shepard (More) walking across Trafalgar Square en route to his new job at the Admiralty. Shepard is a bitter man as his wife has been killed in a German air raid and his destroyer was sunk by Lütjens who is now commander of the *Bismarck*.

Meanwhile Gunther Lütjens, like Shepard, is also an embittered man. After Germany's loss in World War I, he believes that he has received no recognition for his efforts in the war and been forgotten. In this conflict he is therefore determined to be both remembered and recognised, thus as a character he is set up as the arch Nazi villain.

The plot revolves around the fact that in 1941 British convoy routes in the Atlantic were being decimated by U-Boat and surface raider attacks. They were cutting off vital supplies that Britain needed to continue its war against Germany. In May, British intelligence discovers that the *Bismarck* and the heavy cruiser *Prinz Eugen* are attempting to make a breakout into the North Atlantic to raid convoys. Thus the hunt begins with Shepard (More) directing operations from London. It's a cat and mouse game which culminates in the final destruction of the *Bismarck* by several British ships.

Classic stuff, reminiscent of comics like the *Victor* and commando stories that we all grew up with, and there is even a suggestion of a bit of romance at the end as the hero and the Wren emerge from the control room and he asks her if she would like to eat.

Just like *The Cruel Sea*, another classic we've all seen a million times, we all know More is going to pick up the model of the *Bismarck* from the table as he leaves the control room but we all still sit there glued to the screen.

Never has the cliché 'they don't make them like that any more' ever been truer.

The Bridge on the River Kwai

Made in 1957 and directed by one of Britain's greatest film directors, David Lean (*Great Expectations*, *Brief Encounter*, *Lawrence of Arabia*, *Doctor Zhivago*, *A Passage to India* and many more) this film should be compulsory viewing for all. I didn't realise but this classic British movie is actually based on a French novel, *Le pont de la rivière Kwai* by Pierre Boulle.

The movie is set during the construction of the Burmese Railway in 1942–43 and stars Alec Guinness, Jack Hawkins and William Holden. Unlike the war films above, it is largely a fictional story but to me, along with *The Great Escape*, it is as big a part of Christmas as Morecambe and Wise and the Nativity.

I won't bore you with the plot as we all know it so well that we could almost recite the dialogue in unison. In fact you only have to mention the title and most true Brits will start whistling the Colonel Bogey tune, remembering the opening sequences when the British troops enter the camp led by Alec Guinness.

The film has a particular resonance with me because two of my mum's relations were actually captured by the Japanese and forced to work on the railways. They both survived but I can remember as a young boy my Uncle Arthur in particular exploding in a rage if we ever left any food on our plates. Uncle Arthur's story – whether myth, part myth or completely factual I'm not sure – was that after his ship had been torpedoed he and a few others had survived in a life raft for days before being picked up by the Japs and then taken to the camp. After nearly starving he couldn't abide waste and although like most men who have been through such horror he never spoke about his wartime experiences, there would be these vicious tableside rants if we were faddy or wasteful.

The Battle of Britain

Made in 1969 and to me it only feels like yesterday that me, Dad and my brother Simon were queuing outside some fleapit in Coventry to see this great war movie. I can even remember telling my mates about the scene where the pilot gets shot through the eyes and the blood is all over his goggles.

This has got to be not only one of the greatest British war movies but also one of the best of its genre in the world. It's got a great cast, a real story without too much jingoism or fiction, great aircraft, superb dogfights and of course a superb stirring soundtrack largely written by Ron Goodwin who also did the music for *633 Squadron*.

Simply it's the best of British, starring Laurence Olivier, Trevor Howard and a very young Ian McShane, and it's still a movie I would stay in to watch if it was on the box.

In fact the cast is a Who's Who of the Best of British film acting with Michael Caine, Ralph Richardson, Michael Redgrave, Edward Fox, Christopher Plummer, Susannah York, Robert Shaw and of course Kenneth More.

And 'I say, I say', look out for a young Fred Elliot (John Savident in *Corrie*).

Obviously it tells the story of the RAF's finest hour in 1940 when every aircraft and every airman was mobilised to halt the invasion of Britain by the Nazis. By and large the film is historically accurate and has some of the most thrilling aerial cinematography I have ever seen. When you consider this was achieved without the use of computer technology, it is even more remarkable.

I also love the way the movie pays tribute to the contribution of the Polish pilots who fought with the Brits during this period and I love the part the late Barry Foster (Van der Valk) plays in the movie.

Clearly the Battle of Britain was a major turning point in the war which led to Hitler's abandoning Operation Sealion and the invasion of our green and pleasant land and that it why it is so apt that this classic war movie ends with the famous Churchill speech about 'Never in the field of human conflict has so much been owed by so many to so few . . .'

Other movies that could have made it

- *Get Carter* – who can forget the scene on the car park roof?
- *The Loneliness of the Long Distance Runner* – cracking book and script from Alan Sillitoe and superb performance from top Brit actor, Tom Courtenay.
- *The Thirty-Nine Steps* – I like both versions of this classic British thriller, Hitchcock's and the one with Robert 'Jesus' Powell.
- *Kind Hearts and Coronets* – the Ealing Comedy with Alec Guinness playing all the roles.
- *The Lavender Hill Mob* – another British black and white comedy that never ever dates, with a young Sid James amongst the cast.
- *Kes* – my favourite film as a kid and the book is just as good; watch out for Ivy Tilsey out of *Corrie* as Casper's mum.
- *The Ladykillers* – another Ealing classic that definitely didn't need to be remade by Hollywood. Get your Yankee hands off our heritage!

- *Whisky Galore* – this film was so good it's still being ripped off in adverts today. Every Scotsman's fantasy – a beach full of whisky.
- *The Full Monty* – great performance from a truly superb British cast including Robert Carlyle and Tom Wilkinson.
- Any of the *Carry On* movies (camp and dated but so British and so funny).

I could carry on but I think that I have proved the point that when it comes to movies Britain really is great. Most of all, isn't it great to see a film list that doesn't rely on *Notting Hill*, *Four Weddings and a Funeral* and bloody *Bridget Jones*!

40

Four British things I would travel a million miles to see

1. Red Falcons parachute team

I have a vivid memory of these heroes parachuting in not only at events in Coventry but at numerous days out at places like RAF Mawgan Porth in Cornwall and at RAF Cosgrove and even at the Royal Show in Stoneleigh on the outskirts of Coventry when I was a kid. If you've never seen them perform, you are missing one of the greatest British displays of military courage, skill and teamwork and it is almost a crime not to expose your children to their aerial mastery.

The Falcons are based at RAF Brize Norton in Oxfordshire and have been performing displays for over 40 years and perform at least 70 events every year. Depending on weather conditions, they'll jump from 2,500 to 12,000 feet, performing manoeuvres at speeds of over 120mph.

All team members are specially selected from the Parachute Jumping Instructor section of the Physical Education Branch of the RAF. Although the displays are important, the primary role of all selected members is the parachute training for all of the UK's Armed Forces. Each team member spends three years honing their skills, enabling them to become Military Freefall Instructors responsible for training certain elite elements of the British Airborne Forces.

The eleven-person non-contact canopy stack is an amazing, jawdropping, ice-cream-melting spectacle to behold, especially when the old red, white and blue smoke canisters which they wear on their ankles are in full flow. The way they all manage to land in quick succession on a drop zone which can be as small as 50 yards by 75 yards is truly amazing and will keep your kids talking about it for weeks.

The best thing is that the members are always willing to chat with the kids afterwards and pose for the inevitable photos.

You can find details of all the displays and air shows that they are appearing at by going to their website at http://www.raf.mod.uk/falcons/.

2. The White Helmets Motorcycle Display Team

So I'm sitting cross-legged on the grass, I'm nine maybe ten, Dad's smoking and I'm enjoying the smell even the taste as it mingles with my 99 ice cream, it's a special day, the sun is shining. Mum's licking a Mivi and we're at the Royal Show or is it the Memorial Park – I can't remember and it doesn't matter, it's the late Sixties and it's a perfect day as we wait for the motorbikes to be announced over the overloud tinny public address system. Then before you know it they roar into the arena, thirty 750cc Triumph motorcycles with soldiers astride them wearing the traditional open-faced helmets. This is Britain, this is Great Britain.

The Royal Signals White Helmets are the oldest and best-known motorcycle display team in the world, founded in 1927 as a combined display of horsemanship and motorcycle riding skills by Royal Signals dispatch riders.

It's a team of thirty volunteer soldiers from the Corps that tour Britain from April to September every year, demonstrating all the personal qualities demanded of the modern Royal Signals soldier and to this day it's a display that still makes me and thousands of others feel proud to be British.

To become a member of the team you have to be a qualified tradesman in the Corps and successfully complete a tough induction process in the winter. Then you earn the right to wear the white helmet. The thrilling display is meant to show how you need teamwork, courage, trust, strength and agility if you want to be part of the best army in the world, the British Army.

It's a fantastic display of man and machine in perfect harmony and again it's a must do and a must see for every child and their parents if you haven't seen it when you were a kid.

Find out more and all the dates of the displays at http://www.army.mod.uk/signals.

3. The Wall of Death

A bit like the first time you go to watch a speedway meeting, you either love it or hate it and if it's the former the adrenaline rush and unique pure smell of the event never leaves you. I must have been ten or eleven when I first climbed up the steps on the outside of the wall of death and watched in absolute awe as the riders far below kick-started their machines and then roared up the wall. Absolute magic.

Of course the walls are in steep decline with only one or two still touring the country but again it's a tradition that you have got to expose your children to. I don't know whether it's a pure British tradition, I guess it started out in the States, but it's part of the landscape of Britain and country fairs and carnivals that is fast disappearing.

There are only three walls of death in Great Britain today, and Graham Crispey, Ken Fox and Allan Ford own these.

4. RAF Dog Display Team

'Ladies and gentlemen, mums and dads, boys and girls, I would like to present to you a display of obedience, agility and specialised training by the Royal Air Force Police and their dogs.'

Doesn't that bring back memories of long hot hazy afternoons and of dogs jumping through hoops of fire or the bit where one instructor acts like a thief and has a specially padded arm that the dog chases and grabs and pulls him to the floor?

I was amazed to find out that the official RAF dog team which had been set up in the Forties was actually disbanded in 1994 and as a result of this unpopular decision many RAF police dog sections decided to volunteer their spare time to provide men and dogs for the massive demand that was still out there to see these displays of canine agility and bravery.

There is still a great team made up of dogs and handlers from RAF Brize Norton, Oxfordshire, RAF Waddington, Lincolnshire and the

Defence Animal Centre, Leicestershire. The team is now one of the biggest of its kind within the RAF, and has provided displays throughout the UK, helping heighten the RAF's profile once again.

Due to operational requirements the team were unable to attend any events in 2008 but they are hopeful they will be able to get back to the displays, thrilling young and old, in 2009.

41

'It's the way I tell 'em': top British stand-up comics

1. Billy Connolly

The Big Yin was born in 1942 and started out as a boilermaker before becoming a folksinger in a band called The Humblebums with Gerry Rafferty who also went on to major success with his hit 'Baker Street'. Connolly's distinctive monologues started life as interludes between his folk and comic banjo songs. Gradually the stories became longer and Billy really broke through into the mainstream in 1974 with his second album originally titled *Solo Concert*.

I can still remember a ginger-haired Scottish mate of mine, Steve Marnoch, bringing in this album to school in Coventry and whispering that we all had to listen to it but not when our parents were about. It was amazing and within what seemed like minutes we were all reciting the Crucifixion routine. Of course many radio stations banned this and Billy was made!

The other breakthrough moment was of course his brilliant first appearance on *Parkinson*, which along with the Rod Hull and Emu sketch must be the most memorable Parky ever.

There's been a lot of talk in recent years about comedy being the new rock and roll but I am afraid Jimmy Carr, Ross Noble and Peter Kay can forget it, because the Big Yin has already been there and got the T-shirt.

I still love the way he spins a yarn and the fact that he doesn't really tell jokes and that no two performances will ever be the same. I also love the fact that unlike modern comedians his act doesn't rely on TV jokes or comments to work. It is pure observation and wild flights of fancy with a good dollop of obscenity thrown in for good measure. For those who say he swears too much, get a life. As far as I'm concerned, Billy has turned using the word fuck into an art form. With his dexterity it can be both the most brutal and sensitive word and everything in between. The man is a comic genius.

Recently he has reinvented himself as an actor and although he has made a couple of turkeys, his movie about Queen Victoria with Judi Dench, *Mrs Brown*, is a classic British film which I can watch again and again.

Where's the fucking knighthood?

PS check out his website at Billyconnolly.com – it's a classic.

2. Eddie Izzard

I must be the only person in Great Britain who remembers Eddie before he started wearing frocks. I was running my cabaret club in a snooker hall in Coventry when I was persuaded by a contact to try out a new comic who he reckoned was going to be mega. How many times had I heard that and how many times had some bright young thing come up from London and died in front of what has to be said was a very hostile and demanding crowd who liked nothing better than to shout out the Tic Toc Club catchphrase, 'Fuck off and Die', to anyone who couldn't raise a titter?

So I argued over the fee and eventually agreed to pay this newcomer forty quid as long as he did twenty minutes. I needn't have worried. He may have turned up looking like a Noel Edmonds clone complete with beard but he stood on stage and did at least forty minutes of the most surreal and funny material I had ever heard. It was something about dropping custard on the Germans in the Second World War and just like Connolly it was clear that it was no set routine but just a flight of fancy that perhaps even he didn't know where it would end.

The Coventry crowd adored him and he is one of the few people I have ever met – Clive Owen, Simon Le Bon are two others – who could perform the cliché of lighting up a room as they entered.

He's now moved into TV, films and dresses but if you ever get the chance to see him live, especially in a small club, don't miss it.

3. Frank Skinner

The first time I met Frank Skinner he was actually called Chris Collins and he was a geeky, alcoholic part-time teacher with an act that in my view was as funny as haemorrhoids. We were running our club in Coventry and he and a mate were trying to get a comedy club off the ground in of all places Tipton in the Black Country.

We went over to see him one night and I reckon the Tipton Taliban would have raised more laughs. Frank/Chris was, to put it mildly, crap, the only saving grace of his act was a witty tribute song to Kenneth Williams.

However the next week we were short of a compere for our club so we offered Frank the princely sum of twenty quid to warm up the crowd. I've always joked that the fee was £19.99 too much but the truth is he didn't go down too badly. I liked the bloke and I actually took my theatre company over to his college to perform our play *Hooligans* and I was also booked to carry out some drama workshops with his students. One thing led to another, more gigs followed, we became friends and I gave him the chance to perform in one of my venues at the Edinburgh Fringe.

In his autobiography Frank talks about how he performed to one man and his dog and implies that he lost money on the venture. What he fails to do is tell his readers that I gave him the deal of a lifetime on the booking and also got him to compere our comedy club where he got his first chance to mix with the new big beasts of British comedy.

This was to prove, in my opinion, the catalyst for his career to take off as on his return to the Midlands he started to go to London for gigs and then he was asked to take over Birmingham's most successful comedy club. At this point he had to join Equity and as someone already had the name Chris Collins he changed his stage name to Frank Skinner, the name of one of his dad's dead mates, and the rest is comedy history.

Years later when I was working at BBC London I interviewed him down the line about a massive gig he was doing with the unfunny David Baddiel. I was really disappointed with him because he didn't acknowledge our history and so to stitch him up at the end of the interview I asked, 'Whatever happened to Chris Collins?' Without missing a beat he replied, 'He died.'

Chris might have done and Frank may have forgotten those who helped him but there's one thing for sure – this comic will never die on stage, as he is a natural. Good luck to him.

4. Bernard Manning

I don't care what anyone says, Bernard Manning was the greatest British gag-teller of all time. The way he could hold and work an audience was a master class for anyone who ever wanted to be a comedian. I remember back at the birth of new comedy in the early Eighties several of the new comedians held a mock funeral for Bernard and suggested that his form of comedy was now dead and buried. Of course the fat bastard had the last laugh on all of them as his career, despite a virtual TV blackout, continued long after their poxy glitter-suited routines on *Saturday Night Live*.

Bernard had crafted his routine over years on the toughest circuit of all, the British working men's clubs, and when he first appeared on Granada's groundbreaking TV series *The Comedians* in the early Seventies he was an instant star and household name.

Without a doubt Manning was the star from day one and for the next thirty years he simultaneously outraged and wowed his audience by often just saying what they were thinking but afraid to voice.

Manning may have effectively been banned from TV but was one of the most hard-working comedians ever, performing every night but always making sure he returned home to sleep in his own bed.

When he died, fellow comic genius Frank Carson remarked, 'He was a wonderful man. If I had to write his gravestone I'd put: "Here lies Bernard Manning, comedian, who died 76 years old." Underneath that I'd put: "What a pity, he had a booking next week."'

Lisa and I saw him perform in an Edinburgh nightclub back in 1992 and I can quite honestly say he was amazing and apart from Ken Dodd I don't think anyone has made my ribs actually physically ache after a gig.

Of course when discussing the genius that was Manning the racist question has to be addressed. Well, for the record I don't think Bernard was a racist. He dealt in stock characters and stereotypes but that's a tradition you can trace back to the origins of theatre itself. When we saw him, there were perhaps three jokes which made myself and Lisa wince, I remember thinking, *Why does he need to do those jokes?* but was I offended? No.

Years before, when Skinner was first breaking through, I remember a very right-on comedian, who shall remain nameless and unfortunately for him pretty anonymous apart from having a few Radio Four listeners, remark that Skinner's act was just Manning's without the N or C word and the mother-in-law jokes. What this no-mark was demonstrating, however, was his complete ignorance of Manning's act because Manning never told a mother-in-law joke in his life. He was probably accurate though about the basic origin of Skinner's act.

There is a brilliant book on Manning written by Jonathan Margolis and if you ever saw the man or are just fascinated by the King of the Embassy club you must read it. It's called simply *Bernard Manning. A Biography*.

5. Ken Dodd

Doddy was born in 1927 and despite a recent health scare is still working most nights of the week up and down the country. If you've never seen him, do so now but book a day off work the next day as Ken is renowned for his shows never ending. Lisa and I saw him in Leamington Spa a few years ago and he did a routine of songs and jokes that went on for hours but seemed like minutes.

Doddy is the last of the great musical hall acts and I feel honoured to have seen him in his prime. He reminds me of when we were in Florida and we saw a poster for a performance by Cab Calloway at a theatre in Naples. I loved Calloway in *The Blues Brothers* so Lisa and I drove over 200 miles to see him perform 'Minnie the Moocher'. Weeks later he was dead but I can say I saw him. Make sure you can say the same about Ken Dodd.

As well as his comedy, of course Ken has had 29 songs in the charts including 'Tears', which sold over a million copies in 1965. When you see him live, put up with the songs and view them as an opportunity for your ribs to recover!

He's got the OBE but here's another true British star that deserves the knighthood.

6. Lee Evans

I first met Lee in 1989 in a grotty snooker hall in Coventry where we used to hold our weekly cabaret club. He was young, nervous and only going to pick up thirty quid even though he had travelled all the way from London for the gig.

The polite nervous guy you now see on stage entertaining crowds in stadiums was exactly the same all those years ago when he was about to entertain about a hundred people in Coventry. I asked him if he wanted anything, meaning a drink, and he replied, 'Er, yeah, er is it possible, if it's er OK, could I use my own microphone lead, er if that's er OK?'

'Yeah sure, have you got it with you?'

He then produces the longest mic cable I have ever seen in my life out of a battered holdall.

'You sure you want to use this?'

'Er yes, if that's OK er with you?'

'Yeah, no problem.'

I went into the hall and connected his microphone. Ten minutes later he connected with our audience like only a few other comedians did or could.

He walked on, tripped over his cable, got his leg tangled around it and then for the next forty hilarious minutes tried to disentangle himself but only succeeded in wrapping the cord more and more around him. He grunted and groaned and half apologised while the audience fell about in tears of laughter. Eventually he was free, sweating profusely, he walked to the mic, told one joke, looked at his watch and left the stage.

Pure comic genius. Pure business genius from Gaunty! Thirty bloody quid and we've just seen a *star* and I don't use that word lightly or very often.

I'm absolutely delighted that he has gone on to be such a name and a film star to boot because as well as being incredibly talented he is a smashing bloke as well.

My editors have been asking why I haven't included any of the new crop of comedians such as Ross Noble, Jimmy Carr, Alan Carr, or any of the other comics who are being gainfully employed on TV at the moment. The simple answer is I don't think any of them are good enough to even wipe the spittle off the microphone of the Comedy Gods I have talked about.

One thing I really hate about list programmes or best-ever album or film charts is when young kids who have no real experience of seeing or hearing greatness just vote for their band/film of the moment and I am afraid I will not fall into that trap.

The stand-ups I have talked about have learned and formed their craft, their material or style is unique and they were in comedy before it became a lifestyle choice or a bloody degree subject.

42

Top ten British museums and art galleries to take your kids to

One of the greatest things about this country is the wealth and variety of our art galleries and museums and one of the worst aspects of modern British life is that too few of us use these facilities after the proverbial school trips. We need to change our attitude and recognise our history because, as I often say on the radio, if you do not know your past how can you understand the present or prepare yourself for the future?

One of the biggest attractions of these fantastic places is that most of them are completely free to get into. So what's stopping you, Great Britain? Let's get in there and wallow in our history, our culture and our superb artistry.

In my list I have deliberately missed out the obvious places such as the Natural History Museum and the others in London as I take the view that most of these are already well known to you.

1. The Coventry Transport Museum

No need to waste words, as this is just the most amazing and extensive collection of cars built by British working-class tradesmen in the UK if not the world. Write off a day to really enjoy this place.

Millennium Place
Hales Street
Coventry CV1 1PN (try CV1 1JD for SatNav)
tel: 024 7623 4270
email: enquiries@transport-museum.co.uk

2. The Tate Gallery, St Ives, Cornwall

Take off your blinkers and remove your prejudice and just go and have a look at some modern art and make your own mind up. Don't be like the little kid who won't eat up his sprouts because 'I don't like them!' Experience it for yourself in the most glorious setting imaginable, right on the cliffs with the rolling waves of the Atlantic in front of you. Well worth a visit even if it isn't raining one day on your holiday.

While you are in town make sure you visit the studio and museum of one of Britain's greatest sculptors, Barbara Hepworth.

Porthmeor Beach
St Ives, Cornwall TR26 1TG
tel: 01736 796226
email: visiting.stives@tate.org.uk

3. The Burrell Collection, Glasgow

Set in the beautiful surroundings of Pollok Country Park, this is a beautiful and architecturally outstanding modern building housing some great art objects from Egypt, Iraq, Greece and Italy. Tapestries, furniture, textiles, ceramics, stained glass and sculptures from medieval Europe and drawings from the fifteenth to the nineteenth centuries are all on display. The best thing is that entry is free, so what's stopping you visiting?

Pollok Country Park
2060 Pollokshaws Road
Glasgow G43 1AT
Scotland
tel: 0141 2872550

4. The Wilberforce Museum

It's important that adults as well as children understand the full horror and barbarity of slavery where blacks were treated as subhumans and we need to know the part we played in it as well as acknowledging those brave men like Wilberforce who fought for its abolition.

Wilberforce House
23–25 High Street
Hull HU1 1NQ
tel: 01482 613 924

5. The Roald Dahl Museum and Story Telling Museum

This is a cracking little museum, which won the Best Small Visitor Attraction in 2008. Years ago I made a small TV documentary about this fascinating museum dedicated to one of Britain's best-loved children's writers and I took my girls with me to star in the film; they loved the place and I'm sure your kids will too.

81–83 High Street
Great Missenden
Buckinghamshire HP16 0AL
tel: 01494 892192

6. The Imperial War Museum at RAF Duxford

Again no amount of words would do this place justice, as it is quite simply the greatest aviation museum in Europe, if not the world. It was recently awarded the Enjoy England Tourism Gold Award for Large Attraction of the Year and it's no surprise as this former airfield has a brilliant collection of planes including a Mosquito, Lysander, Lancaster, TSR-2, Lightning, Canberra, York, Vulcan, Swordfish, Spitfire Mk. 24, Sunderland, Oxford, Anson, Harrier, Buccaneer and Tornado. There's even Duxford's very own Concorde, which you can actually walk around.

There's also one of the finest collections of tanks, military vehicles and naval exhibits in the country and a separate museum dedicated to the bravery and sacrifice of the 30,000 Americans who gave their lives to defeat the Nazis.

It's just a brilliant day out and every year the attractions and exhibits grow and grow. Try and tie in your visit with one of the days when they are having an air show and you will give your children one of those special days they will never ever forget. Simply the best.

Cambridge
Cambridgeshire CB22 4QR
tel: 01223 835000
duxford.iwm.org.uk

7. The Scottish National Gallery of Modern Art

This is an absolute 'Must do' if you are visiting Edinburgh for the Festival Fringe. Just fifteen minutes from the hustle and bustle of Princes Street but set in the most magnificent countryside grounds, this is a great afternoon out.

Great sculptures by amongst others Moore and Hepworth, great visiting modern art, go on, stretch your taste buds and a surprise around every corner. All I can say is that I love this gallery and that I have been surprised and challenged every time that I have visited the place.

75 Belford Road
Edinburgh EH4 3DR
email: gmainfo@nationalgalleries.org

8. The Ashmolean Museum

Leave your car on the outskirts of Oxford and jump on the park and ride and prepare yourself for a visit to one of the greatest museums in the world. This isn't a day trip, this is a place which demands visit after visit as there is so much to see and learn. Opened in 1683 and still expanding and developing today, this was the first university museum. There are too many rooms and exhibits to describe here so check out the website at www.ashmolean.org and plan your visit or visits.

Making sure of course you leave plenty of time for a wander round this beautiful city and the opportunity to recuperate in any of the fantastic pubs last frequented by Morse. By the way, the museum itself was actually used as a location in the episode, 'The Wolvercote Tongue'.

Beaumont Street
Oxford OX1 2PH
tel: 01865 278000
www.ashmolean.org

9. Bletchley Park

Like most people I guess I didn't know anything about Bletchley Park and the part it played in winning the war until I moved to Milton Keynes in 1990 to work on the radio. There was a campaign at the time to save both the mansion and the huts where Alan Turing and his team of boffins used the Enigma machine to crack the German codes that led to the Nazi defeat.

There was a plan to turn the whole place into a massive housing estate and of course that would have led to this vital piece of our history being forgotten about for ever. A dedicated group of enthusiasts managed to save the Mansion but the site is still under threat and in fact please follow this link to a petition where you can add your voice to the Save Bletchley Park Campaign at:

http://petitions.pm.gov.uk/BletchleyPark

It's a great day out and you really do feel the atmosphere of a place that was so secret during the war it was codenamed Station X.

To my mind it is a national disgrace that Bletchley Park is still fighting for its very survival and we must all do our bit to save it. Go and visit it today.

The Mansion
Bletchley Park
Milton Keynes MK3 6EB
tel: 01908 640404
www.bletchleypark.org.uk

10. Black Country Living Museum

This is a brilliant interactive museum set in the heart of the Black Country and is essentially an urban heritage park to which buildings from throughout the Black Country have been relocated and are brought to life to tell the story of the area's rich industrial heritage. Kids and adults can take a trip down a coal mine, use an outside loo or take a ride on a tram, trolleybus or narrow boat. It really brings to life our industrial past and with the addition of costumed staff the museum is another must do when the kids are younger.

Tipton Road
Dudley DY1 4SQ
www.bclm.co.uk.

I know there's loads of other places I could have included but I trust I have given a flavour of what is on offer right across our green and pleasant land and have whetted your appetite, so that the next time the kids say, 'Dad, I'm bored,' you've got a few more ideas than just switching on the box.

43

Twelve greatest events in the British calendar

We may have cocked up the budget for the Olympics, and the Dome may have been the biggest flop since Frisbee but the bottom line is we've still got some great events in this country and we usually know how to organise them despite the British weather. These are my top events, which any self-respecting True Brit should try to do before they die. I'm about halfway through the list. How about you?

1. Trooping of the Colour

Just the greatest piece of pageantry not only in Great Britain but also surely anywhere in the world and an absolute must do for any Brit to attend at least once in life.

2. Glastonbury

The greatest rock festival in the country even if it has become 'Glastonbury Lite' in recent years and a bit of a brand festival rather than band festival. The Festival started in 1970 with only 1,500 people attending (if you can remember it you clearly weren't there!), and has grown to be a major event in the cultural diary of Britain.

I've been a few times and my theatre company even performed there and I think it was probably better when it was little bit more disorganised and most people bunked in over the fence. It went downhill during the 'Madchester' years with the arrival of the dance scene and the associated drugs and thugs.

This year hit an all-time low with the headlining act of Jay Z. I'm sorry, I like rap but please not in a field in Somerset. You need anthems, you need singalong choruses and by the end of the Mud Fest a bloody good bath and an empty loo.

A rite of passage though for every teenager.

3. Wimbledon

I'm not a tennis fan but I have been to Wimbledon on a corporate do with the BBC. Another good use of your licence fee and I must say I enjoyed it. There's still a bit of snobbery though, of course, as the game is still dominated by the middle class and more needs to be done with Lottery money to open the sport up to working-class kids.

I hated that Andy Murray with his racism against the English but even I was hooked when he actually started to win at Wimbledon. In true English media style, now that he's becoming a genuine contender they've started calling him British not Scottish!

4. British Grand Prix

An absolute must do at least once in your life.

I took Lisa a couple of years ago and we even got into Alonso's garage and saw and heard the engine being revved up. Everything – and I mean everything – in your body shakes and it's just so thrilling. Watching the race on the TV doesn't get anywhere near what the real experience feels like, it's just so exciting, glamorous and even Lisa who has no interest in sport of any kind came away as a complete convert.

It is a disgrace that the midget former second-hand car salesman Bernie Ecclestone is moving the Grand Prix to Donington Park from 2010 as Silverstone is its spiritual home, and the amount that it generates for the local economy is staggering. Of course most Formula 1 teams are based in the UK and the industry is worth millions to the UK economy.

I nearly bought a house close to the track and I asked the guy who was selling it if the noise from the track bothered him. As with most locals his reply showed the affection we have for motor sport: 'That's not noise, that is opera.'

We Brits are the technical whiz kids and engineers behind these cars and this sport and now hopefully at last we have a true British hero to match our technical expertise in the shape of Lewis Hamilton.

5. London Marathon

Let's face it, marathon runners are bores but even a cynical couch potato like me has to accept that it takes guts, courage and determination to take part in this race and the money they raise is phenomenal and impossible to criticise.

Started in 1981 by British athlete Chris Brasher after he completed the New York Marathon, the first event attracted 20,000 applicants with a final starting line-up of nearly 8,000.

Since then this annual event, which is usually run in April with the greatest city in the world and its landmarks and icons as a backdrop, has grown to become an event where now 46,500 runners start off from Blackheath Common and Greenwich Park each year. It is now internationally recognised as one of the greatest marathons in the world and the runners raise the most money out of all races in the world for charity, a staggering £41 million.

6. Chelsea Flower Show

You know summer's on the way when it's Chelsea Flower Show week in mid-May. This is Britain's greatest flower show and is organised by the Royal Horticultural Society and held in the grounds of the Royal Hospital Chelsea.

First held in 1886 in the RHS garden in Kew, it moved in 1913 for what was meant to be one year only to the hospital grounds where it has subsequently stayed ever since, apart from a cancellation in 1917–18 and for the duration of the Second World War when the grounds were used as an anti-aircraft site.

The event is always a complete sellout months in advance and the numbers that visit are only restricted to 157,000 because of the cramped nature of the site.

I have never been to the show and more importantly neither has Lisa who has now taken to asking 'why?' in a much more aggressive manner since I have developed a friendship with Britain's greatest gardener Alan Titchmarsh.

'Surely he can get us a ticket, Jon?'

'Yeah, yeah, maybe next year, love.'

7. Remembrance Sunday

'Remembrance Sunday' is the day traditionally put aside to remember all those who have given their lives for the peace and freedom we enjoy today. On this day people across the nation pause to reflect on the sacrifices made by our brave servicemen and women.

The above words are from the Royal British Legion and more than adequately sum up what this day is all about.

Held on the second Sunday in November, usually the Sunday closest to 11 November, which of course is the day the Armistice was announced in the First World War, it is also the culmination of Poppy Week and all the thousands of pounds that have been raised, which in 2007 was over £30 million. Of course it is vital to remember that the week and Remembrance Sunday is a day and a moment to remember all those lost in war and conflict and is not just a commemoration of the two great wars nor in any way a celebration of victory.

I believe the significance of the symbol of the poppy and the vital work of the Legion is more important today than ever and it is absolutely incumbent upon every parent to teach their children about the sacrifice of our brave armed forces. I have no time for those who refuse to wear a poppy or don a white one. Grow up and show some respect.

The national event held at the Cenotaph each year with the Royal Family in attendance is one of the most moving events that I have ever experienced, but of course there are thousands of services all over Britain and the Commonwealth at exactly the same time.

As a kid and a boy scout we would march through Coventry in crisp and newly pressed uniforms with the old boys resplendent in their berets and caps, their medals proudly displayed on their chests, and then we would attend the service in the City's Memorial Park.

8. FA Cup Final

Simply the greatest club competition in the world. What more can I say, apart from the fact of course that did I mention the mighty Sky Blues won it in 1987?

9. Isle of Man TT

Yeah, yeah, I know strictly speaking the Isle of Man isn't in Britain, but let's face it the TT holds a very special part in most Brits' lives and although I am not a great motorcycle fan myself, apart from my absolute love of speedway, I can still understand the pull and attraction of this uniquely British event.

Now entering its second centenary, the TT, which is held on 37 and three-quarter miles of the island roads, is quite simply the greatest road race in the world and attracts some of the finest motorcycle road riders the planet possesses.

10. Edinburgh Festivals

The official Festival and its larger bastard offspring the Fringe is still going strong every August and is still the largest and greatest arts festival in the world and it's in Britain. Enjoy!

11. England v Scotland Rugby Union

Whether it's at Twickenham or Murrayfield this has to be the clash of the Home Countries and there are not many sporting events that can match it for atmosphere, rivalry and at the end – win, lose or draw – the camaraderie of both fans and players.

12. The Grand National, the Derby, Cheltenham Festival and Royal Ascot

Four of the greatest horse race meetings in the world. The National with those fences – and can the animal-rights brigade please shut up? The Cheltenham Festival with the Irish, the craic, the greatest horses in the world and the Gold Cup and that magnificent oval course. The Derby with its tradition, even if it has moved to a Saturday, and of course Royal Ascot where the blokes can lose their shirts but the ladies have to be reminded to put their knickers on. And they call it the sport of kings!

44

Four times five: top 20 players for the Home Championships

After England's dismal failure to qualify for the European Championships in 2008 my radio station, talkSPORT, launched a campaign to bring back the Home Championships and most true football fans and I backed them all the way.

I loved these blood and guts fixtures as a kid and I was really surprised that this competition that started in 1883 actually finished way back in 1984. It only seems like yesterday that we were arguing over offside decisions and laughing at the Scots' inability to find a goalie that could catch a ball.

There were a number of reasons for the tournament being dropped, including its gradually being overshadowed by the World Cup and the European Championship. However, it is also true to say that the rise in hooliganism and the Troubles in Ireland – don't forget the 1980–81 games had to be cancelled due to the unrest during the IRA hunger strikes – also contributed to the demise of a fine British sporting tradition.

However, I think the restoration of this competition could go a long way to actually reuniting this Disunited Kingdom and put a bit of pride back into our home-grown football players. Who knows, maybe the Jocks will even return the crossbar and the pitch they nicked from Wembley in 1977! (Put down the phone, cancel that email, I'm joking.)

All of the four nations love nothing better than taking on the others, especially the English, and it is this intense but hopefully peaceful rivalry that we need to recapture. There is still nothing to beat a rugby union international between say Scotland and England at Murrayfield and we desperately need to restore that unique atmosphere in football.

Recently in his column in the *Sun* – and I must admit I wondered if he had had too much sun – Ian Wright suggested that perhaps we should have a Great Britain side. I couldn't believe what I was reading from one of the greatest living Englishmen and a true patriot like Wrighty. I told him in no uncertain terms that although this summer was depressing and that we were all fed up of the succession of bozos who have managed us, surrender was never and can never be on the agenda. The bottom line is we Brits love the rivalry and anyway Wrighty what would we sing if we were united?

So in a tribute to this championship and a direct challenge to Ian I asked talkSPORT listeners to nominate their top five players of all time for each national side.

England

Bobby Moore

England's captain from 1963 until 1973 and still the most capped England outfield player with 108 England caps, although Beckham is now breathing down his neck, this is the man who lifted the World Cup for us in 1966. Bobby was the only player that not one single listener disagreed with. Everyone nominated him in their Top Five. He was a true English hero who was sadly taken from us at too young an age when he died of cancer in 1993 at the age of 51.

Bobby Charlton

Of course Sir Bobby is another hero of '66 and European footballer of that year. Capped 106 times by England and remembered as one of the survivors of the Busby Babes, he still holds the record for most goals scored for both England and Man United.

Deservedly knighted in 1994 but one still has got to ask the question: what about the other heroes of '66?

Also a cultural icon who single-handedly invented the combover!

Gazza

This nomination produced vicious debate but the truth is Gazza was one of the most gifted players of his generation who should be remembered for his brilliant goals like the flick over Colin Hendry's head and the volley that buried Scotland in Euro '96. Unfortunately the goal celebrations straight after this piece of mastery are just one of the excesses that Paul is more likely to be remembered for. Remember how he lay on the floor and Teddy Sheringham poured water into his mouth in a clear re-enactment of the drinking session they had all enjoyed in the infamous dentist's chair on their tour of Singapore? The obvious drink problem and the urban myths, half-truths or real stories of his excesses continued, including of course his beating of his wife and the infamous photo with Danny Baker and Chris Evans outside that kebab shop.

When I worked with Danny he said the press got this whole story wrong and that he wasn't out all night with Gazza and that he was home in bed just after midnight just after the photo was taken because he had to do the school run in the morning and who am I to argue with the Candy man?

Fergie reckons he could have rescued Paul if he had signed for United at 21 rather than Spurs and moved to Manchester rather than the bright lights of London. Who knows if that would have been the case, as Manchester didn't seem to help George Best did it, but one thing's for certain there is a dreadful inevitability about Paul's story and I just pray the denouement isn't the one we all dread but are scared to voice.

One thing is for sure: 57 caps and 10 goals for England only tells half the story of this troubled football genius.

Jimmy Greaves

It's a shame that Jimmy will always be remembered as the man who Sir Alf left out of that final in 1966. Greaves was ever-present in the team until he was injured in the last group game against France and had to sit out the second round match against Argentina. Geoff Hurst was given the shirt and took his chance with both hands or should that be feet and scored the winner. As a result he kept his place for the semi against Portugal and despite the fact that Jimmy was fit again for the final, and the British press demanding he should be picked, Sir Alf would not be swayed and Hurst kept his place and created his place in history.

Jimmy played three more times for England and despite saying that he didn't take his place for granted, the fact that he left immediately after the final for a holiday and didn't take part in any of the celebrations speaks volumes.

He scored 44 times for England and was awarded 57 caps but for many kids like me of the Seventies and Eighties he will always be remembered as half of the successful Saint and Greavsie double act that graced our TV screens during that period.

Gordon Banks

Without a doubt in his prime Banksy was the greatest goalkeeper of his generation and no one will ever forget *that* save from Pele in 1970, which is recognised as the greatest save of all time.

Of course one of his 77 caps was also won in the final in 1966 but despite being part of that World Cup team he was released by Leicester City just a year later and moved to Stoke. The reason for his release? Simple. Leicester's new seventeen-year-old signing refused to join unless he was number one. Who was that demanding precocious talent? No other than Peter Shilton, who of course went on to claim the England jersey and finish his international career with 125 caps.

The debate still rages over who was the best keeper between these two superb athletes and the row was mighty on the airwaves over this nomination but in the end I plumped for Banks, largely as a result of the Pele save and the fact that his career was so tragically cut short after his car accident when he lost an eye.

Scotland

Denis Law

Eleven years at Manchester United and 236 goals in 409 appearances justly earned him the nickname The King from the Old Trafford faithful.

Law started his professional career at Huddersfield Town in 1956 before going to Manchester City in 1960 for a season and then becoming the highest valued player to be transferred between England and Italy when he signed for Torino for a figure of £115,000.

After a year in Italy he returned to Manchester but this time for the Reds, scored in the first seven minutes of his debut against the Baggies and the rest is history.

Denis played 55 times for Scotland and probably his most satisfying goal was against the new world champions, England, in 1967 when Scotland beat the old enemy 3–2.

A year later a nagging knee injury sustained in a game against Poland in 1965 returned and meant he missed the semifinal and of course the final of the European Cup in 1968 when Matt Busby's team lifted the trophy for the very first time.

Jimmy Johnstone

Jinky was voted the greatest-ever Celtic player by the club's fans in 2002 and few impartial observers would disagree with their assessment.

Born in 1944 in Lanarkshire Jimmy was to become an integral part of the Lisbon Lions who lifted the European Cup in 1967 and nine successive Scottish championships between 1966 and 1974.

If you want to know what a classical winger is meant to do, then get out the videos of Jimmy in full flow and watch as he exhibits brilliant ball control and runs defences ragged.

Further confirmation of his genius if needed can be found by listening to the words of Emlyn Hughes, who was destroyed by him in a home international: 'Scotland beat us 2–0 one year, and I was embarrassed to come off the pitch. Jimmy Johnstone absolutely crucified me. Alf Ramsey came up and said, "You've just played against a world-class player today. He can do that to anybody."'

Jimmy was a hellraiser off the pitch as well and forget about Freddie Flintoff and the pedalo affair, Jimmy was the originator of such incidents when after a drunken night at the Scottish training camp for the World Cup in Largs in 1974 he decided it was a good idea to nick a rowing boat and ended up having to be rescued.

Jimmy's international career was sporadic and he actually only played 23 games for Scotland.

I also love the way that Jinky explained where his skills came from. 'Football was the greatest part of our lives, just like the boys from Brazil and Spain. They lived in poverty, like us, and that's where all the great players came from – the street.'

What a pity today's streets aren't full of more Jinkys.

No story about Jimmy would be complete without talking about his tragically early death from motor neurone disease at the age of 61. The way he dealt with his diagnosis in 2001 was typical of the wee giant; he dedicated himself to finding out more about the disease and to raise both awareness and money for research into it, most notably by releasing a record of 'Dirty Old Town' with Jim Kerr of Simple Minds.

Kenny Dalglish

King Kenny was born in 1951 and was the first man to score 100 goals in both the Scottish and English top flight and the first to win a hundred caps for Scotland.

Despite being a Rangers fan from childhood he signed for archrivals Celtic and Jock Stein in May 1967 after having trials and being turned down by both West Ham and Liverpool. He became Celtic's most prolific goal scorer under the tutelage of Jock Stein and got his first full international cap off Tommy Docherty in 1971 against Belgium. By 1976 he was scoring the winning goal against England at Hampden by putting the ball through Ray Clemence's legs and the following year he scored again as Scotland and he beat Ray Clemence 2–1 and of course in celebration the fans took the pitch and the goalposts.

By the time of his transfer to Bob Paisley's Liverpool on 10 August 1977 for £440,000 he had made 269 appearances and scored 167 goals for the hoops.

Bought as a direct replacement for Kevin Keegan, Dalglish claimed the number 7 shirt for himself and set about making himself a legend on Merseyside. He scored both on his League debut for Liverpool against Middlesbrough and on his baptism of fire in front of the Kop against Newcastle United.

That season ended with a goal tally of 31, including the winner against Bruges in the European final at Wembley. The success continued with more goals (he also holds the record of 30 goals for Scotland jointly with Denis Law), cups and individual awards, and culminated in his blistering partnership with Ian Rush who joined the club for £300,000 in 1980.

After Heysel he became player manager and won the double in his first season in the role. The success just kept coming and it's hard to argue with a record that includes:

515 appearances, 172 goals, 307 games in charge of the Reds, 8 League Championships, 2 FA Cup wins, 3 European Cup wins, 4 League Cup wins, 1 European Super Cup win, 5 Charity Shield wins, 1 Football Writers' Footballer of the Year award, 1 PFA Player of the Year award, and 3 Manager of the Year awards.

He also showed great dignity after both the tragedy of Heysel and the Hillsborough disaster where 96 Liverpool supporters lost their lives.

He retired from Liverpool on health grounds in February 1991 but returned to football later that same year with second division Blackburn Rovers.

He took them from the second division to winning the Premiership in 1994–95 with the help of Alan Shearer and Chris Sutton, whom he had signed for record fees. Looking at his record, I am now wondering whether he should have also been in my top list of British managers as well. Kenny has also managed at Newcastle for twelve months and of course was caretaker manager at Celtic after John Barnes was sacked in 2000.

Many fans and not just Scottish ones can't wait for Kenny to be back in football one day and maybe it might just happen.

Peter Lorimer

As a kid and admirer of Revie's Leeds United we always used to talk about hot-shot Lorimer and the fact that he allegedly had the hardest and fastest shot in football. I seem to recall a *Grandstand* programme where it was recorded that the ball travelled at 70 miles an hour.

Born in 1946 in Dundee he made his debut for Leeds at the incredible age of fifteen. He was a cultured attacking midfielder who scored 168 goals in 525 appearances in two distinct spells for Leeds United.

Lorimer was capped 21 times for Scotland, scored 4 goals and represented his country at the 1974 World Cup in Germany.

Billy Bremner

Bremner was another of the Revie legends up at Leeds United. Who wouldn't want this fiery, aggressive red-headed midfield dynamo in their side? In total he made over 500 appearances for his club and is immortalised in bronze outside the Elland Road gates whilst his tough, never give up, performances are ingrained on the memories of those who saw him play. Even his little scuffle with Keegan in the 1974 Charity Shield can't diminish the talent that he possessed. Capped 54 times for his country, he is inducted in to both the Scottish and English Football Halls of Fame.

Wales

Neville Southall

Born in 1958 in Llandudno and arguably the greatest keeper of his generation. Big Nev's record speaks for itself with 750 appearances for Everton and 93 caps for Wales between 1982 and 1997.

His career didn't start so brightly when he had unsuccessful trials for Crewe and Bolton, so got a job as a builder and hod carrier while playing non-league football until he was bought for six grand by Bury in 1979. Just two years later Howard Kendall paid £150,000 and brought him from the building sites to Goodison.

After a couple of months Big Nev made the number one shirt his own and helped Everton win the League Championship in 1985 and 1987, the FA Cup in 1984 and 1995 and the European Cup Winners Cup in 1985.

In 1985 he was also voted player of the year by the Football Writers Association and he was awarded an MBE for services to football in 1995.

For such a big bloke he had tremendous reflex skills and a totally dominating and formidable presence in the Everton box.

Ryan Giggs

Born in Cardiff in 1973 Giggs was the player most Welsh fans on talkSPORT nominated for best-ever Welsh player. They also wanted to make sure that I mentioned he is the most decorated player ever in the Premiership and of course he is a Welsh and Manchester United legend, having played all his professional football with the Red Devils.

As a club player he has won every medal in the game and he played 64 times for Wales until he retired from international football in 2007.

A natural winger and some would say the greatest these islands ever produced, his appearance in the Champions League final in 2008 made his total appearances for Man Utd a staggering 759.

John Charles

Probably the greatest all-round footballer Great Britain has ever had who could play at centre forward or centre half. Apart from his versatility, he was comfortable with either foot, possessed a delicate first touch and had great stamina and strength. How much do we pay modern footballers and how many of them could actually fulfil those skill criteria?

Charles also had a fantastic disciplinary record, having never been cautioned or sent off in his entire career. Are you listening, Mr Rooney?

He was born in 1931 and started playing for his country at 18 and was capped 38 times and scored 15 times. He started his club career at Leeds in 1948 with a short break for national service between 1950 and 1952. He scored 150 league goals in eight years for Leeds, including 42 goals in the 1953–54 season.

In 1957 he was one of the first British players to play for a foreign team when he joined Juventus for a fee of £65,000. The Juventus fans loved him, nicknaming him the Gentle Giant and voting him their best foreign player of all time in 1997, quite an achievement when you consider that Michel Platini has also played for them.

After 150 appearances with Juventus and 93 goals Charles 'made the biggest mistake' of his life when he returned to Leeds for another much less successful spell. He went back to Italy with Roma but injuries and personal problems dogged the end of his career.

After his football career ended he went down the usual route of ex-footballers and became a pub landlord but still attended every Leeds home game. There was a massive campaign to get John a knighthood, which he really deserved, but it failed and he was awarded a CBE instead. He died in 2004.

John Toshack

Born in 1949 John would go on to manage Wales twice after a fantastic playing career at Cardiff, Liverpool and Swansea.

He was the youngest player at 16 to come off the bench and score on his debut in 1965 and he held that record for 42 years until Aaron Ramsey broke it in 2007. He played 162 games for Cardiff in four years and scored 74 goals in a lethal strike partnership with Brian Clark before he was signed by the legendary Bill Shankly for Liverpool in 1970 for £110,000. Toshack was already a full international by this time and went on to win 40 caps and score 12 goals for his country.

When Kevin Keegan joined Liverpool in 1971 it was the start of another deadly strike force that saw Toshack setting up goal after goal for Keegan to put away. His 246 games for Liverpool with a goal tally of 96 are the bare bones of why Toshack became an Anfield legend but his career as a manager in Europe is also worthy of note.

His management career started at Swansea and he worked wonders at the Vetch Field, moving them from the Fourth Division to the First Division in just three years. Then in 1984 he was appointed manager of Sporting Lisbon where he only lasted a season, but he found much more success in Spain with Real Madrid twice, Real Sociedad three times, Deportivo La Coruna and Real Murcia.

Ian Rush

Born in 1961 Ian actually made his Welsh debut in May 1980 against Scotland before he officially became a Liverpool player. He went on to gain 78 caps and score 28 goals for his country.

However, Rush shares an unfortunate record with both George Best and Ryan Giggs in that all three never played in a major international tournament during the period that they were at their best as their respective national sides consistently failed to qualify.

That said, Ian has won every club honour going with Liverpool including the following: First Division Championship 1981/82, 1982/83, 1983/84, 1985/86 and 1989/90, FA Cup 1986, 1989 and 1992, League (Milk/Coca Cola) Cup 1981, 1982, 1983, 1984 and 1995, European Cup 1984, Charity Shield 1982, 1986 (shared), 1989, 1990 (shared), Screen Sport Super Cup 1987.

On a personal level he has also picked up the following:

1983 PFA Young Player of the Year
1984 PFA Players' Player of the Year

1984 FWA Footballer of the Year
1984 European Golden Boot

Ian was bought from Chester by Bob Paisley for £300,000 in 1980, which was the largest amount ever for an 18-year-old, and he went on to be one of Liverpool's most prolific scorers in two spells for the club (1980–1987 and 1988–1996). In between times he spent a pretty unhappy time at Juventus. Many believe that this move to Italy was partly to restore good relations between the two clubs after the tragedy of Heysel. The transfer fee was £3 million but Rush failed to repeat his Anfield goal-scoring feats and only managed eight in 29 games.

He returned to Anfield on 18 August 1988 for a British record fee at the time of £2.75 million. In this spell at Anfield, which lasted until his departure to Leeds in May 1996, he scored 90 goals in 245 appearances to add to the 139 he had scored in 224 games in his previous spell. Like many at Anfield Ian also showed tremendous courage, bravery and compassion during the tragedies of Heysel and Hillsborough.

Ian Rush retired in 2000 at the age of 38 after spells at Leeds, Newcastle, Sheffield United, Wrexham and Sydney.

Vinny Jones

I know we are only meant to have five players for each national side but I just felt that I had to mention Vinny. So many fans phoned up saying that although he wasn't the most skilful player ever to pull on the red jersey of Wales Vinny was everything a player should be when representing his country and played with a real passion and a complete love for the shirt.

To a certain extent I agree and I wish there were more who played with his grit and patriotism playing in the home sides today.

Northern Ireland

Pat Jennings

Born in Newry in County Down in 1945, Pat played a record 119 games for Northern Ireland in an international career that lasted an incredible 22 years. He shares his international debut with George Best in a home international against Wales on 15 April 1964 when he was just eighteen. Incredibly his international career ended twenty-three years later at the age of 41 against the mighty Brazil in the 1986 World Cup.

He is famous of course for that goal that he scored for Spurs against Manchester United in the 1967 Charity Shield game at Old Trafford, when he booted the ball straight from his hands and bounced it over the head of one of his archrivals Alex Stepney.

Jennings is of course famous for his spells at North London rivals Tottenham Hotspur and Arsenal but his career started at Newry before he moved to Watford in 1963 and then on to Spurs at the end of that first season (1963–64) for the princely sum of £27,000.

Pat spent thirteen years at White Hart Lane, playing 591 games in all and winning along the way the following: the FA Cup in 1967, the League Cup in 1971 and 1973 and the UEFA Cup in 1972.

In August 1977 he moved to Arsenal and helped them to three FA Cup finals and one win in 1979. In total Jennings made 327 appearances for Arsenal in eight years before he retired in 1987.

Spurs fans must have been spitting feathers as when they sold him eight years previously they thought he was nearing the end of his career!

George Best (1946–2005)

Simply the greatest player these islands if not the world has ever produced.

No statistics needed, no eulogies required and certainly no dissection of his character or weaknesses from me as it has all been said before. Simply get the video, any video, and rejoice in his skill.

The only thing I can add is that it was listening to Rodney Marsh talking about George and his life on the day he died on talkSPORT that was the catalyst for me wanting to broadcast on that station.

George may be gone but he will never be forgotten.

Derek Dougan

Doog was a real footballer and a real character, the likes of which we will never see again. He was a part of my childhood and a permanent feature, even though he was primarily a Wolves player, but growing up in the Midlands you were always aware of his presence either on the pitch or in later years on the box.

Without a doubt Dougan was one of the most colourful and controversial figures ever in British football. He is the man largely responsible, in his position as a vociferous campaigning chairman of the Professional Footballers' Association, for pushing hard for freedom of contract, which was achieved in 1978.

But he was always outspoken, aggressive, even arrogant, and some would say this held his career back until he found his natural home at Molineux and the adoring Wolves fans for whom he could do no wrong. Perhaps his flamboyant character – remember when he shaved his head, saying it made him feel fresh? – sometimes obscured the fact of just what a good centre forward he was.

Born in 1938, after a succession of clubs Derek arrived at Wolves in March 1967 for fifty grand and went on to make 323 appearances and scored 123 goals for them starting with a hat trick on his home debut against Hull City, and in his first season at the club he helped them gain promotion to the top flight.

Dougan won 43 caps and scored 8 goals for his country. However, he was also one of the main players in the Shamrock Rovers team who played an exhibition match against Brazil in 1983. This was effectively an all-Ireland team, which the footballing authorities were completely against, and although he blames his participation in this game for the end of his international career Dougan remained a controversial supporter of a united Ireland team until his death in 2007. Wrighty, are you listening?!

He was of course also one of the pallbearers at his teammate George Best's funeral, along with Rodney Marsh and Denis Law.

Danny Blanchflower

Not just a footballer but a football manager and journalist who captained Spurs during their double-winning season of 1961. One of the great tacticians in the history of the game, renowned for his passing and as an outstanding right half.

A great quote to sum up a great man is the following; 'The great fallacy is that the game is first and last about winning. It is nothing of the kind. The game is about glory, it is about doing things in style and with a flourish, and about going out and beating the other lot, not waiting for them to die of boredom.'

Don't you wish this had been written on the dressing room wall of both teams in the recent Italy and Spain match at the Euro championships and loads of other negative games that we have all had to endure?

Born in 1926, Danny spent ten years at Spurs after moving from Aston Villa in 1954 and played in 337 games, scoring 15 goals but being remembered as one of the most gifted and tactically aware right backs ever.

Obviously the highlight of his playing career has got to be captaining the double-winning side in 1961.

Internationally he won 56 caps for Northern Ireland and in 1958 was the captain when they reached the World Cup finals. Blanchflower was also manager of Northern Ireland (1976–79) and Chelsea (1978–79). He died in 1993.

Sammy McIlroy

The last of the Busby babes by dint of the fact that he was the last youth player signed by Sir Matt Busby in 1971, who at the age of 17 scored on his debut at Maine Road in a derby against City. He went on to score 57 goals in 342 appearances over the next ten years before being sold – some would say discarded – by Big Ron Atkinson to Stoke for a fee of £330,000.

Sammy played 88 times for Northern Ireland including the World Cup in 1982 where the team beat the hosts Spain and in 1986 when he captained the team.

Sammy was a great player with a natural instinctive ability and twinkling feet which he used to great effect in the 1979 cup final against Arsenal when he danced through the defence, nutmegged a player and sweetly slotted the ball past Pat Jennings to score a great equaliser.

Well, that's mine and my listeners' choices but I am sure, as always in football, there's still room for more discussion and rows. The only surprise is that if we have produced so many world-class players, how come we can only point to one major trophy in all these years and even I as an Englishman am fed up of talking about '66. I also can't believe that the massive uncontrolled influx of foreign players into our domestic game can possibly do anything but continue to weaken our international standing further.

45

The best British wheels: top five cars

One thing we can be rightly proud of in this magnificent country is our car industry and more particularly we should really be proud of our brilliant designers and skilled workforce.

Coming from the Midlands I am bound to say this, I know, but the simple plain truth is that we have a motoring heritage that is second to none. I know that we no longer have a truly British marque but we still have a proud tradition of making some of the greatest cars in the world.

If you don't believe me, take the kids for a full day out to the British Transport Museum in Coventry and just marvel at our motoring heritage.

Yes of course we could talk about the bad old days of British Leyland in the Seventies and the industrial strife led by people like Red Robbo at Longbridge. Or we could comment on the managerial incompetence that led to me spending three months, before I went to university, working at the Standard Triumph factory in Coventry pushing cars off the track and into storage because they were missing vital parts.

However, instead I've decided to accentuate the positive and celebrate in my own subjective and biased way the best cars in Britain.

1. The Mini

No list would be complete without this classic designed by Sir Alec Issigonis and first driven off the assembly line in 1959.

It quickly became the most popular British car of all time. This is all the more remarkable as it was only designed as a direct reaction to the Suez oil crisis and it was only intended as an unpretentious run-around.

It's a design classic and its space-saving front wheel design meant that 80 per cent of the floor plan was available for the passengers and luggage, even if that meant that the engine had to be inserted sideways.

I guess the car, along with the mini skirt, Twiggy and The Beatles, summed up the Swinging Sixties and with the success of the Mini Cooper S in the Monte Carlo rallies of 1964, 1965 and 1967 the Mini was firmly placed in the hearts and minds of millions of Brits.

I've never had one but always fancied owning this great car. However, Lisa reckons I would need a matching crowbar to get my considerable bulk in and out!

Of course with the sale to BMW the redesigned Mini is still turning heads and is still built by skilled British workers at Oxford.

2. The Rover 95

Forgive me this one indulgence but, believe it or not, this was the first car that Lisa and I owned. When we were setting up our theatre company back in 1984 we rented a very small industrial unit in the old Renold Chain Factory in Coventry. Underneath the arches of the nearby railway line a bloke restored these magnificent old beasts and one particular car in burgundy with pale blue leather seats caught my eye.

I knew nothing and still know nothing about cars but in a moment of pure madness I just knew that I had to have this motor. I think it cost us two and a half grand but I just loved this car and we had plenty of great trips down to Cornwall in it. It had been restored magnificently and once when we were at Harlyn Bay in Cornwall someone turned up in another 95. This guy was a real enthusiast and bound over to ask me if he could have a look under the bonnet. Yes I did know how to open it. He then proceeded to bore me with details about the car until my silent response clearly illustrated he was talking to a motoring moron. He left slightly disgruntled because I actually think my motor was nicer than his.

When I call it a beast I am not exaggerating: the 95, which was the successor to the 90, weighed one and a half tons. In fact it was so heavy that once when we broke down in Cornwall the RAC couldn't tow it as they reckoned it weighed more than a Transit van.

Introduced in 1963, only 3,680 of these cars were produced and it was commonly known as the working man's Rolls-Royce.

We held on to it until I went bust in 1992 and to this day I still know where the old lady I once owned now is.

3. Ford Cortina

First produced in 1962 and sold for twenty years until it was replaced by the first of the jellybean cars, the Ford Sierra, this was every working-class lad's dream motor, immortalised of course in Tom Robinson's song 'Grey Cortina'.

Wish I had a grey Cortina
Whiplash aerial, racing trim
Cortina owner – no one meaner
Wish that I could be like him

Twin exhaust and rusty bumper
Chewing gum at traffic light
Stop at red but leave on amber
Grey Cortina outa sight

Wish I had a grey Cortina
Whiplash aerial, racing trim
Cortina owner – no one meaner
Wish that I could be like him

Furlined seats and lettered windscreen
Elbow on the windowsill
Eight track blazing Brucie Springsteen
Bomber jacket, dressed to kill

Wish I had a grey Cortina
Whiplash aerial, racing trim
Cortina owner – no one meaner
Wish that I could be like him

Never cop a parking ticket
Never seem to show its age
Speed police too slow to nick it
Grey Cortina got it made

Wish I had a grey Cortina
Whiplash aerial, racing trim
Cortina owner – no one meaner
Wish that I could be like him.

Superb!

All you needed now was the furry dice hanging from the rearview mirror and the green sun visor with your name spelled out in white lettering on the driver's side and your bird's name, usually Sharon, on the passenger's side.

Seriously though this was a mass-market car which had massive appeal. Everyone wanted one, especially the Mark II, and between 1972 and 1981 it was Britain's best-selling car.

4. Jaguar – any Jag

I can still remember standing in the rain trying to get shelter under one of the huge trees that line one of the poshest roads into Coventry, the Kenilworth road, when a white E-Type Jaguar raced past myself and my older brother Simon.

We had been fishing at Leek Wooten and we were waiting for my dad to pick us up and it was bucketing down.

'I'm going to have one of those when I'm older.'

'Dream on, it'll never happen.'

But it did.

It is of course every Cov Kid's dream to own a Jaguar and I just knew that one day by hook or by crook I would drive the greatest car down that very same road.

The son of the owner of the VG shop across the road from where I grew up had a red E-type that my mates and me would peer into at every opportunity until he screamed from the bedroom window, 'Get your mucky mitts off my motor, you brats.'

Twenty-odd years later it actually happened for me when I won a raffle at Highfield Road and got the keys to a racing-green Jaguar XJS.

Let me tell you it's not until you have actually turned the ignition key in a Jaguar that you realise just what a magnificent beast the Cat is. From its sumptuous leather seats through to the immaculate walnut burr of that dash and then of course the growl of the engine.

When I first drove that car I thought I was the dog's bollocks and I was.

Subsequently I have been able to buy my own Jags and still they hold the same allure to me. I could have a Lexus, a Beamer or the Merc but I'm sorry, nothing quite matches up to the Jaguar.

It's a car that is still made by craftsmen, Coventry craftsmen, and now skilled men in the rest of the Midlands and Liverpool and yes I know it's no longer owned by Brits but it's still a classic British design and an undoubted British marque. We shouldn't knock those who by sheer hard work and determination end up owning one. We should celebrate achievement and not indulge in the politics of envy. The story of Yanks applauding someone who owns a Jag, Roller or Cadillac in the States while those in Britain would scratch it may be a cliché but it's born out of fact.

We are too quick in this country to knock those who achieve something in life rather than aspiring to be like them and be motivated by their success to work harder to achieve the same results.

I'm not one of these people who say buy British for the sake of it, but when we produce one of the best motors in the world, why would a true Brit buy anything else? Why go for the dull uniformity of the Germans or Japs? Why not stand out from the crowd and defiantly state where your allegiance lies.

I know the Jags used to be plagued by mechanical problems but that is no longer the case and now they are a proud testimony to the skill of our own manufacturing heroes.

I've just had my new Jaguar XKR delivered and I feel like the cat that has got the cream. It's a beast of a machine with 4.2 supercharged litres under the bonnet and the body curves of a young Barbara Windsor and, my God, when you floor it does the cat roar!

This is British engineering at its best, this is a car that this country should be proud of and I don't care if you think I'm bragging. I'm chuffed to bits that all my hard work means I can drive the car that that little fat Cov Kid dreamed about in the rain all those years ago.

5. Great British engineering

Now here's the point where I could choose to talk about a Roller or an Aston or any other cliché British super car but I am going to resist that temptation and just say that what we actually need to do is celebrate British engineers and British motor engineering in general.

Toolmakers and skilled car workers have never got the recognition that they deserve in this country. There's always been a class-driven attitude of looking down at manual or skilled car workers. I hate that attitude and I think it has held the country back. In Germany engineers are revered and respected but here we might boast about Brunel, Stephenson and now and again if pushed celebrate the genius of people like Frank Whittle who invented the jet engine, but nine times out of ten these people's successors are largely forgotten. Britain isn't the worldwide centre for training car designers or the home of Formula 1 by mistake or a freak accident. It's because we do have some of the most skilled and talented engineers, inventors and designers in the world who are drawing on a rich heritage of design, invention and innovation of previous generations.

Yes I know we've produced some turkeys like the Allegro, the Vectra and the TR7 (remember, you could even get it in shit brown, a bit like the Coventry City kit in the Seventies) but think of everything else from the Triumph TR6 through the Stag (what a car!) through to the humble Transit that we've all owned at least once in our life to the luxury marques of Bentley and Jaguar.

Remember Campbell and the Bluebird or Richard Noble and Thrust One or, for God's sake, the Spitfire, even Concorde (yes I know the French helped us). Then there is Britain's railways and train design or the engineering miracle that is the canal system or our shipbuilding tradition (don't mention the *Titanic*!). All of these are crowning achievements and examples of our engineering and manu-facturing talent and heritage and it is about time they were celebrated more in Great Britain.

That's why I implore you, instead of just reading another car list, get off your arse, get in the car (preferably a British-built one) and get down to the Coventry Transport Museum and teach yourself and your kids the history of the great British motor.

46

Top ten modern-day British politicians

47

Much, much more important than life and death: Britain's greatest football managers

This section was almost called the best Scottish managers as four out of the six are from north of the border. What is with the Scottish and management and how come they can turn out such fine leaders of men but such useless goalkeepers? I'm only joking, but before the influx of foreign managers it has to be said that Scotland did seem to lead the way in terms of leaders of football men.

Although I welcome the introduction of fabulous coaches like Mourinho, Wenger and even Rafa at Liverpool I do worry, just as I do about the number of foreign players, where our British-born managers and coaches are going to come from or get their experience if this foreign invasion continues.

Of course our Premiership is the greatest league in the world but the issue of foreign player quotas has to be addressed. England's and indeed the other home nations dismal failure to qualify for the European championships in 2008 is surely ample proof of this.

Likewise young British coaches like Paul Ince and older figures such as Harry Redknapp and even Stuart Pearce need to be given time and opportunity to develop and learn their craft.

I am not necessarily against the national team being managed by a foreigner but call it xenophobia if you will – I still feel that it is better if a national side should be coached by someone from that country.

1. Sir Alex Ferguson (b. Govan, 1941)

Without doubt Sir Alex is the greatest British manager of all time and his record speaks for itself. He has won more trophies than any other manager and has been in charge at Old Trafford for over 1,000 matches and for 21 years. At Manchester United, Alex has become the most successful manager in the history of English football, having guided the team to eleven League Championships.

In 1999, he became the first manager to lead an English team to the treble of League Championship, FA Cup and UEFA Champions League. As well as being the only manager to win the FA Cup five times. Not only that but he is also the only manager ever to win three successive League Championships in the top flight in England with the same club (1998–99, 1999–2000 and 2000–01).

Alex is a bit like Dennis Wise. Every football fan in the country hates him but every fan would actually love them to play or manage their team. Of course he is famous for his hairdryer treatment of players and although his management technique has to be more sophisticated than just shouting at players it is clear that he adopts a 'my way or the highway' approach to handling millionaire superstars. The casualty list speaks for itself; Beckham, Stam, Keane and Strachan, to name but a few.

I personally love his arrogance, his self-belief and his uncanny ability never to see when his player is at fault.

2. Brian Clough (b. Middlesbrough, 1935; d. 2004)

I know it's a cliché but I don't care. Cloughie was the greatest England manager we never had.

As a young boy I used to love watching him on *Sportsnight* or on ATV giving it large and putting the world to right. I loved his arrogance, his outspokenness and his complete self-belief. He wasn't English in that sense because too many of us (not me of course) hide our light under a bushel or suffer from what I call *aspireontitus* – the dreadful British disease of false modesty that holds so many people back. I much prefer the American and Cloughie way of dealing with life: if you're good and you can back it up, tell people and grab the opportunities that come your way, don't sit back and let them pass you by.

We could all learn from some of Cloughie's more outrageous quotes:

'I certainly wouldn't say I'm the best manager in the business, but I'm in the top One.'

Or how about this quote, 'They say Rome wasn't built in a day, but I wasn't on that particular job.'

And surely every football fan in the land would agree with him about how the long-ball game has ruined British football: 'If God had intended for us to play football in the clouds he wouldn't have put grass on the ground.'

I also love the way he reacted to the fact that he was never given the England job:

'They thought I was going to change it lock, stock and barrel. They were shrewd because that's exactly what I would have done.'

So instead we got the Turnip, the Swede and the Wally with the brolly, and the buffoons in the blazers still run the FA and ruin our national game.

I also love this quote from Cloughie about his upbringing in Middlesbrough, 'Everything I have done, everything I've achieved, everything that I can think of that has directed and affected my life – apart from the drink – stemmed from my childhood. Maybe it was the constant sight of Mam, with eight children to look after, working from morning till night, working harder than you or I have ever worked.'

What a pity more modern British footballers can't think like this. What a pity more managers don't treat players like this. 'If a player had said to Bill Shankly, "I've got to speak to my agent", Bill would have hit him. And I would have held him while he hit him.'

Cloughie was a brilliant manager and a great player whose own playing career was tragically cut short by a knee injury after he had only played two games for England. As a manager of course Old Big Head will be remembered for successful spells at Derby and the two European cups at Nottingham Forest as well as for his infamous 44 days at Leeds after he replaced the traitor that was Revie.

But Cloughie was more than just a great footballer or brilliant manager, he was also a one-off, a British eccentric, who fought back after injury to become even more successful at his second career.

This final quote sums up the man and should act as a mantra for us all who wish to succeed in life: 'If anyone wants to see my O-Levels and A-Levels, I'll get my medals from upstairs and put them on the table. They're my O-Levels and A-Levels.'

3. Sir Matt Busby (b. Lanarkshire, 1909; d. 2004)

Sir Matt is still the longest-serving manager in Manchester United's history although Sir Alex Ferguson is now breathing down his neck and has actually managed the team for more games.

Busby, who managed the team from 1945 to 1969 and again for a brief spell in the 1970–71 season, will of course always be linked with the Busby Babes – the young team whom he moulded into what would have been world-beaters if it hadn't been for the tragic events of 6 February 1958 when seven players, three club officials and thirteen other people died as their plane crashed on the tarmac at Munich airport on the return from a game against Red Star Belgrade.

Busby himself suffered appalling injuries and was actually administered the last rites on two occasion but pulled through and three months later left hospital and took over the managerial reins again the next season.

He rebuilt the team around the survivors including Bobby Charlton and of course drafted in the legendary Denis Law and discovered the Belfast Boy himself, George Best. And the rest is history, including of course the European Cup triumph of 1968.

He retired as manager the following year, only to return on a temporary basis when Wilf McGuiness was sacked in 1970. Eventually he was made President of the club.

4. Sir Alf Ramsey (b. Dagenham, 1920; d. 1999)

England manager, 1963–74. Won England the World Cup. What else do we need to say?

5. Jock Stein (b. Lanarkshire, 1922; d. 1985)

Stein was the first non-Catholic manager of Celtic and he went on to win the European Cup, ten Scottish League Championships, eight Scottish Cups and six Scottish League Cups.

What I love most about Stein though is that his Lisbon Lions who won the European Cup in 1967 were all born within thirty miles of Glasgow. Also let's not underestimate the achievement. This was the first time in history that a British club had lifted this trophy and the achievement is best summed up by fellow Scots legend Bill Shankly who told Stein shortly after this remarkable achievement, 'Jock, you're immortal now.'

Every football fan must love this quote from the big man, 'We did it by playing football. Pure, beautiful, inventive football' (Lisbon, 1967).

Or how about this one? 'Football is nothing without fans.'

Football is nothing without men like Jock Stein.

6. Bill Shankly (b. Ayrshire, 1913; d. 1981)

Shanks would be pleased to be regarded as Liverpool's greatest manager by their fans as he was a working-class man who really valued the fans more than anything else. In fact he thought he was just the same as those who followed the team. 'I'm just one of the people who stands on the Kop. They think the same as I do, and I think the same as they do. It's a kind of marriage of people who like each other.'

He also believed that if his team lost, they were truly letting the fans down:

'If you are first, you are first. If you are second, you are nothing.'

Shanks' most famous quote sums up his attitude to the game, even if he did later say it was just an off-the-cuff remark: 'Some people believe football is a matter of life and death. I'm very disappointed with that attitude. I can assure you it is much, much more important than that.'

I thought long and hard about including Shanks and argued with my talkSPORT audience about whether we should include Bob Paisley who of course won more silverware, but after hours of rows I decided to go for Bill because he is the man who is constantly voted by Liverpool fans as their greatest-ever manager. He was also the man who transformed the club from Second Division also-rans into the world-beaters that Paisley was then able to build upon.

Other greats who have to be mentioned

Bill Nicholson: Spurs manager, 1958–74. The first man to win the double in 1961, three FA Cups in total and two League and UEFA Cups.

Sir Bobby Robson: Teams managed include Ipswich, England (1982–9 including getting us to the semi-final of the World Cup in 1990), PSV Eindhoven, Porto, Barcelona and Newcastle. Robson's achievements with England combined with his managing of top European clubs make him a stand-out British manager.

48

'This royal throne of kings': all-time greatest British quotes

There are certain lines and images that all Brits should know and remember. Here are my favourites:

1. William Shakespeare

This royal throne of kings, this sceptred isle,
This earth of majesty, this seat of Mars,
This other Eden, demi-paradise,
This fortress built by Nature for herself
Against infection and the hand of war,
This happy breed of men, this little world,
This precious stone set in the silver sea,
Which serves it in the office of a wall
Or as a moat defensive to a house,
Against the envy of less happier lands,
This blessed plot, this earth, this realm, this England.

King Richard II Act 2, Scene 1

2. Colonel Tim Collins

We go to liberate, not to conquer. We will not fly our flags in their country.

We are entering Iraq to free a people and the only flag which will be flown in that ancient land is their own. Show respect for them.

There are some who are alive at this moment who will not be alive shortly. Those who do not wish to go on that journey, we will not send.

As for the others, I expect you to rock their world. Wipe them out if that is what they choose. But if you are ferocious in battle remember to be magnanimous in victory.

Iraq is steeped in history. It is the site of the Garden of Eden, of the Great Flood and the birthplace of Abraham. Tread lightly there.

You will see things that no man could pay to see – and you will have to go a long way to find a more decent, generous and upright people than the Iraqis.

You will be embarrassed by their hospitality even though they have nothing.

Don't treat them as refugees for they are in their own country. Their children will be poor, in years to come they will know that the light of liberation in their lives was brought by you.

If there are casualties of war then remember that when they woke up and got dressed in the morning they did not plan to die this day.

Allow them dignity in death. Bury them properly and mark their graves.

It is my foremost intention to bring every single one of you out alive. But there may be people among us who will not see the end of this campaign.

We will put them in their sleeping bags and send them back. There will be no time for sorrow.

The enemy should be in no doubt that we are his nemesis and that we are bringing about his rightful destruction.

There are many regional commanders who have stains on their souls and they are stoking the fires of hell for Saddam.

He and his forces will be destroyed by this coalition for what they have done. As they die they will know their deeds have brought them to this place. Show them no pity.

It is a big step to take another human life. It is not to be done lightly.

I know of men who have taken life needlessly in other conflicts. I can assure you they live with the mark of Cain upon them.

If someone surrenders to you then remember they have that right in international law and ensure that one day they go home to their family.

The ones who wish to fight, well, we aim to please.

If you harm the regiment or its history by over-enthusiasm in killing or in cowardice, know it is your family who will suffer.

You will be shunned unless your conduct is of the highest – for your deeds will follow you down through history. We will bring shame on neither our uniform nor our nation.

[*On Saddam's chemical and biological weapons:*]
It is not a question of if, it's a question of when. We know he has already devolved the decision to lower commanders, and that means he has already taken the decision himself. If we survive the first strike we will survive the attack.

As for ourselves, let's bring everyone home and leave Iraq a better place for us having been there. Our business now is north.

Extemporised eve-of-battle speech to his troops in Iraq, 19 March 2003. Copyright Tim Collins, 2003

Love her or loathe her, and over the years I've done both, you can't deny that Mrs Thatcher was a great natural leader, a woman with balls and a woman with an eye for the main chance.

Of course she was heading for election meltdown when she took the decision to fight Argentina and of course it saved or even made her political career but at least she didn't dither or bottle her decision. She knew what the Argies had done was wrong and she decided to show in no uncertain terms that Britain still ruled the waves.

I was at university at the time and even though I was politically miles away from the Tories I can still recall how proud I was when the Taskforce sailed from Southampton and how even as a student leftie I had to admire her response to questions on the steps of Downing Street.

I'm sorry, I now believe even more than ever that this was a great moment for a great nation and of course as I have got older I have appreciated more and more what Mrs T did for this country.

3. Maggie Thatcher

'Rejoice!'

After our forces had recaptured South Georgia in the Falklands war, this was Mrs Thatcher's response, hardly a speech but it captured the mood of a nation but upset some of the liberals who thought it was inappropriate after the deaths in the conflict.

'Ladies and gentlemen. The Secretary of State for Defence has just come over to give me some very good news and I think you'd like to have it at once.'

Then Defence Secretary John Nott stepped forward and said, 'The message we have got is that British troops landed on South Georgia this afternoon, shortly after 4 pm London time. They have now successfully taken control of Grytviken; at about 6 pm London time, the white flag was hoisted in Grytviken beside the Argentine flag. Shortly afterwards, the Argentine forces there surrendered to British forces. The Argentine forces offered only limited resistance to the British troops. Our forces were landed by helicopter and were supported by a number of warships, together with a Royal Fleet Auxiliary.

'During the first phase of this operation, our own helicopters engaged the Argentine submarine, Santa Fé, off South Georgia. This submarine was detected at first light and was engaged because it posed a threat to our men and to the British warships launching the landing. So far, no British casualties have been reported. At present we have no information on the Argentine casualty position. The Commander of the operation has sent the following message:

' "Be pleased to inform Her Majesty that the White Ensign flies alongside the Union Jack in South Georgia. God save the Queen." '

A member of the press shouted out this question, 'What happens next, Mr Nott? What's your reaction . . .?'

The Iron Lady waded in, 'Just rejoice at that news and congratulate our forces and the marines.'

She turned to walk into Number 10.

'Goodnight.'

Someone else in the press shouted out, 'Are we going to war with Argentina, Mrs Thatcher?'

She paused on the steps and said, 'Rejoice.'

Outside 10 Downing Street, 26 April 1982

4. Winston Churchill

Even though large tracts of Europe and many old and famous States have fallen or may fall into the grip of the Gestapo and all the odious apparatus of Nazi rule, we shall not flag or fail. We shall go on to the end, we shall fight in France, we shall fight on the seas and oceans, we shall fight with growing confidence and growing strength in the air, we shall defend our Island, whatever the cost may be, we shall fight on the beaches, we shall fight on the landing grounds, we shall fight in the fields and in the streets, we shall fight in the hills; we shall never surrender, and even if, which I do not for a moment believe, this Island or a large part of it were subjugated and starving, then our Empire beyond the seas, armed and guarded by the British Fleet, would carry on the struggle, until, in God's good time, the New World, with all its power and might, steps forth to the rescue and the liberation of the old.

House of Commons, 4 June 1940

5. James Thomson

When Britain first, at heaven's command,
Arose from out the azure main,
This was the charter of the land,
And guardian angels sung this strain:
    'Rule, Britannia, rule the waves;
    Britons never will be slaves.'

Alfred: a Masque, 1740

6. William Blake

And did those feet in ancient time
Walk upon England's mountains green?
And was the holy Lamb of God
On England's pleasant pastures seen?

And did the Countenance Divine
Shine forth upon our clouded hills?
And was Jerusalem builded here
Among these dark satanic mills?

Bring me my bow of burning gold!
Bring me my arrows of desire!
Bring me my spear! O clouds, unfold!
Bring me my chariot of fire!

I will not cease from mental fight,
Nor shall my sword sleep in my hand,
Till we have built Jerusalem
In England's green and pleasant land.

Jerusalem, 1808

7. The British Grenadiers

Some talk of Alexander, and some of Hercules;
Of Hector and Lysander, and such great names as these;
But of all the world's brave heroes, there's none that can compare
With a tow, row, row, row, row, row, row, for the British
   Grenadiers.

Anon

8. Flower of Scotland

In the past I've slagged this song off, usually just to wind up the
Scottish listeners, but the truth is I'm rather jealous of them and their
song. They have managed to create a new national song that actually
sounds really traditional and when 80,000 of them sing, including their
players at a rugby or football match, we English know there is a
mighty battle about to commence. Perhaps it's time for the English to

find a new song that would have the same effect and that even Wayne Rooney could learn the words to and bloody sing when he is wearing the Three Lions?

O Flower of Scotland,
When will we see
Your like again,
That fought and died for,
Your wee bit Hill and Glen,
And stood against him,
Proud Edward's Army,
And sent him homeward,
Tae think again.

The Hills are bare now,
And Autumn leaves
lie thick and still,
O'er land that is lost now,
Which those so dearly held,
That stood against him,
Proud Edward's Army,
And sent him homeward,
Tae think again.

Those days are past now,
And in the past
they must remain,
But we can still rise now,
And be the nation again,
That stood against him,
Proud Edward's Army,
And sent him homeward,
Tae think again.

O Flower of Scotland,
When will we see
your like again,
That fought and died for,
Your wee bit Hill and Glen,
And stood against him,

Proud Edward's Army,
And sent him homeward,
Tae think again.

Words and Music by Roy M. B. Williamson. © The Corries
(Music) Ltd. All rights reserved. International Copyright secured.
Reprinted by permission

9. The Land of My Fathers

The Welsh are just the same when they sing this or 'Bread of Heaven', there's real passion and pride and again, if I'm really honest, I am jealous of their absolute commitment to their team, country and culture.

The land of my fathers, the land of my choice,
The land in which poets and minstrels rejoice;
The land whose stern warriors were true to the core,
While bleeding for freedom of yore.

Wales! Wales! fav'rite land of Wales!
While sea her wall, may naught befall
To mar the old language of Wales.

Old mountainous Cambria, the Eden of bards,
Each hill and each valley, excite my regards;
To the ears of her patriots how charming still seems
The music that flows in her streams.
My country tho' crushed by a hostile array,
The language of Cambria lives out to this day;
The muse has eluded the traitors' foul knives,
The harp of my country survives.

Evan James, Hen Wlad Fy Nhadau, 1856

10. Land of Hope and Glory

Dear Land of Hope, thy hope is crowned.
God make thee mightier yet!
On Sov'ran brows, beloved, renowned,
Once more thy crown is set.

Thine equal laws, by Freedom gained,
Have ruled thee well and long;
By Freedom gained, by Truth maintained,
Thine Empire shall be strong.

Land of Hope and Glory, Mother of the Free,
How shall we extol thee, who are born of thee?
Wider still and wider shall thy bounds be set;
God, who made thee mighty, make thee mightier yet.
God, who made thee mighty, make thee mightier yet.

Thy fame is ancient as the days,
As Ocean large and wide:
A pride that dares, and heeds not praise,
A stern and silent pride:
Not that false joy that dreams content
With what our sires have won;
The blood a hero sire hath spent
Still nerves a hero son.

A. C. Benson and Sir Edward Elgar, 1902

49

'Clunk click every trip': great British public information films

In the days before multi-platform TV, breaks in transmission were filled with either the occasional *Tom and Jerry* cartoon or, more likely, hours of the test card featuring the girl with the stuffed clown (do you remember that story, probably an urban myth, that if you watched the card for long enough the girl punches the clown – or was that just a Coventry thing?) If we were very lucky though we'd get a public information film.

These films were made by the Central Office of Information and were first broadcast in 1945. There is a brilliant website at www. nationalarchives.gov.uk where you can actually view every one of the films from the past sixty years. It's a great way of wasting a couple of hours and will have you crying and laughing with nostalgia. Here are five of my favourites.

1. Charlie says

This has got to be my favourite although it's weird. I thought there was only one Charlie film about the dangers of playing with matches but actually there were six in total. They warned kids of the dangers of playing by water, hot water in teapots, playing by stoves in the kitchen and talking and going off with strangers.

First launched in 1973, Charlie's mangled speech was a hit with myself and millions of other kids. An added bonus was that the late great Kenny Everett voiced the films. Years later The Prodigy used the voice in their hit 'Charly' in 1991 but I get the feeling they weren't talking about a cat!

2. Joe and Petunia

This fat, thick cartoon couple appeared in loads of films starting in the late Sixties but the one on the beach with the ice cream has to be the most famous.

PETUNIA:	Oh it's ever so nice and peaceful up here, Joe. Nice view, too.
JOE:	Aye, very nice Petunia. And look at that nice little boat. He's having a lot of fun out there in his nice little dinjy. That's what they call them, you know, sailing dinjies.
PETUNIA:	Aren't they nice people at our hotel, Joe?
JOE:	Hey hey! Hello! Now he's splicing his main brace.
PETUNIA:	Though I don't think the man on table six is very nice.
JOE:	Ey, do you think he's in trouble, Petunia?
PETUNIA:	Ooh no, Joe, he's just enjoying himself on holiday.
JOE:	Oh, he's decided to have a swim. Now he's going to climb back again. I expect that water's a bit cold, don't you? Oh, oh, he's changed his mind. Now he's waving to us. Coooeeee! I can't say I recognise him, though.
PETUNIA:	Well he must know us. Maybe it's the gent on table number six?
JOE:	No it's not him, he's much . . . Oh now he's shouting. LOVELY DAY, ISN'T IT?
SAILOR:	HELP HELP! DIAL 999 AND ASK FOR THE COASTGUARD.
JOE:	I can't hear a word he's saying, you know. (*reading*) Dial 999 . . . and . . . ask . . . for . . . the . . . coast . . . guard . . . Well I never!

> VOICEOVER: If you see a boat you think may be in distress, dial 999 and ask for the coastguard.

An absolute classic I'm sure you agree and reproduced with kind permission of HM Coast Guard.

3. 'Clunk Click' – Jimmy Savile

This film first appeared in 1972 and successfully persuaded people to wear seatbelts. It combined the legend that is Jimmy Savile with hard-hitting images and shock tactics of the consequences of not wearing a belt. However, it took ten more years before it became law to wear a belt in the front of a car.

The slogan 'Clunk Click Every Trip' was used until 1993, although there are still crap impressionists using the voice and catchphrase in their acts!

4. Rolf Harris in the swimming pool

What kid of the Seventies can't remember Rolf falling back into the water with his toes waving goodbye, but can you finish the rest of his script?

> Those of you who can't swim yet, just wait over in the shallow end for me. Kids and water, they love it. Rivers, canals, even the lily pond in the garden – you can't keep them away from it. Water has a fascination for children – and I should know. When I was three years old I fell in the river at our place, couldn't swim. Somehow managed to scramble my way to the bank. Frightened the wits out of my mum and dad – and you can bet they had me taught to swim not long after that.

Forget the nostalgia. Rolf's message is as important today as it was then as although the rate of drowning has fallen since the Seventies it is still the third most common form of accidental death for under-sixteens.

5. Green Cross Code – Kevin Keegan and Darth Vader

Dave 'Darth Vader' Prowse in his guise as the Green Cross Man was the face and considerable body of road safety for fourteen years from

1975. He was aided and abetted by, amongst others, Kevin Keegan, whose acting was nearly as wide as his jacket lapels.

Following on from the adventures and messages of Tufty, the campaign had considerable success, with child road deaths falling considerably, but of course it is a message that needs to be constantly reinforced to keep our kids safe.

50

Made in Britain: top five British eccentrics

1. Sir Patrick Moore

The longest serving TV presenter in the world, having presented his programme *The Sky at Night* every month since 1957 except for one occasion when he had a bout of food poisoning. With his portly frame, monocle and appearances on light-entertainment programmes this man made a real academic subject interesting and accessible to the masses. A true British legend.

2. Eddie Waring

Rugby league and *It's a Knockout* owe loads to Eddie 'Up and Under' Waring. Eddie's commentaries were certainly not out of a textbook but they helped to popularise the game all over the UK. His voice has got to be one of the most mimicked in Britain ever with everyone from Mike Yarwood through Lenny Henry to John Culshaw having a bash at it. Another icon of the Seventies sadly missed since he passed away in 1986.

3. Stuart Hall

Of course Eddie's co-presenter on *It's a Knockout*, but I love him for his soccer reports with his constant references to Shakespeare and

Greek classics. He never uses one word when there are fifty available! The man is a genius and the only thing worth listening to on BBC Five Dead.

4. Professor Heinz Wolfe

Before you start shouting that he isn't British let me tell you that he moved to Britain from Germany when he was ten years old, on the day when war broke out, so as far as I'm concerned he's one of us. Most famous now I guess because of the TV programme *The Great Egg Race* but I grew up with him on programmes like *Young Scientist of the Year* that we all watched in the Seventies. I loved the clipped German accent, the bow ties and the almost Einstein standing-up hair. The eccentric look and the accent, however, made him eminently watchable and there must be millions of kids who were turned on to science by him.

5. John Noakes

The ultimate *Blue Peter* presenter and a British Legend to a whole generation of Brits like me. This was your favourite uncle mixed with a dash of hero-worship. John was the longest serving *Blue Peter* presenter, joining the programme in 1965 and leaving in 1978. Of course it was the Noakes, Singleton and Purves team that is probably the most famous line-up of all time. I loved them but I could have done without the recent revelation from Val that she and Peter used to do things without the aid of sticky-back plastic!

Noakes was everyone's favourite, largely due to his daredevil exploits. Remember his record-breaking free-fall jump and of course his catchphrase, 'Get down, Shep.' I also loved his follow-up series, *Go with Noakes*. There was something slightly mad – even dangerous – about John. He was the ultimate mad uncle who could either spin a fanciful yarn or go off on wild adventures of his own.

51

'Careful with that axe, Eugene': top five most stupid British haircuts of all time

1. The Purdey

Based on Joanna Lumley's character from *The New Avengers* (ITV, 1976–77). Every girl I knew in the era just before punk had this pudding bowl cut. What a mess but it looked great on the legendary Joanna Lumley.

2. The Charlie Nicholas

Champagne Charlie's barnet was copied right across the country. Straight at the front with a perm at the back – prat!

3. The Mullet

He and we might like to think of David Bowie as a style icon but let's not forget it was this man who introduced us to the infamous mullet during his *Ziggy Stardust and the Spiders from Mars* phase.

4. The Skinhead and the Suedehead

Being a copper's son I was never allowed this but, by God, did I want the cut, the Crombie, the Sta-Press and the Docs or Brogues. Despite the fascist/racist overtones I still think the skinhead or suedehead look is the most authentic and stylish working-class subculture uniform.

Do you remember the Skinhead and Suedehead book series by Richard Allen? If you were like me, you would have read them by torchlight under the bed covers with Radio Luxembourg playing on a tinny trannie through a minute earpiece so that you didn't wake your parents.

5. Any haircut started by Beckham

Nuff said.

52

Five things you will only find in Britain

1. Saucy seaside postcards

Do you remember snatching a sneaky prepubescent look at these outside the gift shop on the prom while at the same time pretending you were actually looking at the buckets and spades? Of course you do! The traditional saucy seaside postcard is as much a part of the traditional working-class British holiday as stripy deckchairs, glamorous granny competitions, fish and chips and rain for a fortnight.

These cards' origins date back to 1894 and were part of the seaside scene for nearly a century until the demise of their most famous producer, Bamforth & Co. in 1990. They relied on traditional stock seaside characters like the fat woman, the big-boobed bird or the sexually frustrated older man. They dealt in double- or even single-entendre and they were just harmless fun with their end-of-pier-style humour. It's really sad that their demise has almost mirrored the decline of traditional resorts like Blackpool.

2. Pantomime

I could get all heavy with you and show off my Drama degree and tell you all about the origins of pantomime from Ancient Greece and Rome, but I won't bother. I'll just concentrate on the UK Panto – an almost uniquely British phenomena.

Panto is most Brits' first experience of live theatre and almost every town has either a professional or amateur show at Christmas. To be honest, Christmas isn't Christmas without a visit to the panto, in my opinion. I love the stories, the stock characters, the conventions – like a bloke playing the dame and a pretty girl with legs up to her eyeballs playing the principal boy. I also love the set routines, like the laundry scene in Aladdin, the ghost scene, the baking scene or the decorating scene. I love the way pop songs of the day are rewritten to suit either the star performer or the plot – and of course I love seeing the panto villain getting his comeuppance. Although there are pantomimes in Australia and Canada, it's still largely a British tradition and a tradition like cricket that the Yanks can't get their heads around, thank God!

I have seen some of the biggest stars in panto and amongst my favourites are Ken Dodd, Stanley Baxter (the best legs in showbiz by the way!), Billy Dainty and Les Dawson. In more recent years, Brian Conley and even Bobby Davro have performed brilliantly.

I even had a go myself a few years ago, playing the Evil Queen's henchman in *Snow White and the Seven Dwarfs* with Vikki Michel (*'Allo 'Allo*) at St Albans. I had a great time but I can tell you after Boxing Day it's a real hard slog and one of the most taxing jobs I have ever done.

'Oh no, it isn't!'

'Oh yes, it is!'

3. Queuing

Just had to mention this. What is it with us Brits and queuing? We must be the most polite nation in the world and not only that but if we see a blooming queue we join it, what's that all about then?

Also the one thing Brits hate more than a queue is a queue jumper. I have travelled the world and no nation queues like us.

4. Saying sorry when someone stands on your foot

This is another British quirk. Why is it that us Brits are always the first to apologise even when it's not our fault? The classic example is when someone stands on your foot and you say sorry first, not them!

5.The fish man coming round the boozer trying to sell you prawns or cockles

In Coventry he was always called Mr Mussels, get it? And he would always arrive without fail as the last orders bell rang out.

I always loved the food, just as I believe no trip to the seaside is complete without a cup of mussels or whelks or prawns with lashings of vinegar which have to be eaten as you walk against the wind on a rain-lashed prom or pier. However, us Brits, for an island race, have a pathetic attitude to fish and shellfish and quite simply don't eat enough of the stuff with most of our best seafood, especially shellfish, being exported straight to places like Spain. I would dearly love this attitude to change, as I love my fish.

53

'Get your trousers on, you're nicked': top British TV coppers

1. DCI Gene Hunt – *Life on Mars* (BBC TV, January 2006–April 2007)

Nearly as funny as the actual series was the British liberal elite trying to make out that we the British public were laughing at the un-PC policing of Gene Hunt rather than laughing with him.

Clearly this series and its hero Gene hit a real nerve with a British public that was fed up to the back teeth with the softly-softly (and I'm not talking about the programme with Barlow and Watts) policing we've had to suffer for the past decade.

Target policing to Gene Hunt meant could he punch his target, the criminal, to get a conviction. Of course no one wants a return to his style of policing (no really, I'm being sincere!) but in the Seventies, as my old man used to say when watching this series, at least we nicked the bad 'uns.

2. Jack Regan – *The Sweeney* (ITV, January 1975–December 1978)

Growing up in the Seventies, I loved everything about this programme from the brilliant theme music, that we all used to sing in the playground, to the car chases with the Ford Granada through to the immortal line from Inspector Regan, 'Get your trousers on, you're nicked.'

Clearly the model for Gene Hunt, the late great John Thaw's portrayal of Inspector Regan has got to be one of the greatest cop creations in British TV history.

3. Jim Taggart – *Taggart* (STV, September 1983–present)

I loved Taggart and when I say Taggart I mean the original Jim Taggart played by the late Mark McManus.

It must be the fact that I was brought up in a police family with a bit of a rough diamond for an old man but so many of these characters resemble people I either met or sat at the top of the stairs listening to while they drank and smoked with my old man in the front room.

Taggart's attitude to villains is brilliantly summed up by this quote from an episode in 1987 when he tells a witness, 'Yer brains'll be on the pavement unless ye help us!'

McManus died while filming an episode in 1994 but the series is still playing today, which is testament both to the superb cast and of course the introduction of another no-nonsense copper in the guise of DCI Matt Burke, formerly of Special Branch (played by Alex Norton).

4. Sergeant Bert Lynch – *Z-Cars* (BBC TV, January 1962– September 1978)

Lynch wasn't a rough and tumble copper like the others above but *Z-Cars* has got to get a mention and if so then it's got to be Lynch played by James Ellis.

He was in the series from 1962 until 1978, starting out as a constable and rising through the 'ranks' to Inspector. So in essence he framed my childhood and was ever present on the box.

I can clearly remember my old man muttering about which bits they got right and were realistic but also often as not stating in no uncertain terms that the real police were nothing like *Z-Cars*.

Strangely, however, if he was at home when it was on he would always watch the episode right to the end.

5.Inspector Morse – *Morse* (ITV, 33 episodes between 1975 and 2000)

John Thaw again, of course, with one of British TV's most popular characters and a complete opposite to Regan.

6. Sir Ian Blair

What do you mean he isn't a fictional TV cop?!

54

Ten things to do in Great Britain before you die

1. Travel through Glencoe in the mist in Europe's last great wilderness

Too many people think that Scotland stops at Edinburgh or Glasgow and while it may be the truth that the bulk of the Scottish population live in the M8 corridor that joins these two magnificent cities there is plenty to see and do further north.

It isn't an exaggeration either to say the Highlands are Europe's last great wilderness and not to visit it is almost a crime, although I write these words with trepidation because on every extended visit to the area it has usually resulted in a row at least or almost divorce proceedings between Lisa and myself.

The starting point for the trouble is the fact is that it such a long way to travel by car and what looks like a short distance on the map and would be by motorway is of course much longer when you are driving on smaller roads. If the weather is great and you can avoid the biting midges the scenery is also magnificent and the air clean and crisp. When we lived in Scotland I used to love walking the dog or pushing Rosie in her pram because the quality of light is just so amazing and so different to the Midlands. Lisa says it's as if the sky goes on forever.

However driving through Glencoe I feel the mist or even a little rain helps the atmosphere. It really is a mystical place with an horrific history.

Many think the name means Glen of weeping, which refers to the massacre of Glencoe in 1692 when 38 men of the Macdonald clan were killed by the Campbells in their homes and over forty women and children died of exposure in the Glen. What made the massacre worse was the fact that the Macdonalds had actually invited the Campbells into their homes and offered them hospitality before they turned on them and the massacre began. This act of betrayal means that even to this day on the door of the great little boozer in Glencoe called the Clachaig Inn there is still a sign saying 'No Hawkers or Campbells'.

Once you get through Glencoe, get up to places like Oban, the village of Plockton where they filmed *Hamish Macbeth*, and if you have enough time over to Skye and the Islands.

2. Stand at the bottom of the Angel of the North

I love modern public art and I am not one of these pillocks who slags off art just because it isn't a landscape or a picture of an animal. Art should be about challenging people's preconceptions and great public art should of course by its nature attract controversy.

Anthony Gormley's steel sculpture, standing on the A1 near Gateshead, certainly got the locals talking when it was unveiled in 1998 but now it is seen as the landmark of the North East of England. Most locals I've spoken to now love the thing and are immensely proud of it.

The steel statue is 66 feet tall and the wings measure 178 feet across. Due to its location it has to withstand winds of up to 100mph so the foundations that anchor the angel are at least 66 feet deep. The whole statue weighs 220 tons and was made in Hartlepool.

The Angel cost £1 million to build and was largely funded by the National Lottery and I believe this was an excellent use of Lottery money. One of the Lottery's uses should surely be to lift our spirits and elevate our minds and I think the Angel does this brilliantly.

3. See all the history plays by the RSC

How anyone can call themselves a patriot and not watch or like Shakespeare is beyond me. These particular plays and productions are both Shakespeare and the RSC at their patriotic best. Don't miss them.

4. Watch your team lift the FA Cup like I did in 1987

After getting married, being at the birth of my two daughters and winning three Sony awards in one night, watching Coventry City win the FA Cup was one of the best days of my life.

I've still got the ticket and it's in a frame in my downstairs loo. Me and a couple of mates paid the grand price of six pounds each to stand behind the goal the day that the Mighty Sky Blues won the cup. Of course we were the underdogs next to Spurs but to use that old cliché, that's the romance of the greatest club football competition in the world.

However, it didn't feel very romantic when Spurs' Clive Allen scored after two minutes, but despair turned to pure joy only seven minutes later when Dave Bennett clinched an equaliser. We went absolutely potty high up behind Oggy's goal and I can remember the whole of the Wembley stand vibrating under my feet.

The game was probably one of the best finals the Old Wembley ever staged and of course it ended memorably for us when Keith Houchen, who only seconds earlier we had been calling a donkey, scored with that fabulous diving header to make it two all. Our winner came from an own goal by Gary Mabbut and I swear there are many men still in Coventry who would sleep with Gary for that gift.

If the atmosphere at the match was good then the journey home and the reception the following day was out of this world. As we drove back up the M1 and got closer to Coventry, people were hanging over the motorway bridges waving any piece of cloth that was vaguely sky blue. I don't think a single pub closed that evening in Coventry as we celebrated and I certainly know that the little Irish boozer we were drinking in at Spon End in Coventry was still serving the black stuff at breakfast time.

That Sunday afternoon the suburbs were deserted as over 350,000 Coventry people welcomed the team and the cup back to Coventry. The Phoenix had risen again and the cup heroics gave the city a morale and economic boost that would last for ages.

That's the beauty of the beautiful game; it's more than just football, isn't it? Winning the FA cup can unite and lift a whole city and that's what it did for my home town and I know I go on about it and I know it's over twenty years ago but when your club and your city do it, you will know exactly how I feel too.

5. Bodyboarding at Croyde, North Devon

I love foreign holidays but I can honestly say that if you get the weather there are some great places to have a family holiday in this country and chief amongst them has to be Croyde Bay in North Devon.

When the girls were younger and money was tighter we spent many happy weeks at Ruda Holiday Park staying in a caravan on the cliffs overlooking the magnificent golden sands and surfing waves of Croyde.

When I was a lad we would go to Cornwall and bodyboard with an old wooden board and only a T-shirt to keep us warm but by the time I introduced Rosie and Bethany to the delights of the surf, things were a little more sophisticated. Foam boogie-boards and wet suits were *de rigueur* but the fun, sense of danger and sheer exhilaration and joy etched on to their faces was the same as when I was their age.

We're not talking Hawaii here or even Bondi Beach with perma-tanned toned bodies standing up on boards. I'm talking about fat blokes, like me, with their head over one shoulder shouting 'Now' as the wave breaks and all three of us trying to dive and catch the next surf. Then if all goes well hitting the beach, standing up, catching your breath as the kids shout, 'Come on, Dad, let's do it again.' Fan-bloody-tastic! Britain at its best.

6. Visit Tintagel and swim out to the island

Tintagel has always had a special hold over me. I remember visiting the place as a kid every August, wrapped up in our woolly jumpers, braving the wind and rain as we walked up and down the steps that lead to the beach.

I love the black sand and the small island that lies off the cove. I know in recent years the place had become a bit more touristy and there's the tacky Camelot's arcade or whatever it's called at the top of the cliffs but Tintagel still has a rugged beauty and an almost magical feel all of its own.

Years ago my dad, my brother and I swam out to the rocky crop that lies just off the beach. I can remember sitting there out of breath waving at Mum who was still on the beach, watching anxiously for us to return.

It was a special moment and Tintagel is a very special place.

7. Visit Orkney and see the Old Man of Hoy and the Standing Stones of Stenness

When I was running my theatre company we were invited to take a production of my play *Hooligans* to the St Magnus Festival on Orkney. I didn't have a clue where Orkney was, let alone what the festival was all about, but I was soon to find out.

A bloke called Sir Peter Maxwell Davies, who was a composer and who is now the Queen's Master of Music, led the festival. It's basically a musical festival but every year they invite one fringe theatre company to perform, so we headed off to Orkney.

Be warned, the ferry trip over is usually a nightmare and myself and the rest of the company spent most of the journey shouting for 'Hughie', but when we arrived in the capital Kirkwall we soon recovered as a result of the locals' hospitality and the fine whisky on offer.

For five inner-city lads just breaking into the world of theatre and the arts, Orkney and the festival was a revelation. The place has a rugged but flat charm and a real absence of trees and it felt a bit how people talk about New Zealand as if we were stepping back into Fifties Britain.

The people were warm and friendly and us Cov Kids found it absolutely amazing that no one locked their car doors let alone their front doors. We did all the usual touristy things like visiting Scapa Flow where the German fleet scuttled their own ships after the armistice in 1918. We also went to visit the Italian chapel that was created by Italian prisoners of war who also built many of the sea barriers that were meant to keep the German fleet out of the channels but now serve as causeways linking the islands, and of course we admired the Old Man of Hoy.

This is a magnificent mind-blowing 450-foot-high red sandstone sea stack that rises out of the sea on the west coast of the Island of Hoy which you get a great view of from the ferry if you are not being too sick! Thousands of climbers have made the pilgrimage to Hoy to climb the Old Man but even if you're not a climber this is something you have to see at least once in your life.

But for me the greatest thing about Orkney was the fact there was hardly any nighttime – it never seemed to get dark. In the summer, when we were there, the sun rises at 3 a.m. and sets at about 11.30 p.m.; there are hardly any stars and no real darkness.

I vividly recall coming out of the Town Hall after a ceilidh, which was another first for us Cov Kids; a dance where people passed on their female partners, everyone drunk and there were no fights! But as we left the dance we decided we wouldn't drive but walk home. Along the way we spotted some pushbikes in a front garden so we nicked them, I am ashamed to say, and cycled drunkenly home to our hotel.

The next morning I woke with a start with a mouth like the inside of a budgie's cage and a raging hangover and the realisation that we had abused people's hospitality by taking the bikes. I raised the boys and we all pedalled furiously back to town to replace the bikes. As we arrived a middle-aged woman came out of the house and expecting the worse I began to apologise.

'I'm sorr –'

'Oh, you must be the English lads doing the play, *Hooligans*, isn't it?'

Shamefaced I replied, 'Yes.'

'Oh yes, we're coming to see you tonight, thanks for bringing the bikes home, I wondered who had borrowed them, are you sure you don't need them any longer?'

It was amazing she really believed that we had only borrowed them and that there was no criminal intent. Is this what New Zealand is like? Was there ever a halcyon day when mainland Great Britain was like this and if so can we ever return to it? Shamefaced and shocked we hailed a taxi and went to prepare for that night's performance.

After the show and the inevitable ceilidh we went at midnight to visit the Standing Stones of Stenness. This is a Neolithic stone circle which is also now a UNESCO world heritage site and is a must see. The place, especially in the half-light of nighttime, has a mystical feel to it. Set on a promontory by a loch, the stone circle is made up of twelve slabs which are about a foot thick with some of them being as high as sixteen feet. Nearby is the Neolithic settlement of Skara Brae, which is a site of ten houses that lay undiscovered under sediment until a huge storm revealed them in 1850.

Again it's a must see but essentially for me it was the atmosphere and the people of Orkney that made my visit, so please go and feel it for yourself.

8. Eat a proper balti at Saleem's Restaurant in Ladypool Road, Birmingham

When I was a student and perhaps looking through rose-tinted spectacles, I seem to remember that you could get drunk on a fiver and still have enough left over for a curry and a nan bread in Saleem's Balti House in Sparkhill.

I call it a balti house but of course back in 1978/79 they weren't called balti houses, they were just cheap curry houses. Yes the food was served in a balti dish but us students didn't know what it was. We just knew it was cheap, filling and made your ring sing in the morning!

Saleem's was situated down a quiet dark road but there was no sense of menace and it was right in the heart of the predominantly Pakistani community. It was very popular with students. There were other cheap 'Indians' at the time but Saleem's was our favourite.

To the right, as you entered the shop, was an old rusty display fridge full of Indian sweets, which years later I would see a white racist be thrown through and land in what was my favourite Indian dessert after consumption of a hot curry, Rasmali, basically a combination of coconut and yoghurt, delicious.

The tables were formica-topped and the lino on the floor was cracked and peeling, the only decoration in the place being a cash and carry warehouse calendar sellotaped to the wall.

There were no knives and forks and part of our sport was watching the uninitiated or 'Saleem virgins' ask for cutlery, to be met with a snort of derision and quite often a spit on the floor from old man Saleem who sat on a wooden chair underneath the public phone. He would sit impassively watching his customers come and go, only stirring himself now and again to help out his white waiter with putting the best pakora or bhajis in the whole of Birmingham into the microwave. This waiter had ginger hair and a goatee and could speak exactly the same dialect as Old Man Saleem and this was I guess multiculturalism at its best.

The menu wasn't exactly extensive: you could have meat curry (lamb) or chicken or vegetarian. All three were served in a metal dish (later called the balti) with several large nan breads plonked next to them to soak up the delicious gravy or help you pick up the hot meat. The toilets were filthy but added to the charm.

This was all years before the City Council recognised the unique flavour, culture and ambience of the area and designated the whole neighbourhood as the 'Balti Belt'. Now it's a tourist area and many more balti houses have opened and the existing ones have upped their game with more extensive menus, cutlery and even clean toilets. But do you know what? Something has been lost amongst all this upgrading and official approval.

In a way Saleem's was a melting pot. It was a very distinct community living within a much larger one and I'm not suggesting that there wasn't racial tensions and deprivation. Of course there was, but this was pre 9/11, pre 7/7 and definitely pre the preachers of hate. We were just ordinary white and black students after a cheap curry, wanting to buy into this ethnic culture and cuisine; it didn't need an official sanction or a tourist rosette to justify its existence. Likewise Mr Saleem and his Pakistani-speaking white waiter just wanted to serve up cheap nutritious food to everyone regardless of race, creed or culture.

Recently I dropped Rosie off at a gig in Birmingham and had a couple of hours to kill before picking her up so I revisited Saleem's.

It was still there, much cleaner, much brighter and a much bigger menu. The food was just the same but old Mr Saleem had long since died and, I don't think it's too dramatic to say, so had the community. I remember driving down the street in the Jag and yes the girls were still working the streets and the area still had a scruffy charm but I also feel that it was very much like entering a different world, a completely separate culture.

Something had died with Mr Saleem and, perhaps with the deaths on 9/11 and 7/7, there has certainly been a loss of innocence. Despite the acres of newsprint, Government initiatives and talk about multiculturalism, I sometimes worry that we will never return to a time when we all just got on with our lives and almost lived in harmony.

9. Visit the Edinburgh Festival Fringe

If you have never visited the Athens of the North why don't you combine a trip to this magnificent city with a visit to the largest arts festival in the world?

I love the Fringe because I promoted theatre, music and comedy there for over fifteen years, but let me tell you, even if you're not that much into the arts this is the place where you can still see the best, funniest and most radical comedy and theatre anywhere in the world.

The scale of it is hard to imagine so let me just give you some facts from the Fringe's own website.

- Fringe 2007 featured 31,000 performances of 2,050 shows in 250 venues.
- An estimated 18,626 performers were on stage at the Fringe in 2007.
- 40 per cent (815) of the shows were world premieres and from the remaining 60 per cent of the programme 236 of the shows were European premieres and 93 were UK premieres.
- 304 shows at the Fringe were absolutely free.
- 1.6 million tickets (1,697,293) were sold during the 2007 Fringe, smashing all arts festival records.
- The Fringe sells 118 per cent more tickets than it did only 10 years ago (776,560 in 1997; 1,531,606 in 2006).
- The Fringe has a 75 per cent market share of all attendance at Edinburgh's year-round festivals and annually generates around £75 million for the Edinburgh and Scottish economy.

All this from an event that started out in an upstairs room of a damp and squalid pub back in 1947 as an alternative to the official Edinburgh Festival that had been created as a postwar arts initiative to reunite Europe through the arts. Essentially too many performers wanted to perform so a fringe festival organically started as a side show to the main event. Over the following 61 years I think it is fair to say that the Fringe has now clearly outgrown and overshadows its official parent.

My association with this mad manic festival started back in 2001 when I and a group of fellow students form Birmingham University, including Simon Le Bon, took a couple of plays up to the festival and lost a load of money as most first-timers do. Until you actually go it is impossible to get your head around the scale of the thing and it takes a couple of visits to learn the tricks of the trade so that you end up performing to more than the proverbial one man and his dog.

Every available space and room is converted into a theatre or a cabaret room and many international household names started their career at this festival including Peter Cook, Dudley Moore, Mike Myers, Hugh Laurie, Harry Enfield and Eddie Izzard.

As well as the performances you have to pay for there's loads of great street theatre which is absolutely free and it's a great place to take a young family as there are so many kids shows and activities for children.

Whatever you do, don't listen to the cynics who say the whole Fringe has become too commercial. They were saying that 25 years ago when I was promoting an unknown Julian Clary; Mike Myers was performing to less than twenty people; and a young comedian out of Birmingham called Frank Skinner was playing to no one most nights in one of my theatres. The truth is you never know who you might see as they make the first steps in their showbusiness career and this, coupled with the brilliant bars, nightlife and restaurants and dramatic architecture of Edinburgh, make this an absolute must do.

The Festival always happens in the first three weeks of August so what are you waiting for? The Best of British talent is waiting, just waiting to impress you!

10. See the Coventry Mystery Plays

Years ago when I was in the Belgrade Youth Theatre in Coventry a couple of mates and I were asked to be extras in a revival of the Coventry Mystery Plays that were going to be performed in the ruins of Coventry Cathedral.

These plays were first performed in 1392 and folklore has it that a young Shakespeare would have seen a performance before the plays were suppressed in 1579. The Belgrade revival of these plays was a massive success and now every other year they reinvent them for new audiences.

The setting is magnificent and near the end of the show after Herod has slaughtered the innocents, there is a magnificent moment when two mothers walk the length of the aisle cradling a dead baby each and sing the Coventry Carol. They are lit by follow spots and are framed by the bombed-out window of the Nave. It always seems to drizzle as the singing begins and this results in one of the most dramatic and poignant scenes I have ever witnessed in a theatre anywhere in the world. You can hear a pin drop as the mothers make their slow progress up the aisle, and the symbolism of the tyrant Herod, the bombed cathedral and the cross of nails speaks volumes about the nature of mankind. The crucifixion scene is also extremely moving.

In between of course, as in all Mystery plays, there are plenty of laughs and stock characters and the whole performance is something so immediate as you stand and walk round the cathedral as the performance unfolds.

This is one of the greatest theatrical experiences in Britain. Do not miss it.

And finally . . .

That's it then. That's *Gaunty's Best of British* and I hope that you have enjoyed my views on this great country of ours.

Now it's time to wrap ourselves in the flag and start working together to put the Great back into Britain.

Because we must all remember, this is Great Britain not Rubbish Britain.

Index